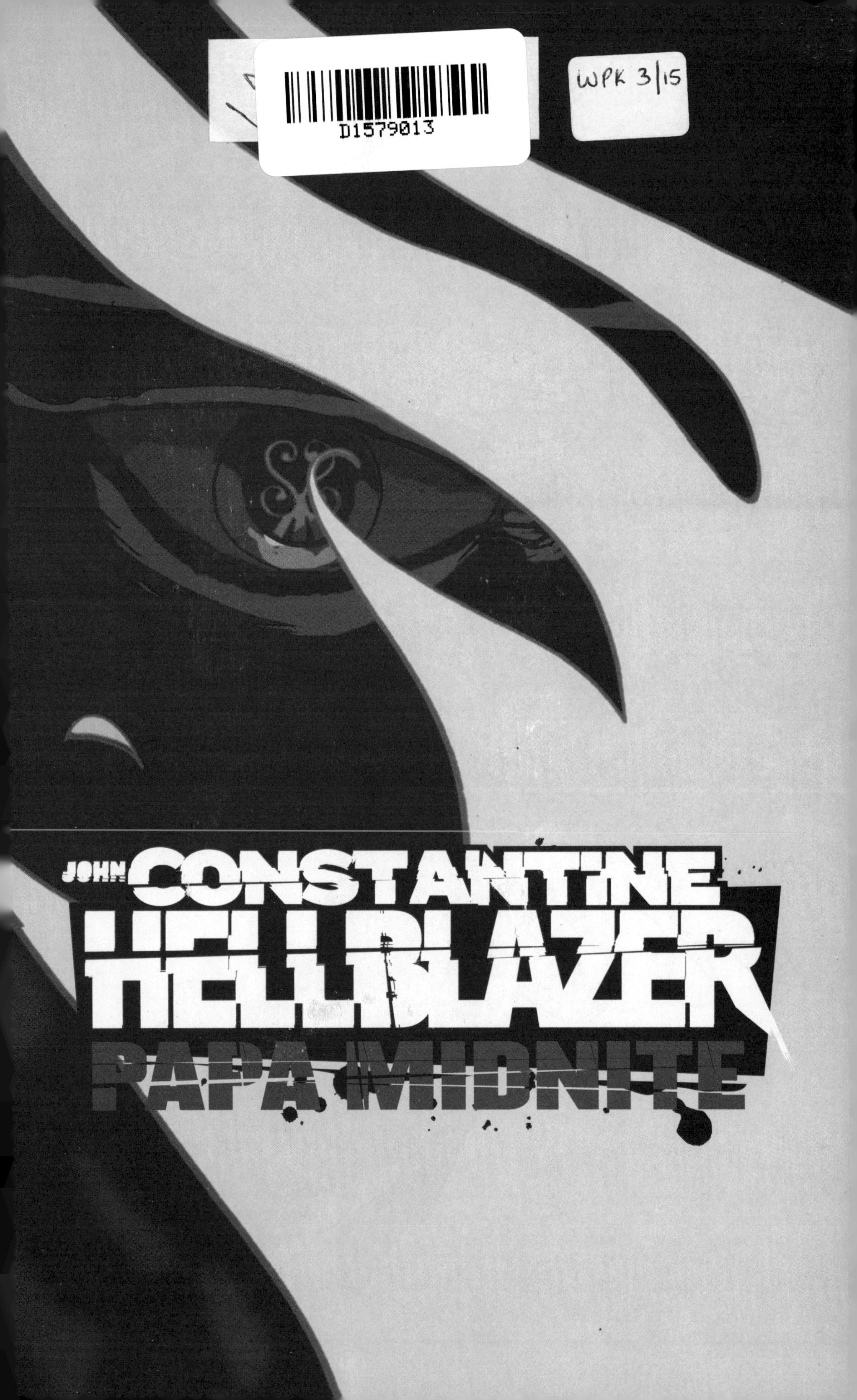
JOHN CONSTANTINE
HELLBLAZER
PAPA MIDNITE

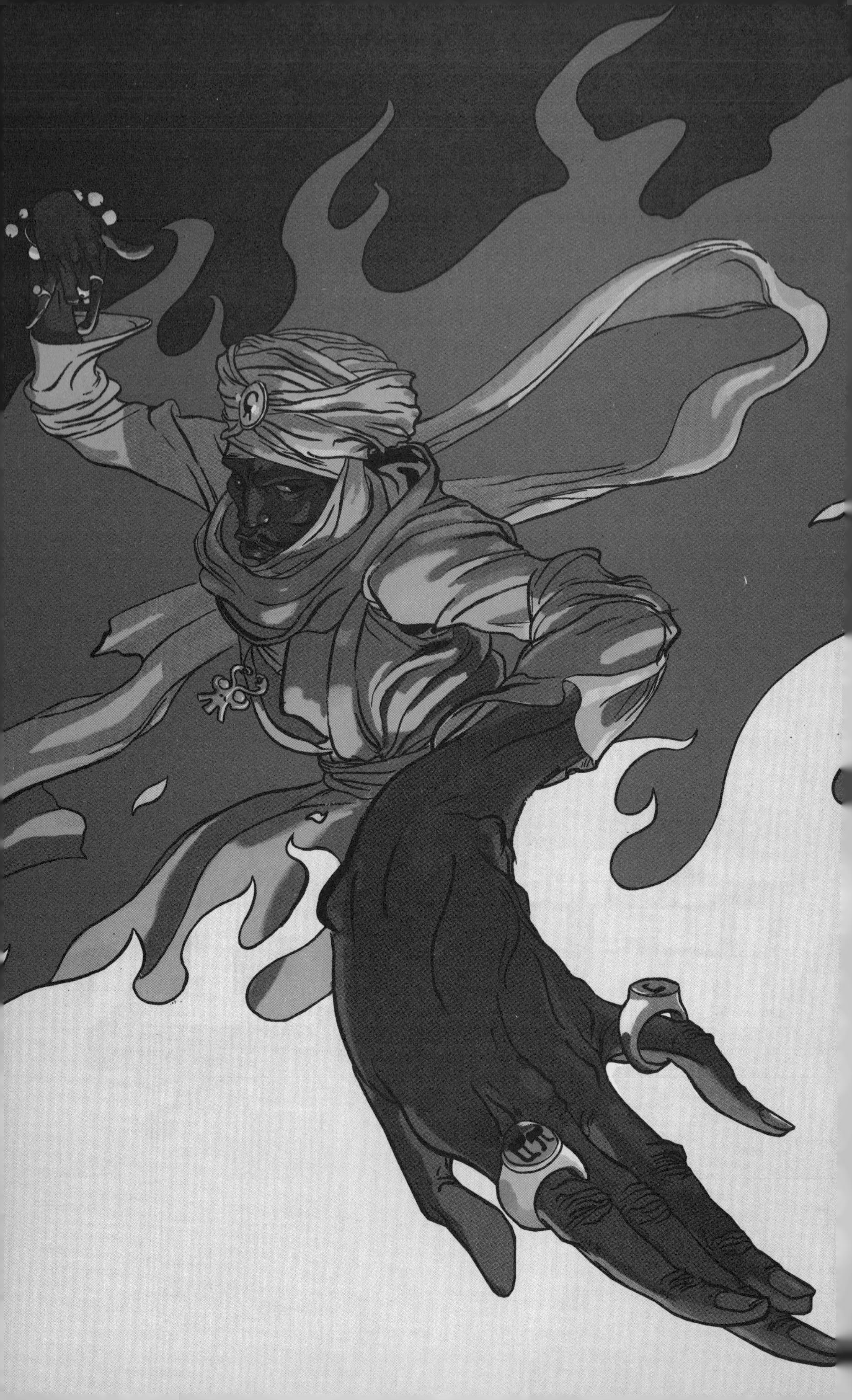

JOHN CONSTANTINE HELLBLAZER

PAPA MIDNITE

Mat Johnson	Writer
Tony Akins	Penciller
Dan Green	Inker
Brian Miller	Colorist
Phil Balsman	Letterer
Ronald Wimberly	Original Series Covers

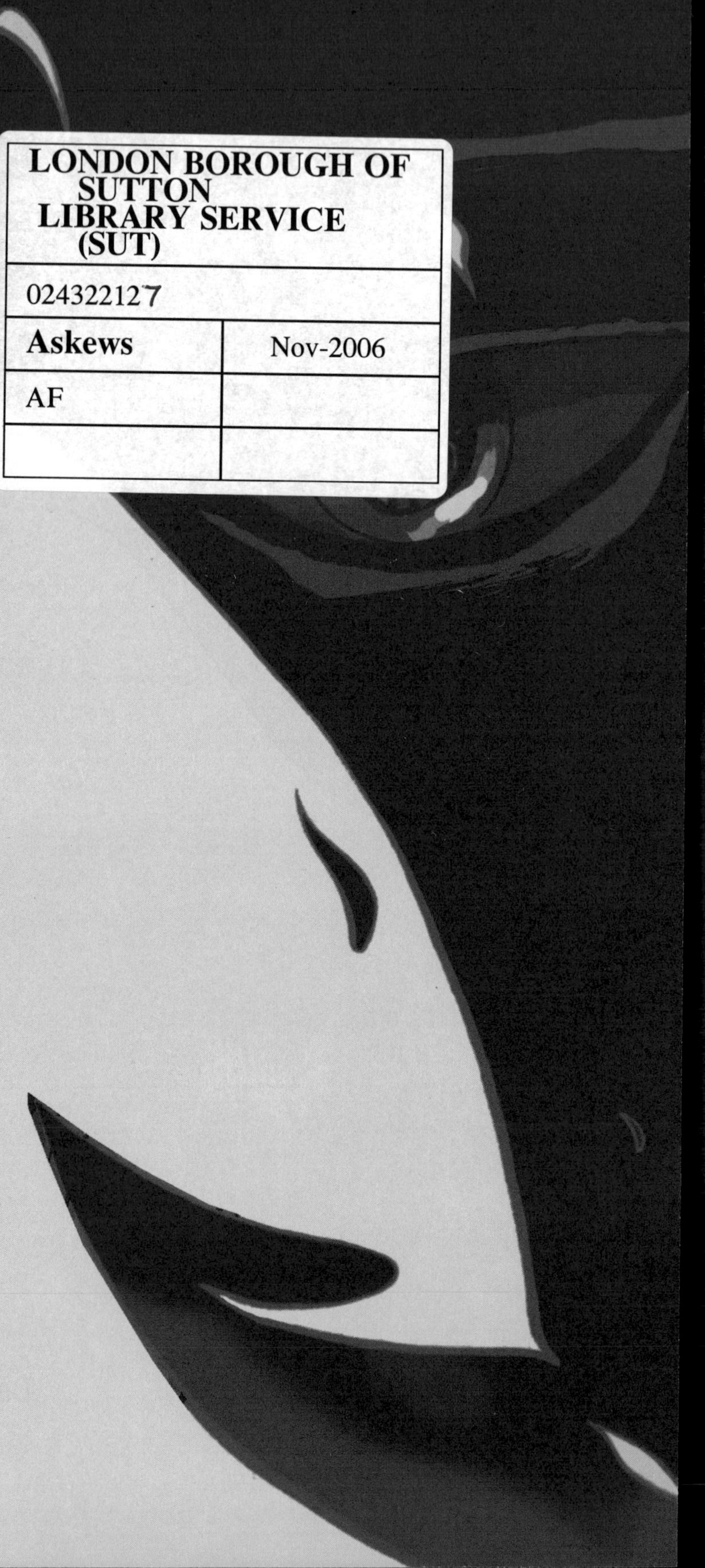

JOHN CONSTANTINE, HELLBLAZER: PAPA MIDNITE

DC Comics, 1700 Broadway, New York, NY 10019.
A Warner Bros. Entertainment Company.
Printed in Canada. First Printing.
ISBN: 1-4012-1003-1
ISBN 13: 978-1-4012-1003-8
Cover illustration by Ronald Wimberly.
Logo design by Nessim Higson.
Publication design by Peter Hamboussi.

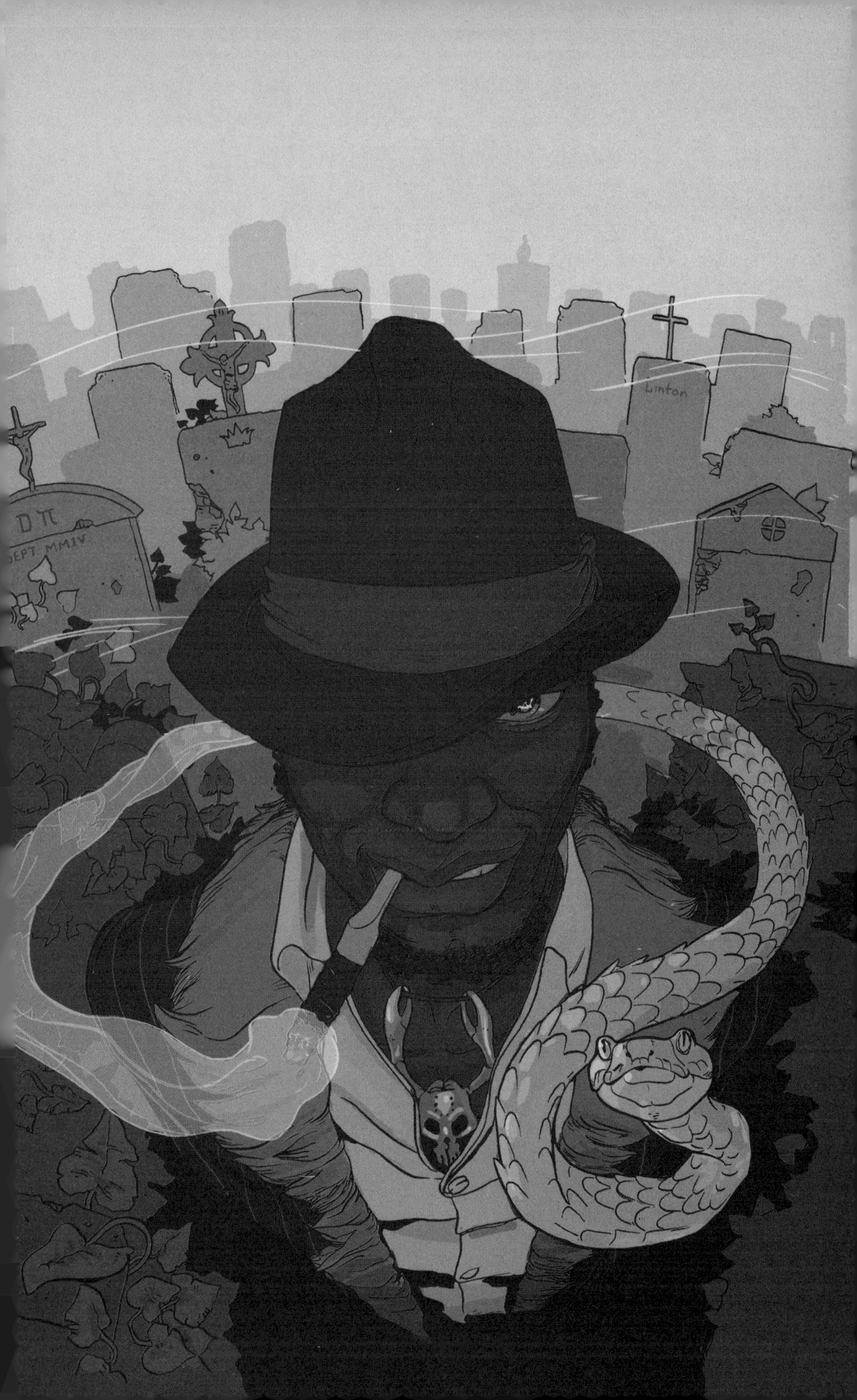
DEPT. MMIV
Linton

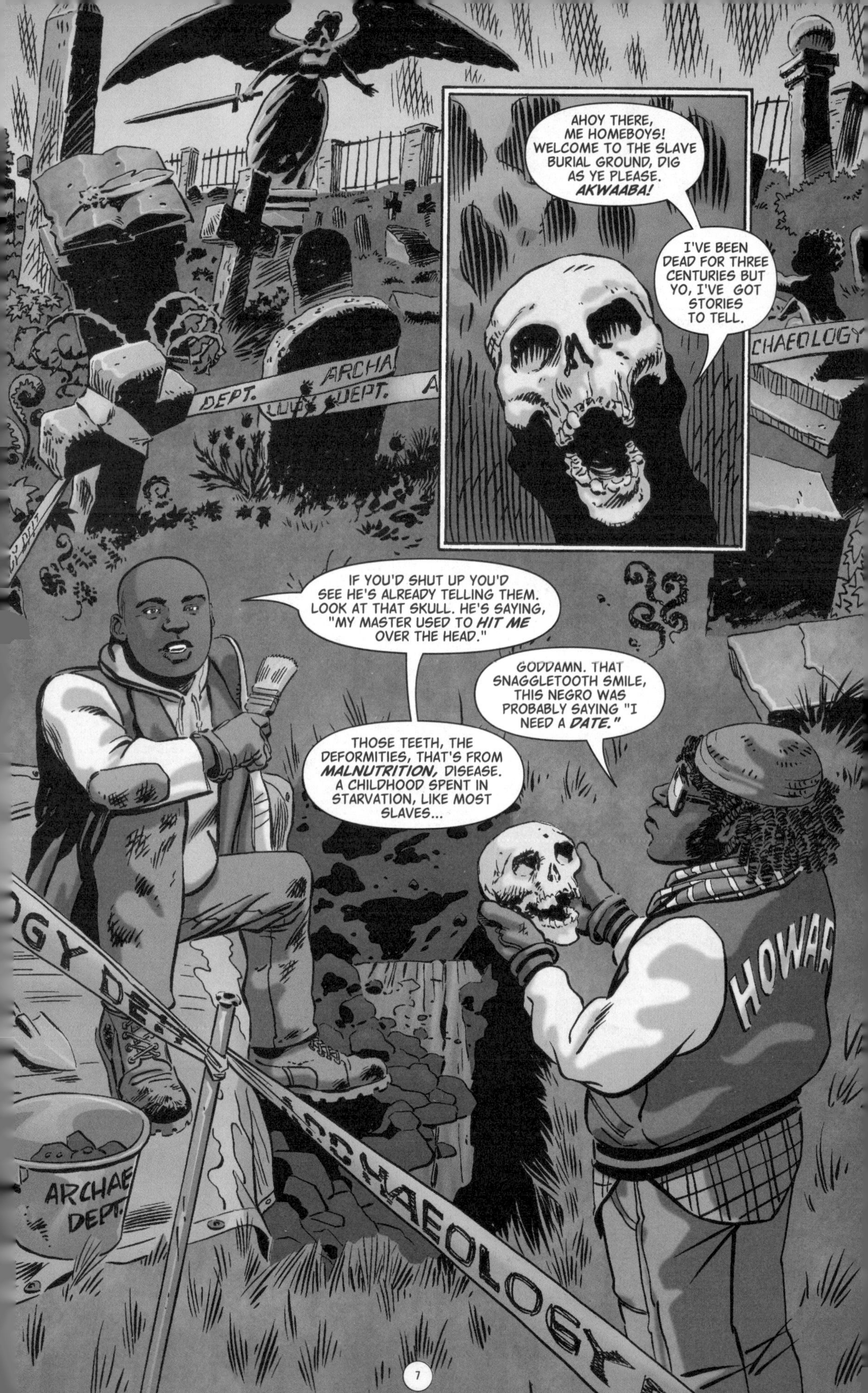
AHOY THERE, ME HOMEBOYS! WELCOME TO THE SLAVE BURIAL GROUND, DIG AS YE PLEASE. AKWAABA!
I'VE BEEN DEAD FOR THREE CENTURIES BUT YO, I'VE GOT STORIES TO TELL.
IF YOU'D SHUT UP YOU'D SEE HE'S ALREADY TELLING THEM. LOOK AT THAT SKULL. HE'S SAYING, "MY MASTER USED TO HIT ME OVER THE HEAD."
THOSE TEETH, THE DEFORMITIES, THAT'S FROM MALNUTRITION, DISEASE. A CHILDHOOD SPENT IN STARVATION, LIKE MOST SLAVES...
GODDAMN. THAT SNAGGLETOOTH SMILE, THIS NEGRO WAS PROBABLY SAYING "I NEED A DATE."
ARCHAE DEPT.
HOWAR

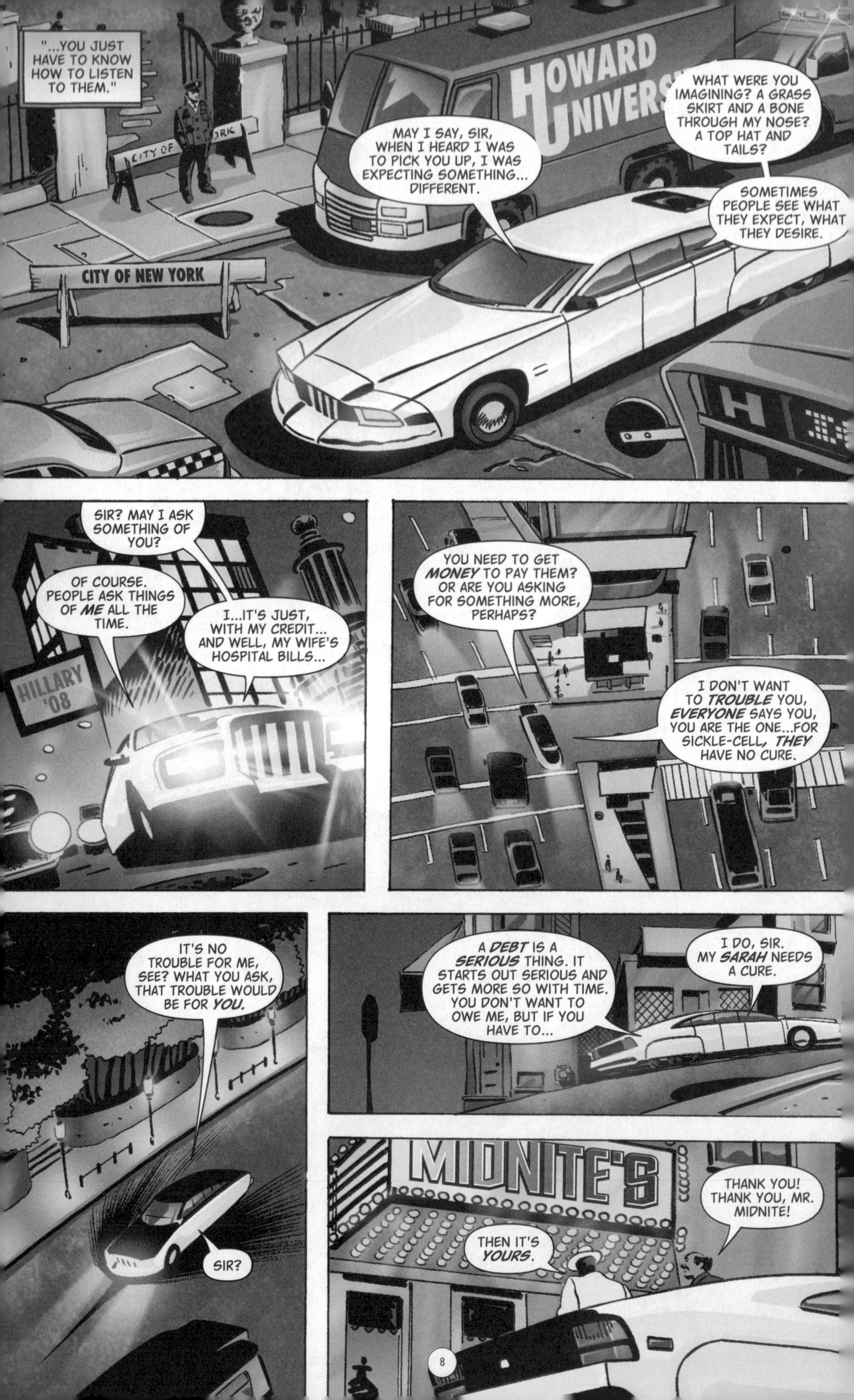
"...YOU JUST HAVE TO KNOW HOW TO LISTEN TO THEM."
HOWARD UNIVERS
CITY OF NEW YORK
MAY I SAY, SIR, WHEN I HEARD I WAS TO PICK YOU UP, I WAS EXPECTING SOMETHING... DIFFERENT.
WHAT WERE YOU IMAGINING? A GRASS SKIRT AND A BONE THROUGH MY NOSE? A TOP HAT AND TAILS?
SOMETIMES PEOPLE SEE WHAT THEY EXPECT, WHAT THEY DESIRE.
SIR? MAY I ASK SOMETHING OF YOU?
OF COURSE. PEOPLE ASK THINGS OF *ME* ALL THE TIME.
I...IT'S JUST, WITH MY CREDIT... AND WELL, MY WIFE'S HOSPITAL BILLS...
HILLARY '08
YOU NEED TO GET *MONEY* TO PAY THEM? OR ARE YOU ASKING FOR SOMETHING MORE, PERHAPS?
I DON'T WANT TO *TROUBLE* YOU, *EVERYONE* SAYS YOU, YOU ARE THE ONE...FOR SICKLE-CELL, *THEY* HAVE NO CURE.
IT'S NO TROUBLE FOR ME, SEE? WHAT YOU ASK, THAT TROUBLE WOULD BE FOR *YOU.*
SIR?
A *DEBT* IS A *SERIOUS* THING. IT STARTS OUT SERIOUS AND GETS MORE SO WITH TIME. YOU DON'T WANT TO OWE ME, BUT IF YOU HAVE TO...
I DO, SIR. MY *SARAH* NEEDS A CURE.
MIDNITE'S
THEN IT'S *YOURS*.
THANK YOU! THANK YOU, MR. MIDNITE!

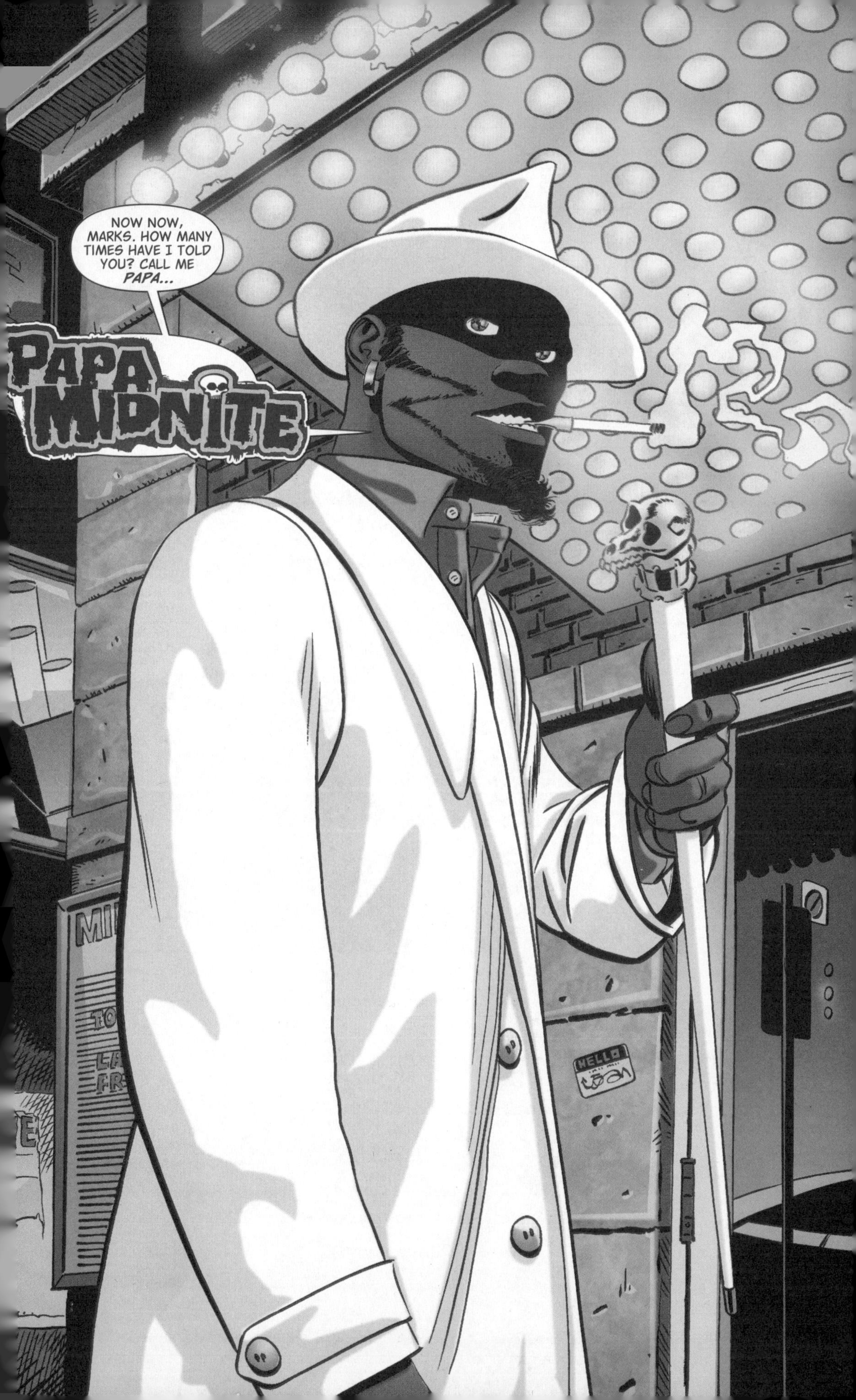
NOW NOW, MARKS. HOW MANY TIMES HAVE I TOLD YOU? CALL ME *PAPA...*
PAPA MIDNITE
HELLO

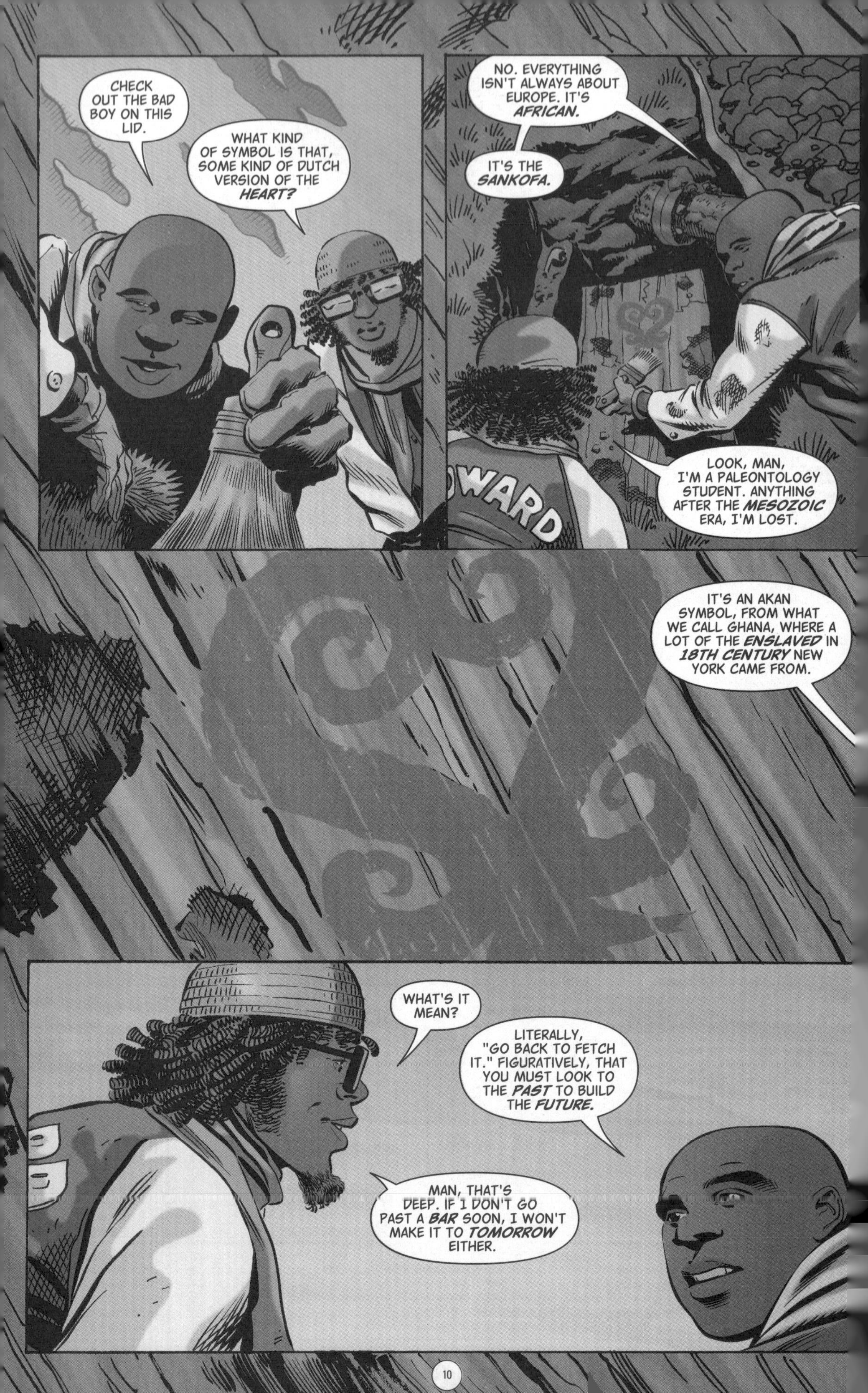
CHECK OUT THE BAD BOY ON THIS LID.
WHAT KIND OF SYMBOL IS THAT, SOME KIND OF DUTCH VERSION OF THE HEART?
NO. EVERYTHING ISN'T ALWAYS ABOUT EUROPE. IT'S AFRICAN.
IT'S THE SANKOFA.
LOOK, MAN, I'M A PALEONTOLOGY STUDENT. ANYTHING AFTER THE MESOZOIC ERA, I'M LOST.
WARD
IT'S AN AKAN SYMBOL, FROM WHAT WE CALL GHANA, WHERE A LOT OF THE ENSLAVED IN 18TH CENTURY NEW YORK CAME FROM.
WHAT'S IT MEAN?
LITERALLY, "GO BACK TO FETCH IT." FIGURATIVELY, THAT YOU MUST LOOK TO THE PAST TO BUILD THE FUTURE.
MAN, THAT'S DEEP. IF I DON'T GO PAST A BAR SOON, I WON'T MAKE IT TO TOMORROW EITHER.

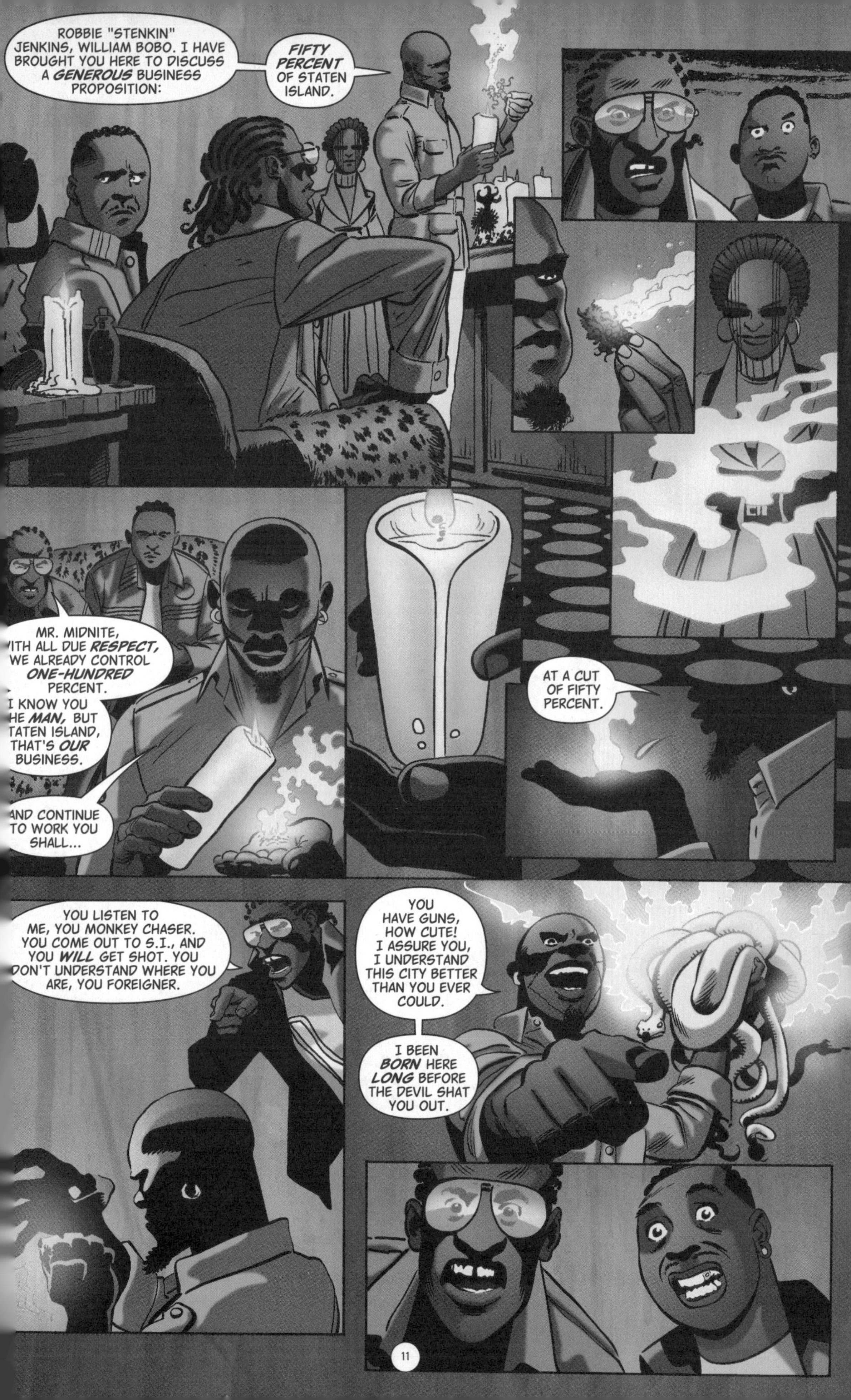
ROBBIE "STENKIN" JENKINS, WILLIAM BOBO. I HAVE BROUGHT YOU HERE TO DISCUSS A GENEROUS BUSINESS PROPOSITION:
FIFTY PERCENT OF STATEN ISLAND.
MR. MIDNITE, VITH ALL DUE RESPECT, WE ALREADY CONTROL ONE-HUNDRED PERCENT.
I KNOW YOU HE MAN, BUT TATEN ISLAND, THAT'S OUR BUSINESS.
AND CONTINUE TO WORK YOU SHALL...
AT A CUT OF FIFTY PERCENT.
YOU LISTEN TO ME, YOU MONKEY CHASER. YOU COME OUT TO S.I., AND YOU WILL GET SHOT. YOU DON'T UNDERSTAND WHERE YOU ARE, YOU FOREIGNER.
YOU HAVE GUNS, HOW CUTE! I ASSURE YOU, I UNDERSTAND THIS CITY BETTER THAN YOU EVER COULD.
I BEEN BORN HERE LONG BEFORE THE DEVIL SHAT YOU OUT.

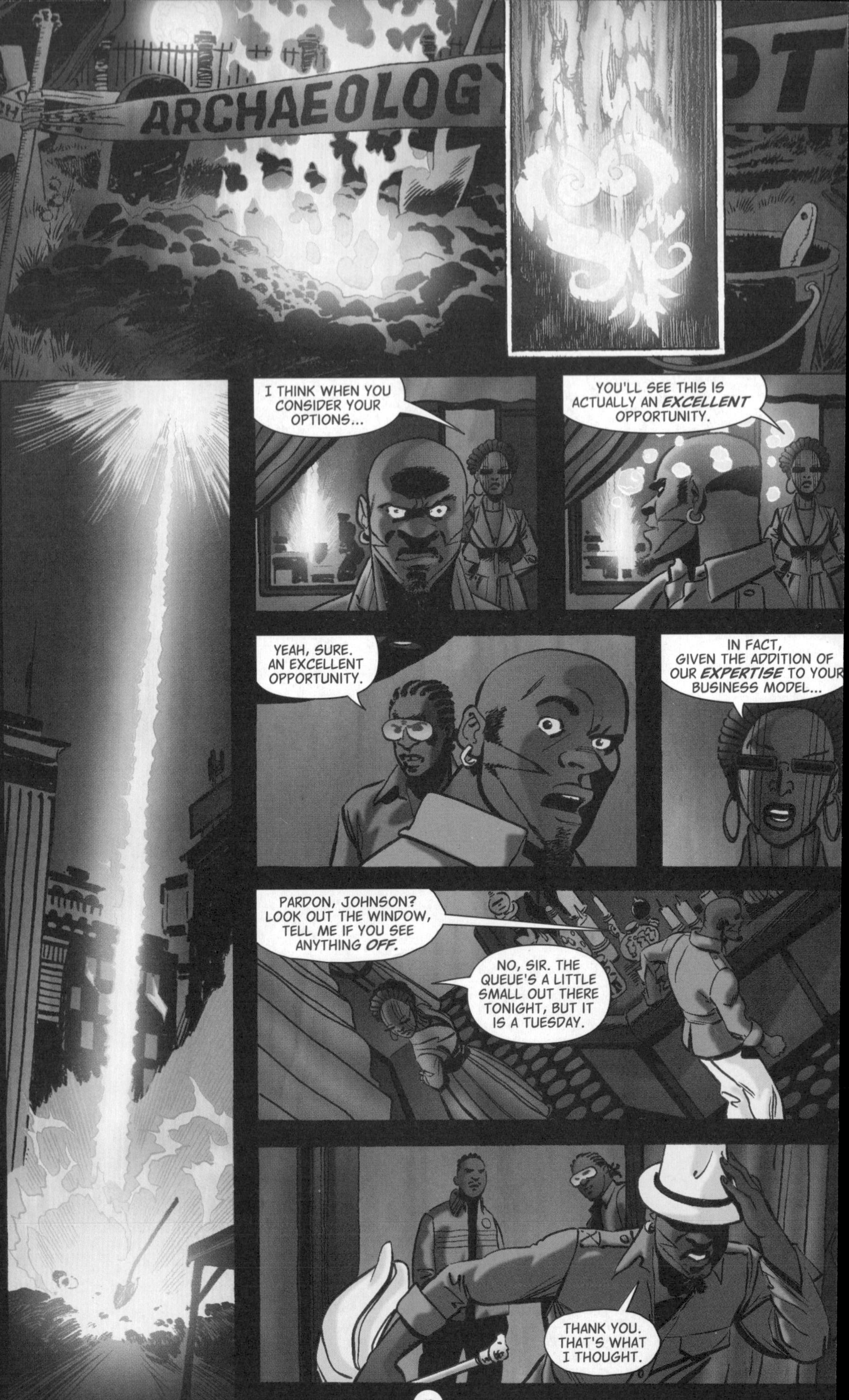
ARCHAEOLOGY
I THINK WHEN YOU CONSIDER YOUR OPTIONS...
YOU'LL SEE THIS IS ACTUALLY AN EXCELLENT OPPORTUNITY.
YEAH, SURE. AN EXCELLENT OPPORTUNITY.
IN FACT, GIVEN THE ADDITION OF OUR EXPERTISE TO YOUR BUSINESS MODEL...
PARDON, JOHNSON? LOOK OUT THE WINDOW, TELL ME IF YOU SEE ANYTHING OFF.
NO, SIR. THE QUEUE'S A LITTLE SMALL OUT THERE TONIGHT, BUT IT IS A TUESDAY.
THANK YOU. THAT'S WHAT I THOUGHT.

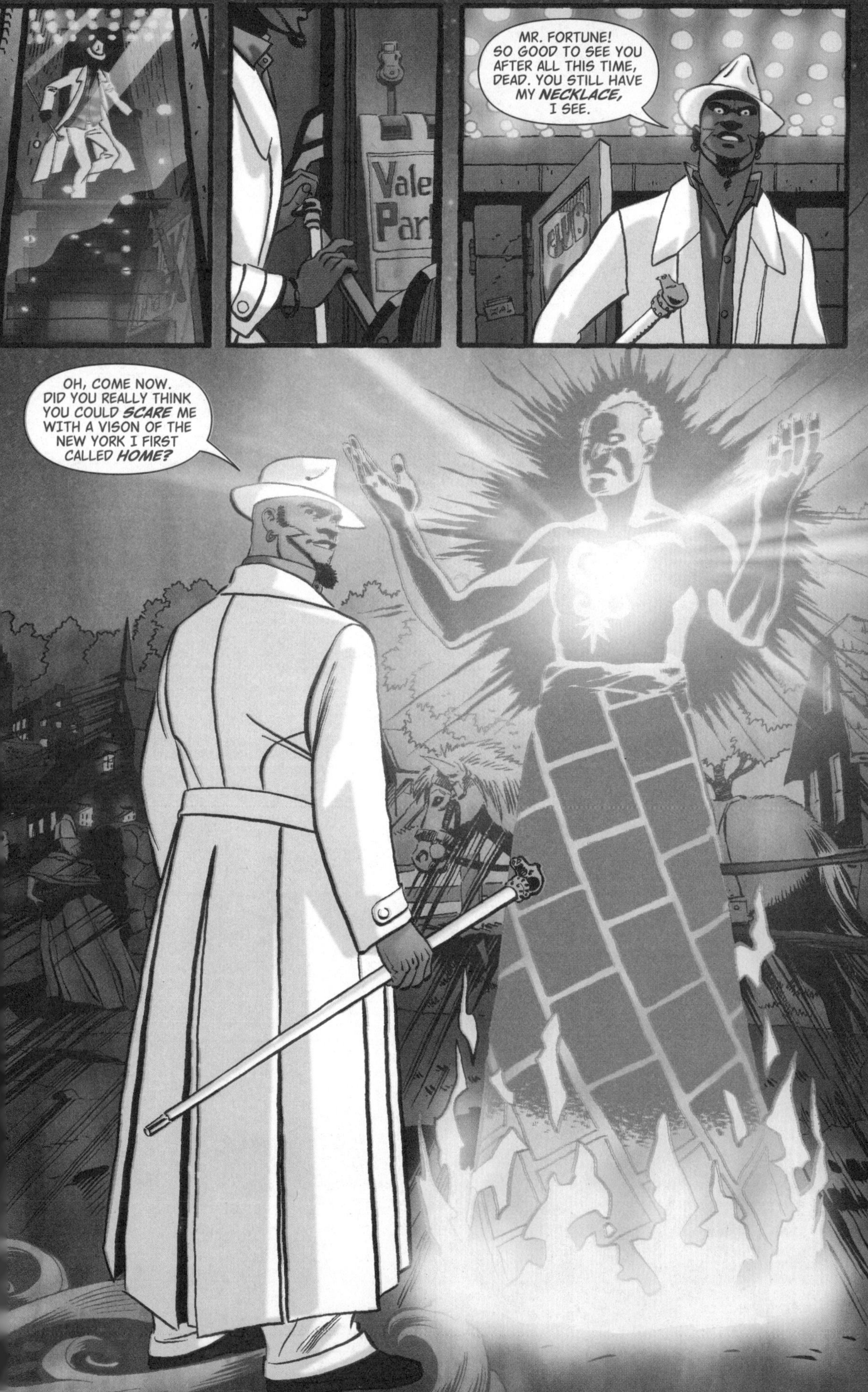
Vale
Par
MR. FORTUNE! SO GOOD TO SEE YOU AFTER ALL THIS TIME, DEAD. YOU STILL HAVE MY NECKLACE, I SEE.
OH, COME NOW. DID YOU REALLY THINK YOU COULD SCARE ME WITH A VISON OF THE NEW YORK I FIRST CALLED HOME?

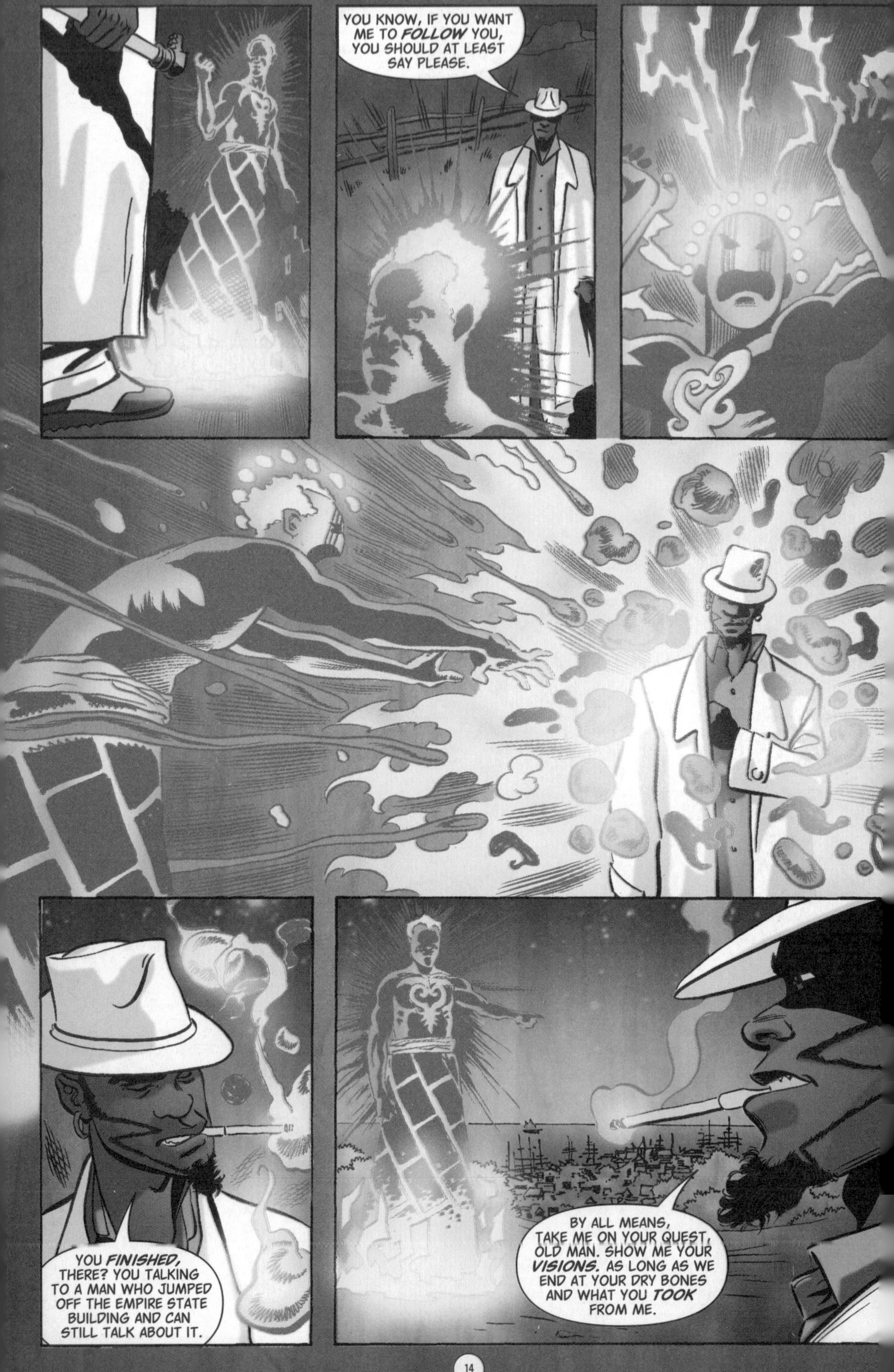
YOU KNOW, IF YOU WANT ME TO FOLLOW YOU, YOU SHOULD AT LEAST SAY PLEASE.
YOU FINISHED, THERE? YOU TALKING TO A MAN WHO JUMPED OFF THE EMPIRE STATE BUILDING AND CAN STILL TALK ABOUT IT.
BY ALL MEANS, TAKE ME ON YOUR QUEST, OLD MAN. SHOW ME YOUR VISIONS. AS LONG AS WE END AT YOUR DRY BONES AND WHAT YOU TOOK FROM ME.

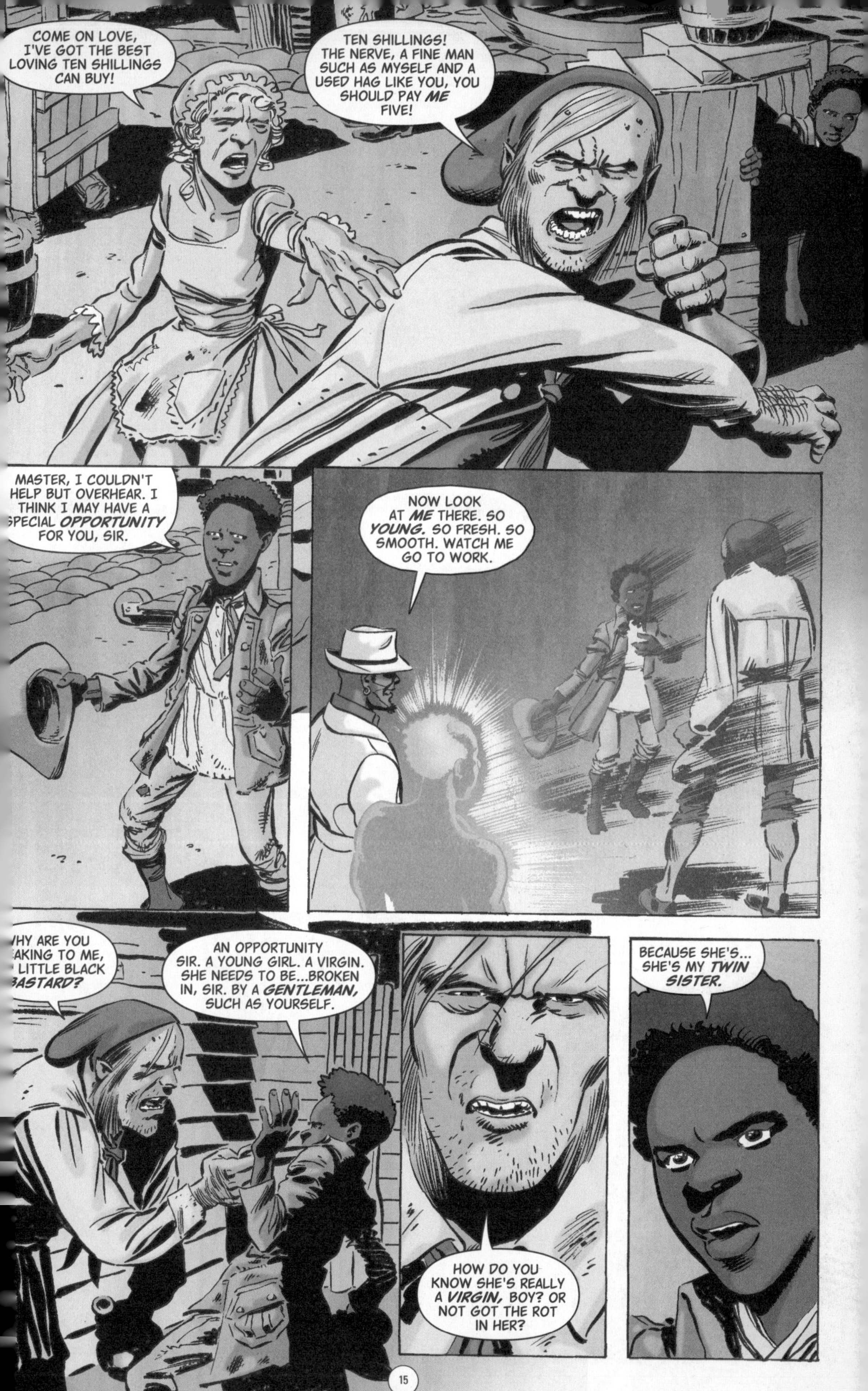

COME ON LOVE, I'VE GOT THE BEST LOVING TEN SHILLINGS CAN BUY!
TEN SHILLINGS! THE NERVE, A FINE MAN SUCH AS MYSELF AND A USED HAG LIKE YOU, YOU SHOULD PAY *ME* FIVE!
MASTER, I COULDN'T HELP BUT OVERHEAR. I THINK I MAY HAVE A SPECIAL *OPPORTUNITY* FOR YOU, SIR.
NOW LOOK AT *ME* THERE. SO *YOUNG.* SO FRESH. SO SMOOTH. WATCH ME GO TO WORK.
HY ARE YOU AKING TO ME, LITTLE BLACK *BASTARD?*
AN OPPORTUNITY SIR. A YOUNG GIRL. A VIRGIN. SHE NEEDS TO BE...BROKEN IN, SIR. BY A *GENTLEMAN,* SUCH AS YOURSELF.
HOW DO YOU KNOW SHE'S REALLY A *VIRGIN,* BOY? OR NOT GOT THE ROT IN HER?
BECAUSE SHE'S... SHE'S MY *TWIN SISTER.*

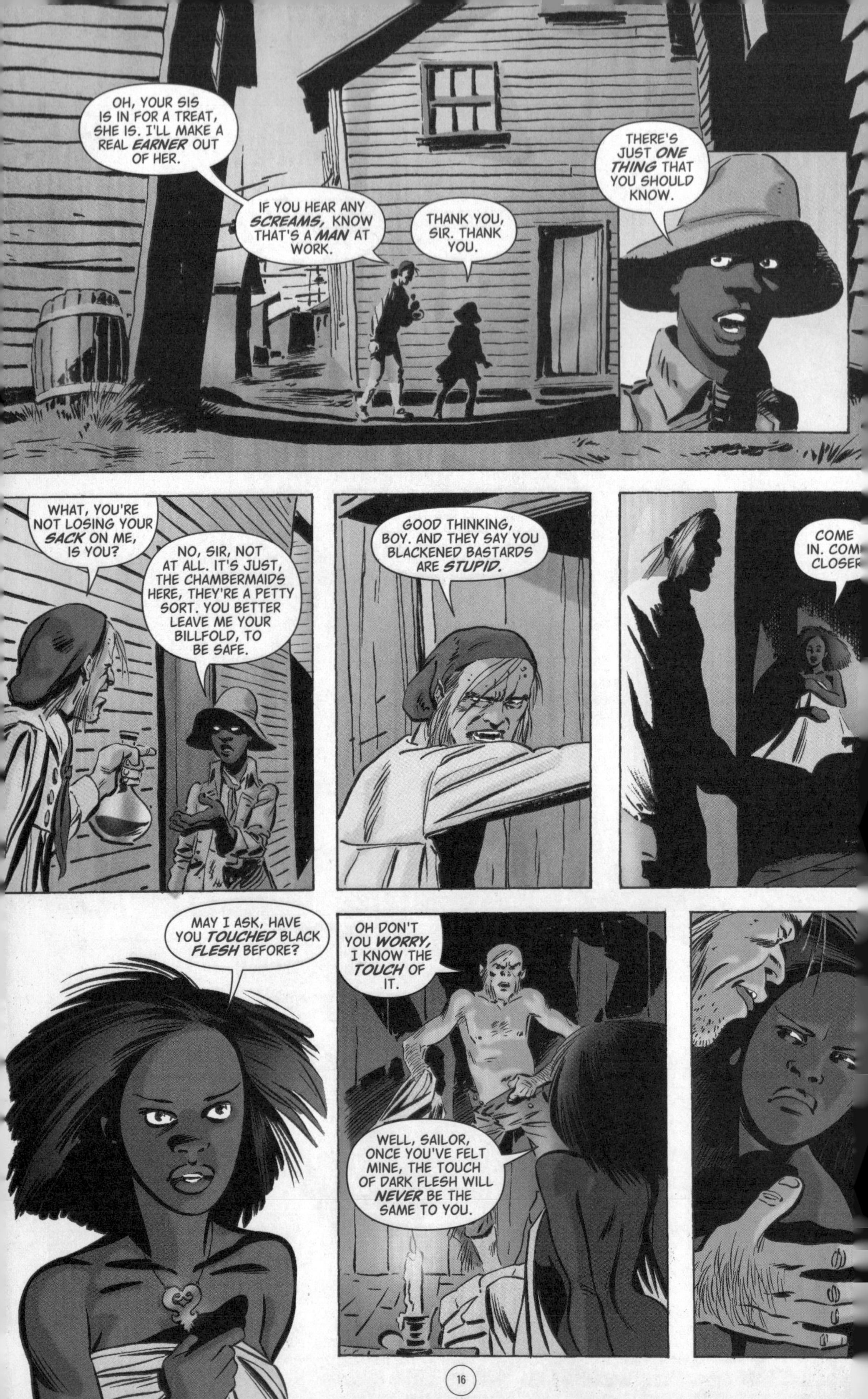

OH, YOUR SIS IS IN FOR A TREAT, SHE IS. I'LL MAKE A REAL EARNER OUT OF HER.
IF YOU HEAR ANY SCREAMS, KNOW THAT'S A MAN AT WORK.
THANK YOU, SIR. THANK YOU.
THERE'S JUST ONE THING THAT YOU SHOULD KNOW.
WHAT, YOU'RE NOT LOSING YOUR SACK ON ME, IS YOU?
NO, SIR, NOT AT ALL. IT'S JUST, THE CHAMBERMAIDS HERE, THEY'RE A PETTY SORT. YOU BETTER LEAVE ME YOUR BILLFOLD, TO BE SAFE.
GOOD THINKING, BOY. AND THEY SAY YOU BLACKENED BASTARDS ARE STUPID.
COME IN. COM CLOSER
MAY I ASK, HAVE YOU TOUCHED BLACK FLESH BEFORE?
OH DON'T YOU WORRY, I KNOW THE TOUCH OF IT.
WELL, SAILOR, ONCE YOU'VE FELT MINE, THE TOUCH OF DARK FLESH WILL NEVER BE THE SAME TO YOU.

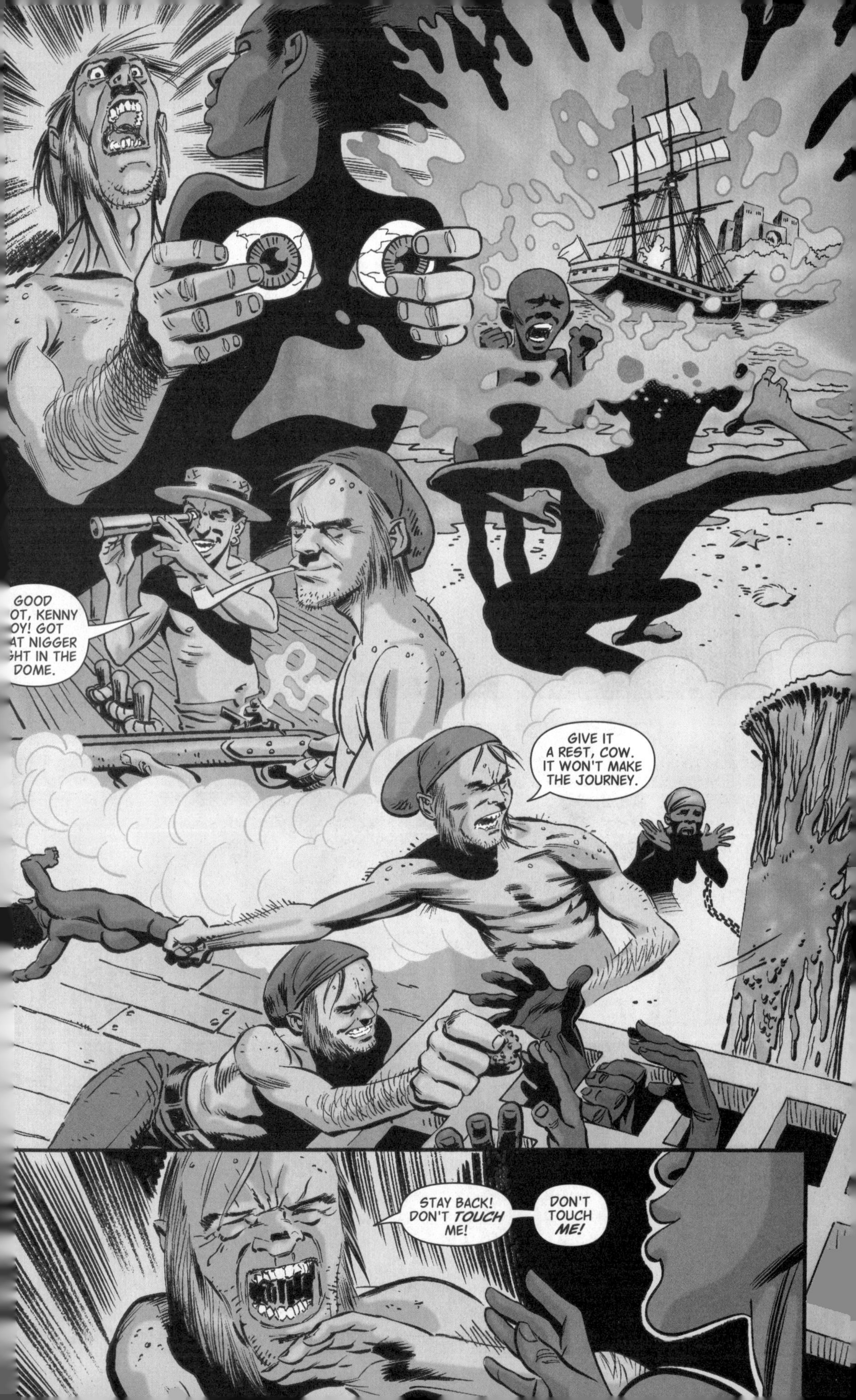
GOOD OT, KENNY OY! GOT AT NIGGER GHT IN THE DOME.
GIVE IT A REST, COW. IT WON'T MAKE THE JOURNEY.
STAY BACK! DON'T *TOUCH* ME!
DON'T TOUCH ***ME!***

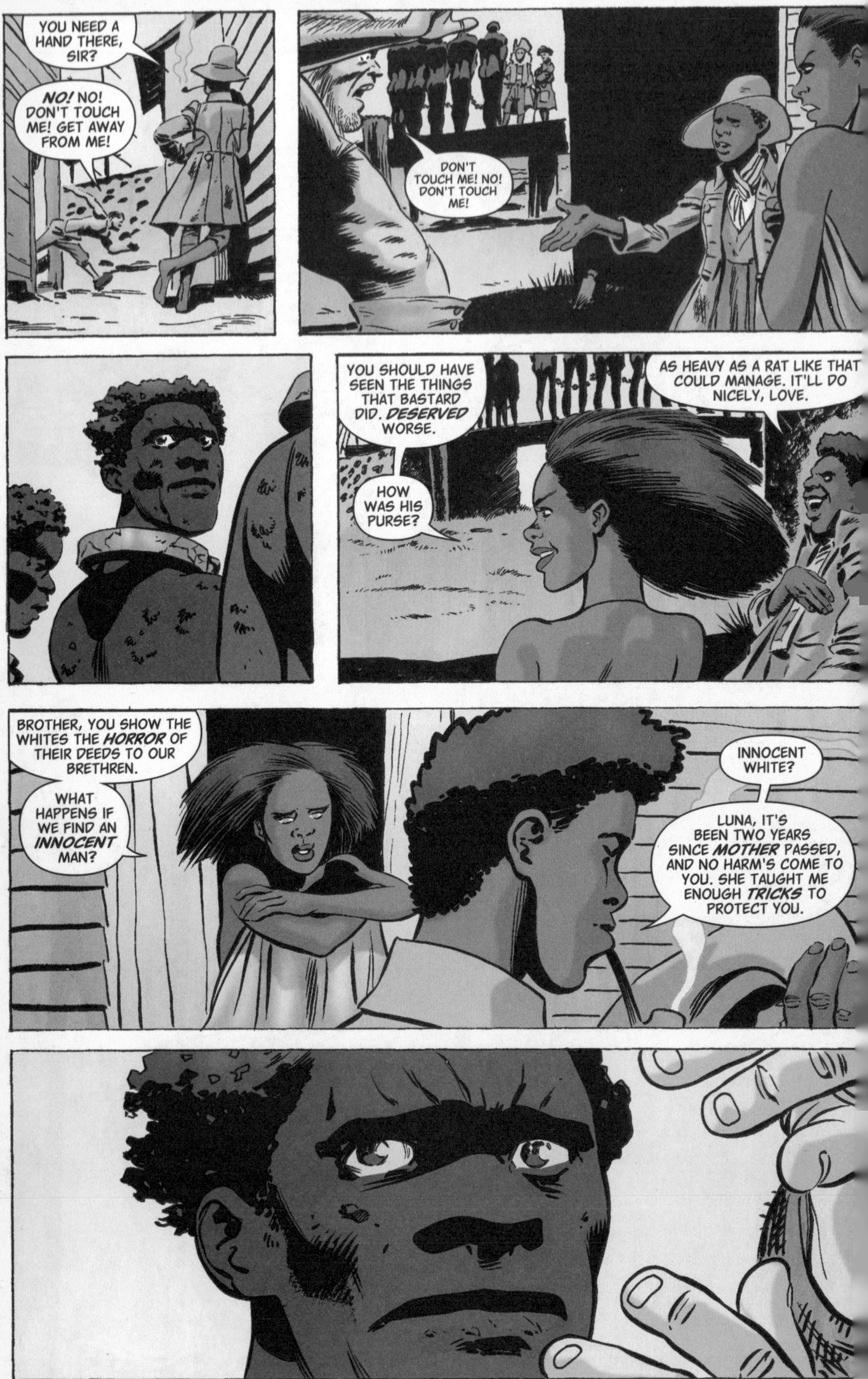
YOU NEED A HAND THERE, SIR?
NO! NO! DON'T TOUCH ME! GET AWAY FROM ME!
DON'T TOUCH ME! NO! DON'T TOUCH ME!
YOU SHOULD HAVE SEEN THE THINGS THAT BASTARD DID. DESERVED WORSE.
HOW WAS HIS PURSE?
AS HEAVY AS A RAT LIKE THAT COULD MANAGE. IT'LL DO NICELY, LOVE.
BROTHER, YOU SHOW THE WHITES THE HORROR OF THEIR DEEDS TO OUR BRETHREN.
WHAT HAPPENS IF WE FIND AN INNOCENT MAN?
INNOCENT WHITE?
LUNA, IT'S BEEN TWO YEARS SINCE MOTHER PASSED, AND NO HARM'S COME TO YOU. SHE TAUGHT ME ENOUGH TRICKS TO PROTECT YOU.

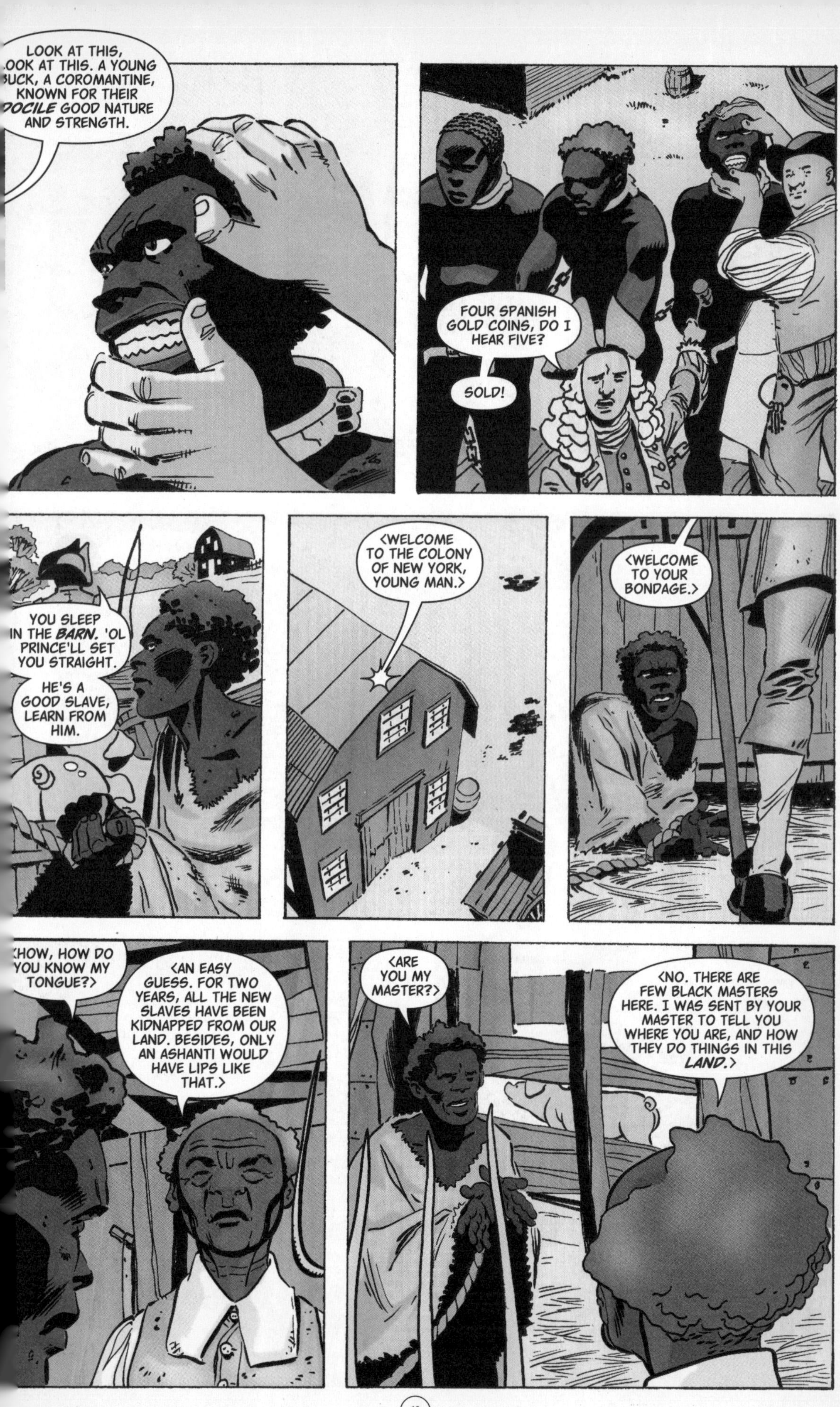
LOOK AT THIS, LOOK AT THIS. A YOUNG BUCK, A COROMANTINE, KNOWN FOR THEIR DOCILE GOOD NATURE AND STRENGTH.
FOUR SPANISH GOLD COINS, DO I HEAR FIVE?
SOLD!
YOU SLEEP IN THE BARN. 'OL PRINCE'LL SET YOU STRAIGHT.
HE'S A GOOD SLAVE, LEARN FROM HIM.
<WELCOME TO THE COLONY OF NEW YORK, YOUNG MAN.>
<WELCOME TO YOUR BONDAGE.>
<HOW, HOW DO YOU KNOW MY TONGUE?>
<AN EASY GUESS. FOR TWO YEARS, ALL THE NEW SLAVES HAVE BEEN KIDNAPPED FROM OUR LAND. BESIDES, ONLY AN ASHANTI WOULD HAVE LIPS LIKE THAT.>
<ARE YOU MY MASTER?>
<NO. THERE ARE FEW BLACK MASTERS HERE. I WAS SENT BY YOUR MASTER TO TELL YOU WHERE YOU ARE, AND HOW THEY DO THINGS IN THIS LAND.>

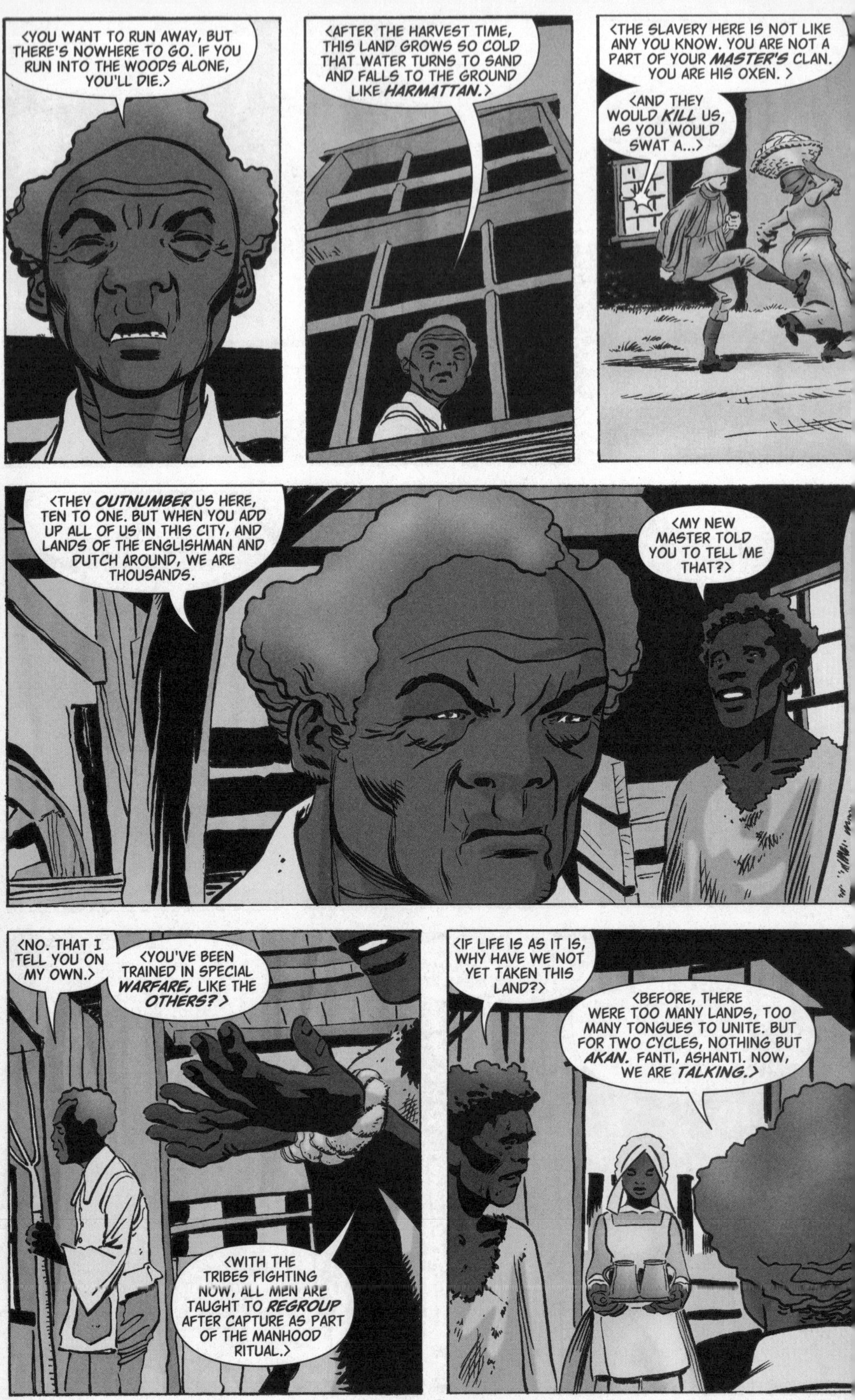

<YOU WANT TO RUN AWAY, BUT THERE'S NOWHERE TO GO. IF YOU RUN INTO THE WOODS ALONE, YOU'LL DIE.>
<AFTER THE HARVEST TIME, THIS LAND GROWS SO COLD THAT WATER TURNS TO SAND AND FALLS TO THE GROUND LIKE HARMATTAN.>
<THE SLAVERY HERE IS NOT LIKE ANY YOU KNOW. YOU ARE NOT A PART OF YOUR MASTER'S CLAN. YOU ARE HIS OXEN. >
<AND THEY WOULD KILL US, AS YOU WOULD SWAT A...>
<THEY OUTNUMBER US HERE, TEN TO ONE. BUT WHEN YOU ADD UP ALL OF US IN THIS CITY, AND LANDS OF THE ENGLISHMAN AND DUTCH AROUND, WE ARE THOUSANDS.
<MY NEW MASTER TOLD YOU TO TELL ME THAT?>
<NO. THAT I TELL YOU ON MY OWN.>
<YOU'VE BEEN TRAINED IN SPECIAL WARFARE, LIKE THE OTHERS?>
<WITH THE TRIBES FIGHTING NOW, ALL MEN ARE TAUGHT TO REGROUP AFTER CAPTURE AS PART OF THE MANHOOD RITUAL.>
<IF LIFE IS AS IT IS, WHY HAVE WE NOT YET TAKEN THIS LAND?>
<BEFORE, THERE WERE TOO MANY LANDS, TOO MANY TONGUES TO UNITE. BUT FOR TWO CYCLES, NOTHING BUT AKAN. FANTI, ASHANTI. NOW, WE ARE TALKING.>

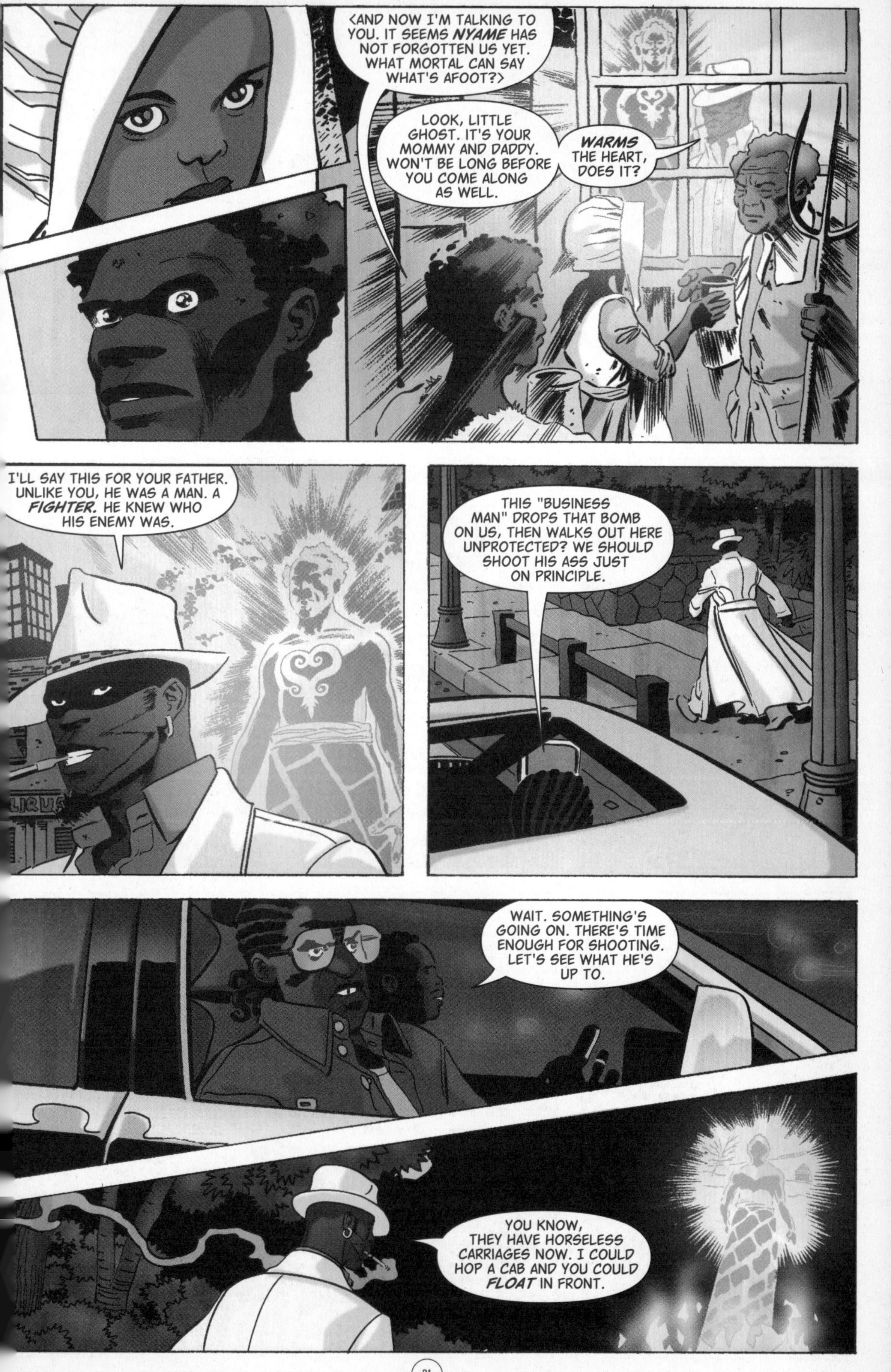
<AND NOW I'M TALKING TO YOU. IT SEEMS NYAME HAS NOT FORGOTTEN US YET. WHAT MORTAL CAN SAY WHAT'S AFOOT?>
LOOK, LITTLE GHOST. IT'S YOUR MOMMY AND DADDY. WON'T BE LONG BEFORE YOU COME ALONG AS WELL.
WARMS THE HEART, DOES IT?
I'LL SAY THIS FOR YOUR FATHER. UNLIKE YOU, HE WAS A MAN. A FIGHTER. HE KNEW WHO HIS ENEMY WAS.
THIS "BUSINESS MAN" DROPS THAT BOMB ON US, THEN WALKS OUT HERE UNPROTECTED? WE SHOULD SHOOT HIS ASS JUST ON PRINCIPLE.
WAIT. SOMETHING'S GOING ON. THERE'S TIME ENOUGH FOR SHOOTING. LET'S SEE WHAT HE'S UP TO.
YOU KNOW, THEY HAVE HORSELESS CARRIAGES NOW. I COULD HOP A CAB AND YOU COULD FLOAT IN FRONT.

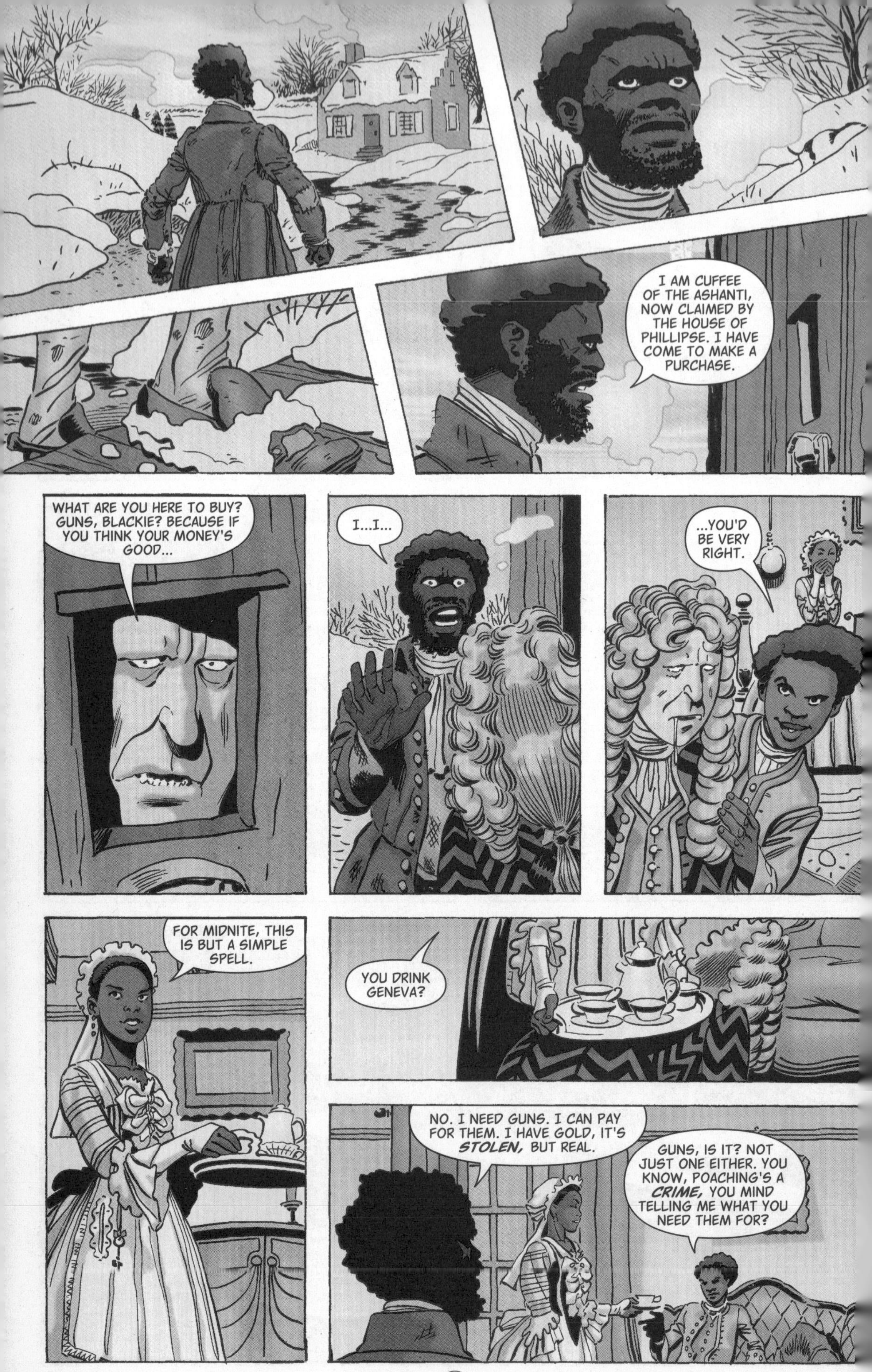
I AM CUFFEE OF THE ASHANTI, NOW CLAIMED BY THE HOUSE OF PHILLIPSE. I HAVE COME TO MAKE A PURCHASE.
WHAT ARE YOU HERE TO BUY? GUNS, BLACKIE? BECAUSE IF YOU THINK YOUR MONEY'S GOOD...
I...I...
...YOU'D BE VERY RIGHT.
FOR MIDNITE, THIS IS BUT A SIMPLE SPELL.
YOU DRINK GENEVA?
NO. I NEED GUNS. I CAN PAY FOR THEM. I HAVE GOLD, IT'S STOLEN, BUT REAL.
GUNS, IS IT? NOT JUST ONE EITHER. YOU KNOW, POACHING'S A CRIME, YOU MIND TELLING ME WHAT YOU NEED THEM FOR?

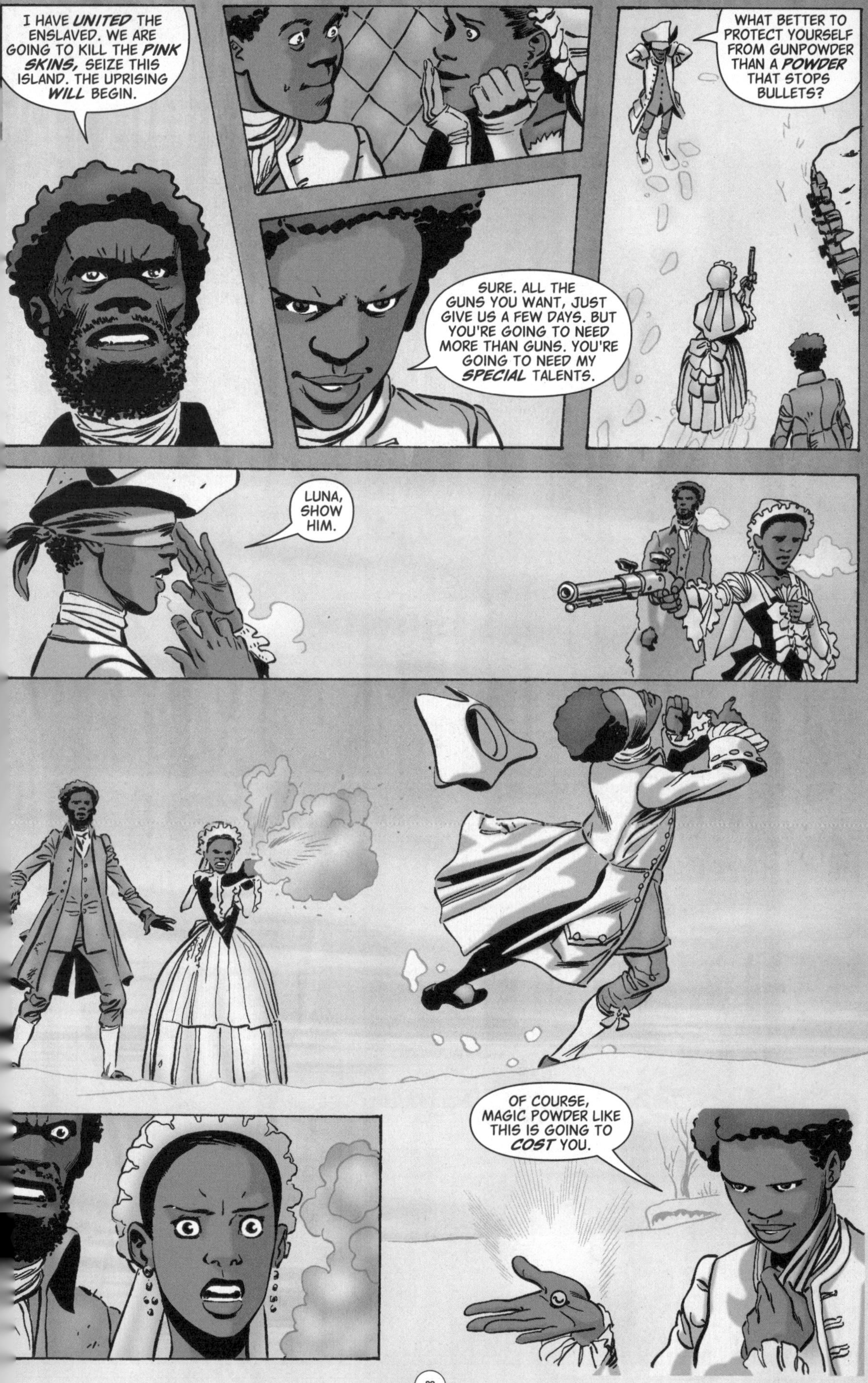
I HAVE UNITED THE ENSLAVED. WE ARE GOING TO KILL THE PINK SKINS, SEIZE THIS ISLAND. THE UPRISING WILL BEGIN.
SURE. ALL THE GUNS YOU WANT, JUST GIVE US A FEW DAYS. BUT YOU'RE GOING TO NEED MORE THAN GUNS. YOU'RE GOING TO NEED MY SPECIAL TALENTS.
WHAT BETTER TO PROTECT YOURSELF FROM GUNPOWDER THAN A POWDER THAT STOPS BULLETS?
LUNA, SHOW HIM.
OF COURSE, MAGIC POWDER LIKE THIS IS GOING TO COST YOU.

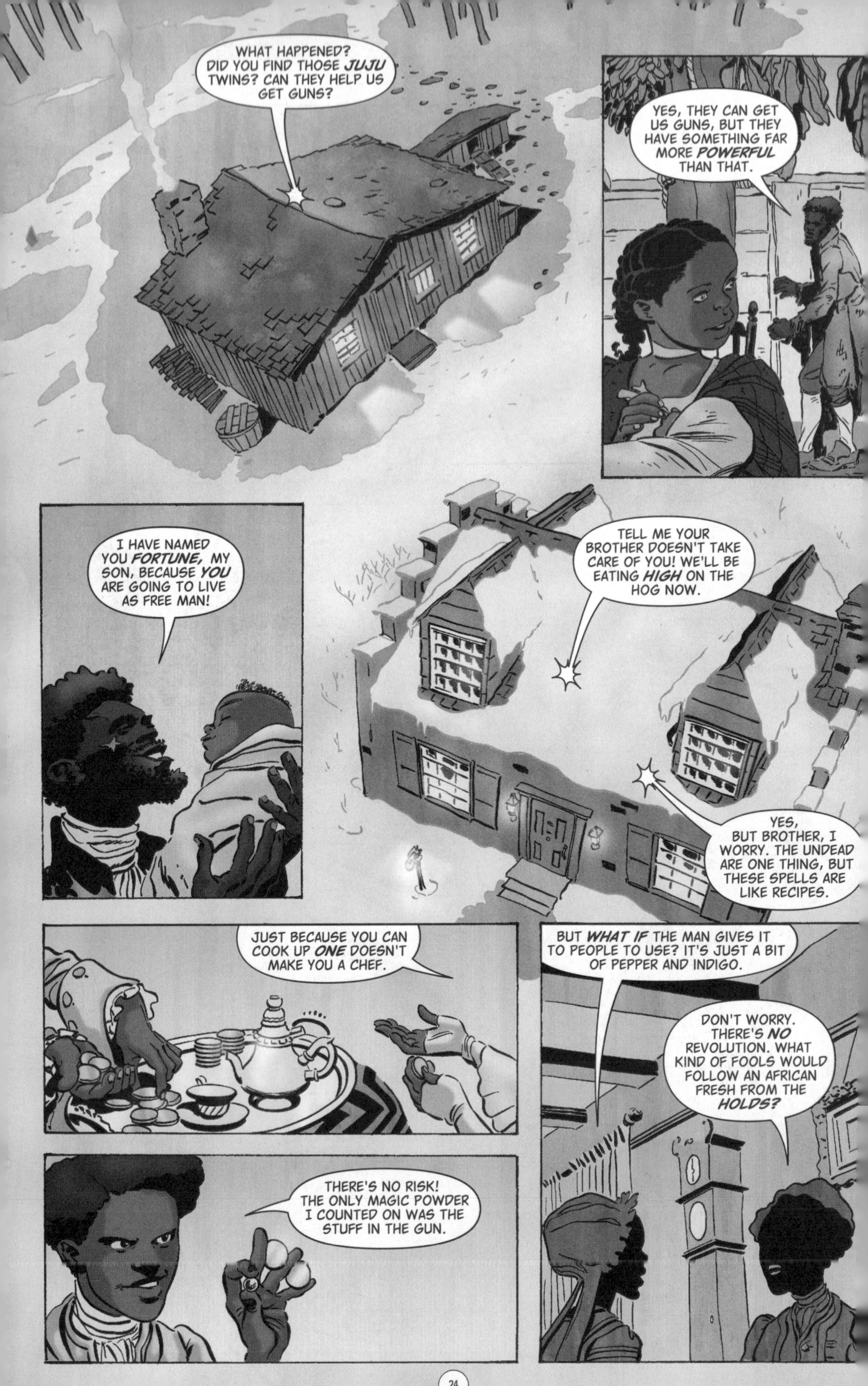
WHAT HAPPENED? DID YOU FIND THOSE JUJU TWINS? CAN THEY HELP US GET GUNS?
YES, THEY CAN GET US GUNS, BUT THEY HAVE SOMETHING FAR MORE POWERFUL THAN THAT.
I HAVE NAMED YOU FORTUNE, MY SON, BECAUSE YOU ARE GOING TO LIVE AS FREE MAN!
TELL ME YOUR BROTHER DOESN'T TAKE CARE OF YOU! WE'LL BE EATING HIGH ON THE HOG NOW.
YES, BUT BROTHER, I WORRY. THE UNDEAD ARE ONE THING, BUT THESE SPELLS ARE LIKE RECIPES.
JUST BECAUSE YOU CAN COOK UP ONE DOESN'T MAKE YOU A CHEF.
BUT WHAT IF THE MAN GIVES IT TO PEOPLE TO USE? IT'S JUST A BIT OF PEPPER AND INDIGO.
DON'T WORRY. THERE'S NO REVOLUTION. WHAT KIND OF FOOLS WOULD FOLLOW AN AFRICAN FRESH FROM THE HOLDS?
THERE'S NO RISK! THE ONLY MAGIC POWDER I COUNTED ON WAS THE STUFF IN THE GUN.

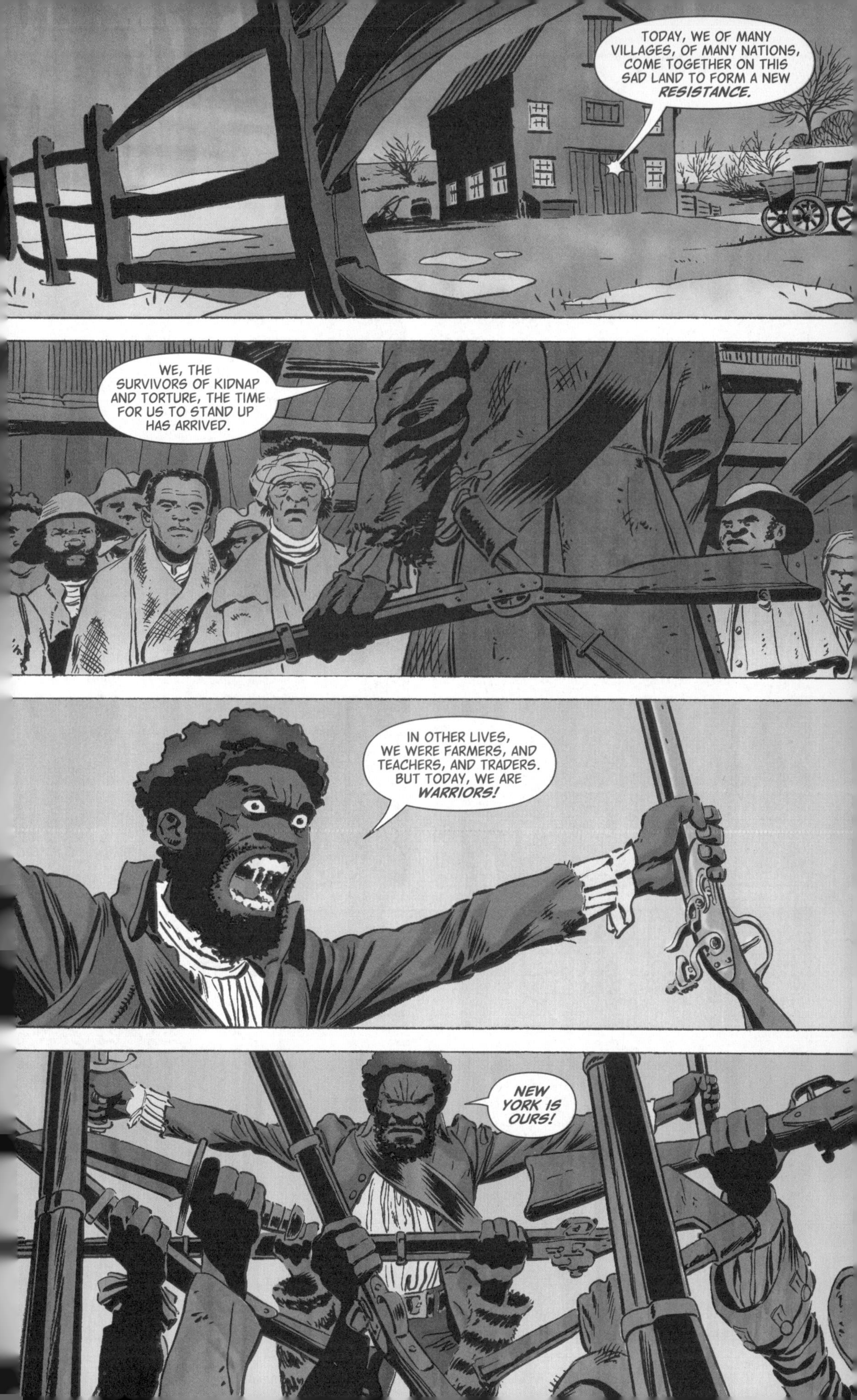
TODAY, WE OF MANY VILLAGES, OF MANY NATIONS, COME TOGETHER ON THIS SAD LAND TO FORM A NEW *RESISTANCE.*
WE, THE SURVIVORS OF KIDNAP AND TORTURE, THE TIME FOR US TO STAND UP HAS ARRIVED.
IN OTHER LIVES, WE WERE FARMERS, AND TEACHERS, AND TRADERS. BUT TODAY, WE ARE *WARRIORS!*
NEW YORK IS OURS!

COLONY LIFE IS SO *STRANGE* TO ME. DON'T YOU GET NERVOUS, WITH THEM AROUND YOU ALL THE TIME?

YOU SEE, THE NEGRO IS *DOCILE* BECAUSE GOD MADE HIM TO *SERVE*.

EXACTLY. JUST AS GOD GAVE US THE *CHICKEN* FOR ITS EGGS.

RIGHT. OR AS GOD GIVES US *LEECHES* TO BLEED OUR ILLS.

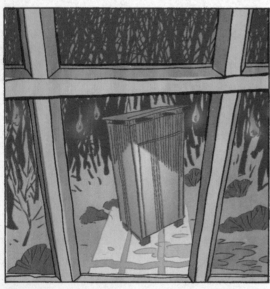

I SAY, IS THAT *NORMAL*?

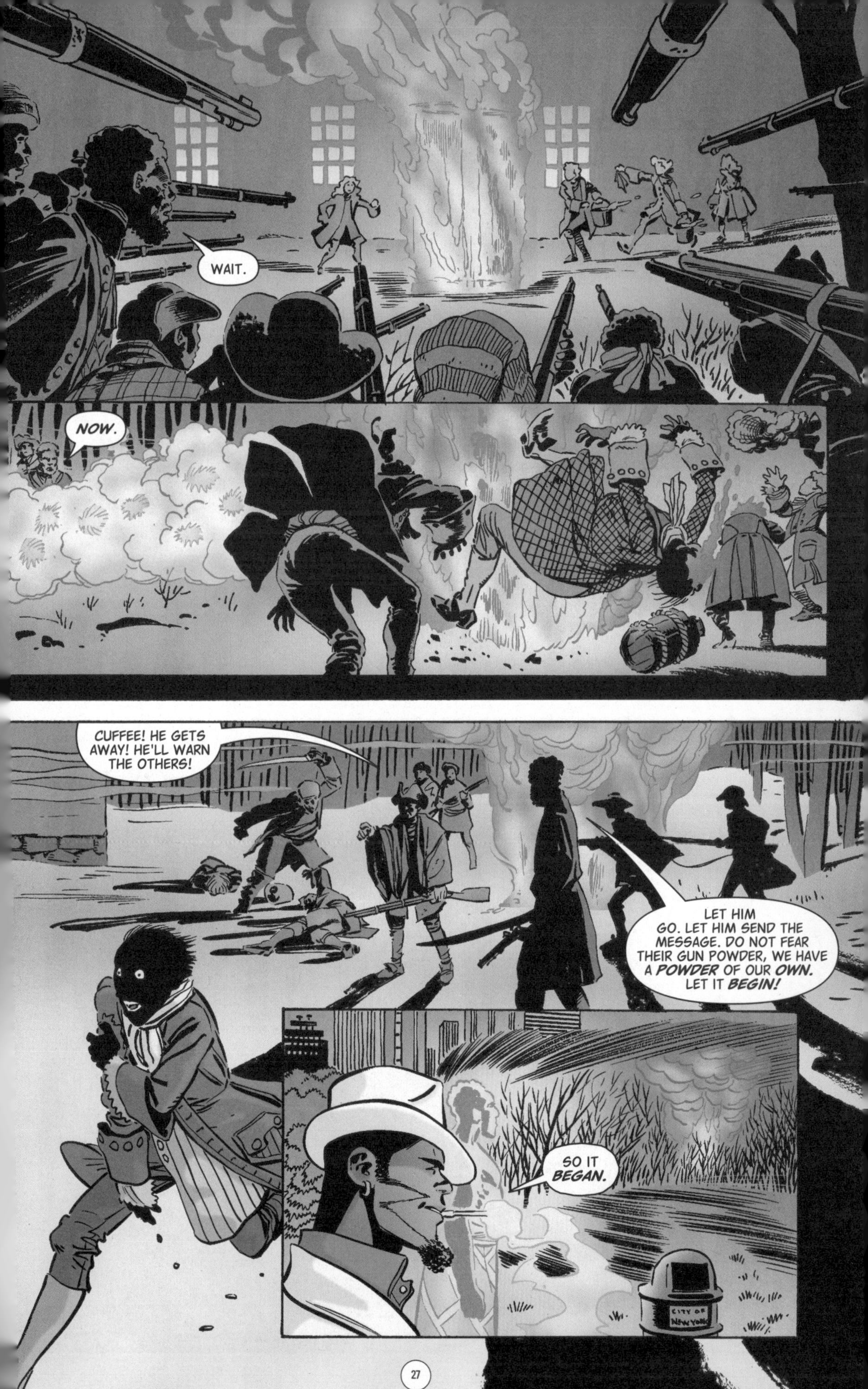
WAIT.
NOW.
CUFFEE! HE GETS AWAY! HE'LL WARN THE OTHERS!
LET HIM GO. LET HIM SEND THE MESSAGE. DO NOT FEAR THEIR GUN POWDER, WE HAVE A POWDER OF OUR OWN. LET IT BEGIN!
SO IT BEGAN.
CITY OF NEW YORK

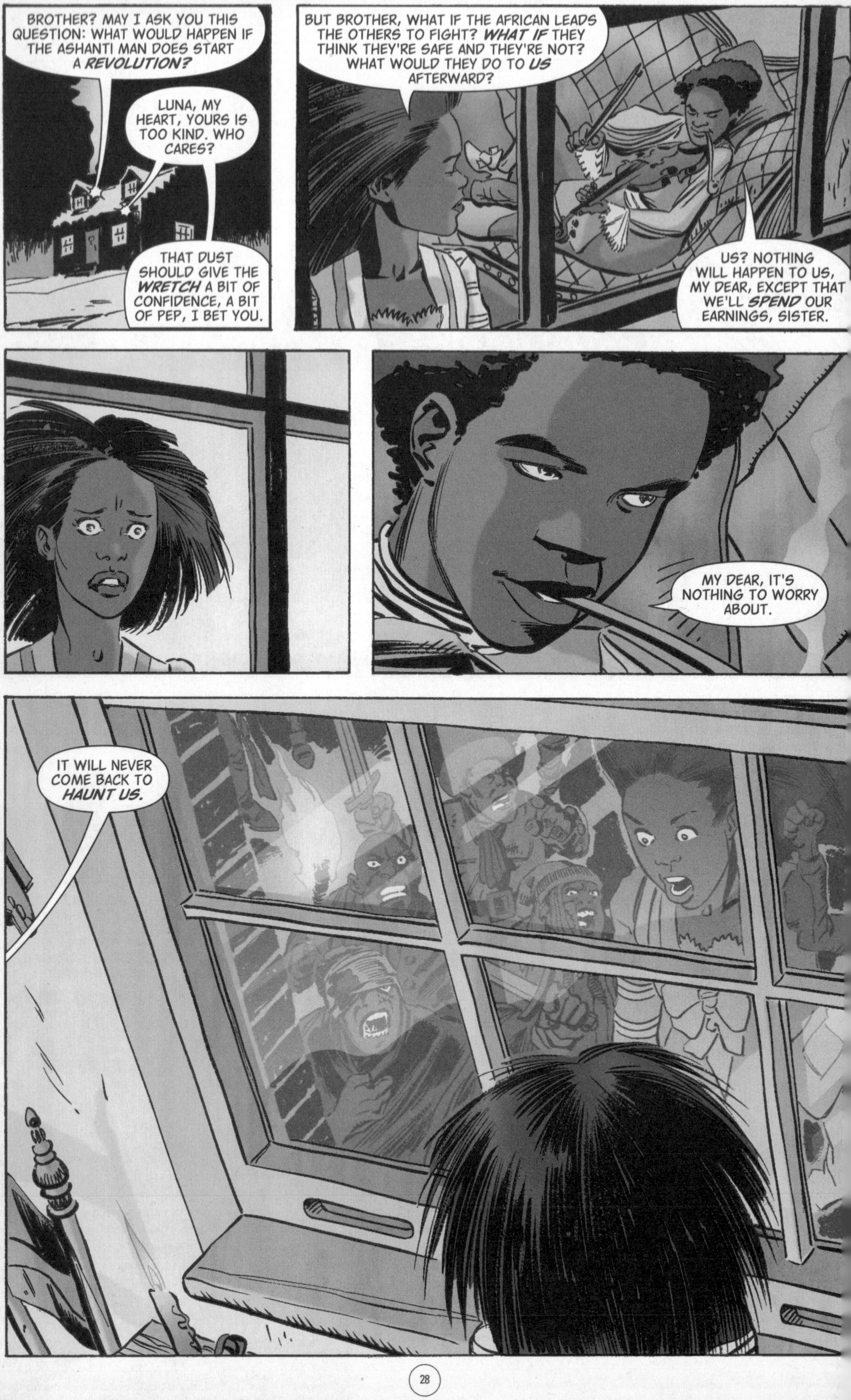
BROTHER? MAY I ASK YOU THIS QUESTION: WHAT WOULD HAPPEN IF THE ASHANTI MAN DOES START A REVOLUTION?
LUNA, MY HEART, YOURS IS TOO KIND. WHO CARES?
THAT DUST SHOULD GIVE THE WRETCH A BIT OF CONFIDENCE, A BIT OF PEP, I BET YOU.
BUT BROTHER, WHAT IF THE AFRICAN LEADS THE OTHERS TO FIGHT? WHAT IF THEY THINK THEY'RE SAFE AND THEY'RE NOT? WHAT WOULD THEY DO TO US AFTERWARD?
US? NOTHING WILL HAPPEN TO US, MY DEAR, EXCEPT THAT WE'LL SPEND OUR EARNINGS, SISTER.
MY DEAR, IT'S NOTHING TO WORRY ABOUT.
IT WILL NEVER COME BACK TO HAUNT US.

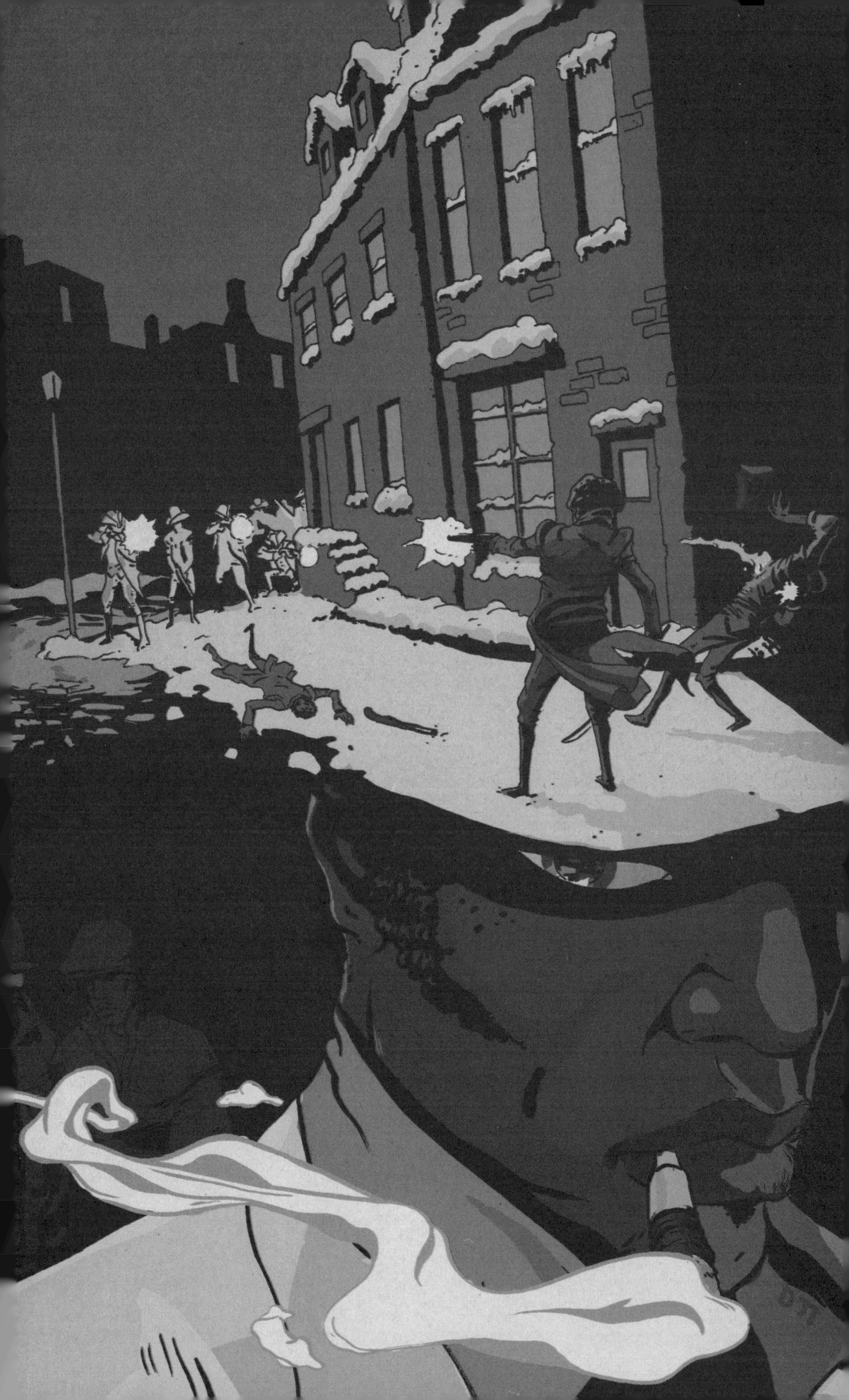

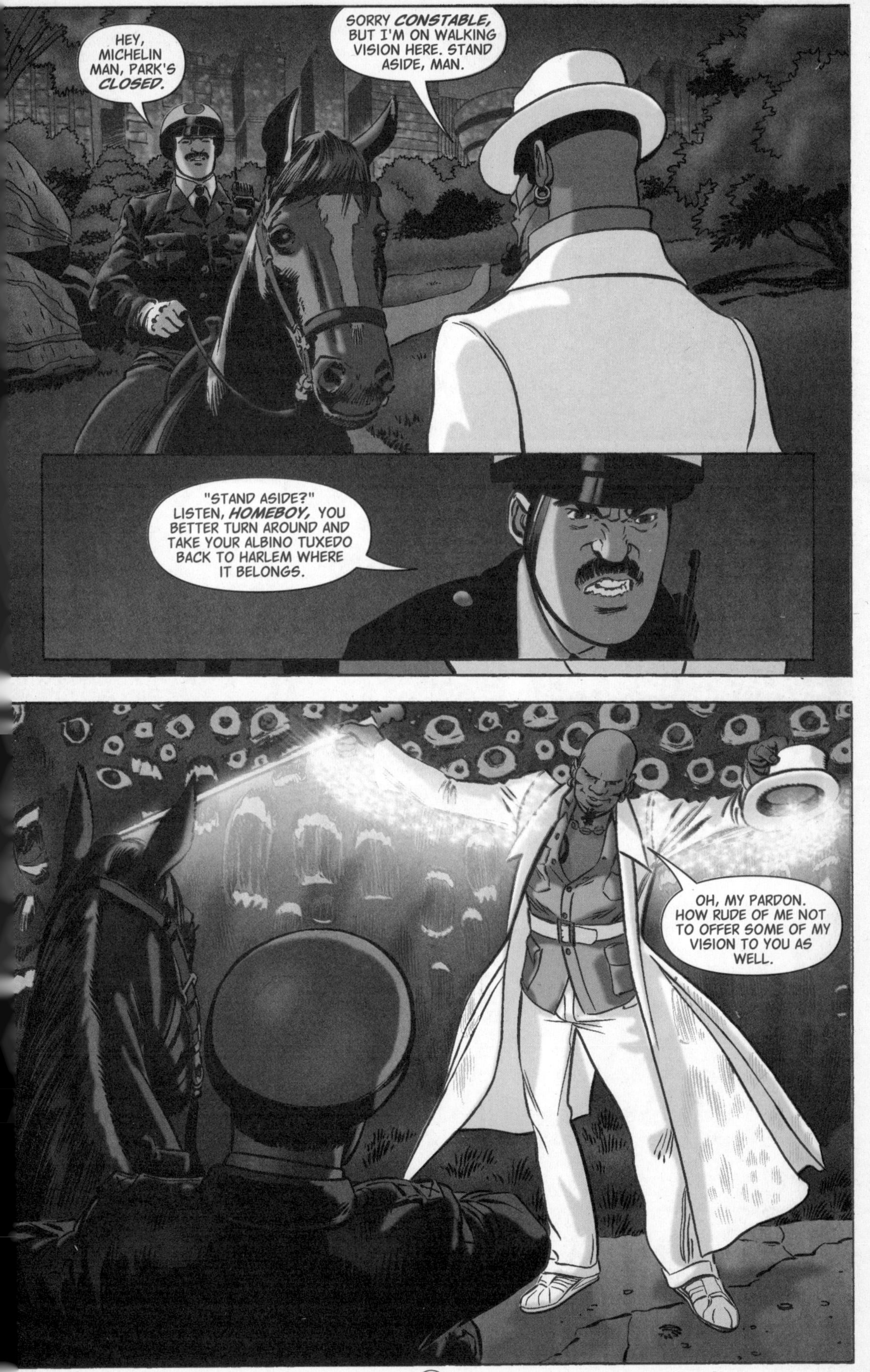
HEY, MICHELIN MAN, PARK'S CLOSED.
SORRY CONSTABLE, BUT I'M ON WALKING VISION HERE. STAND ASIDE, MAN.
"STAND ASIDE?" LISTEN, HOMEBOY, YOU BETTER TURN AROUND AND TAKE YOUR ALBINO TUXEDO BACK TO HARLEM WHERE IT BELONGS.
OH, MY PARDON. HOW RUDE OF ME NOT TO OFFER SOME OF MY VISION TO YOU AS WELL.

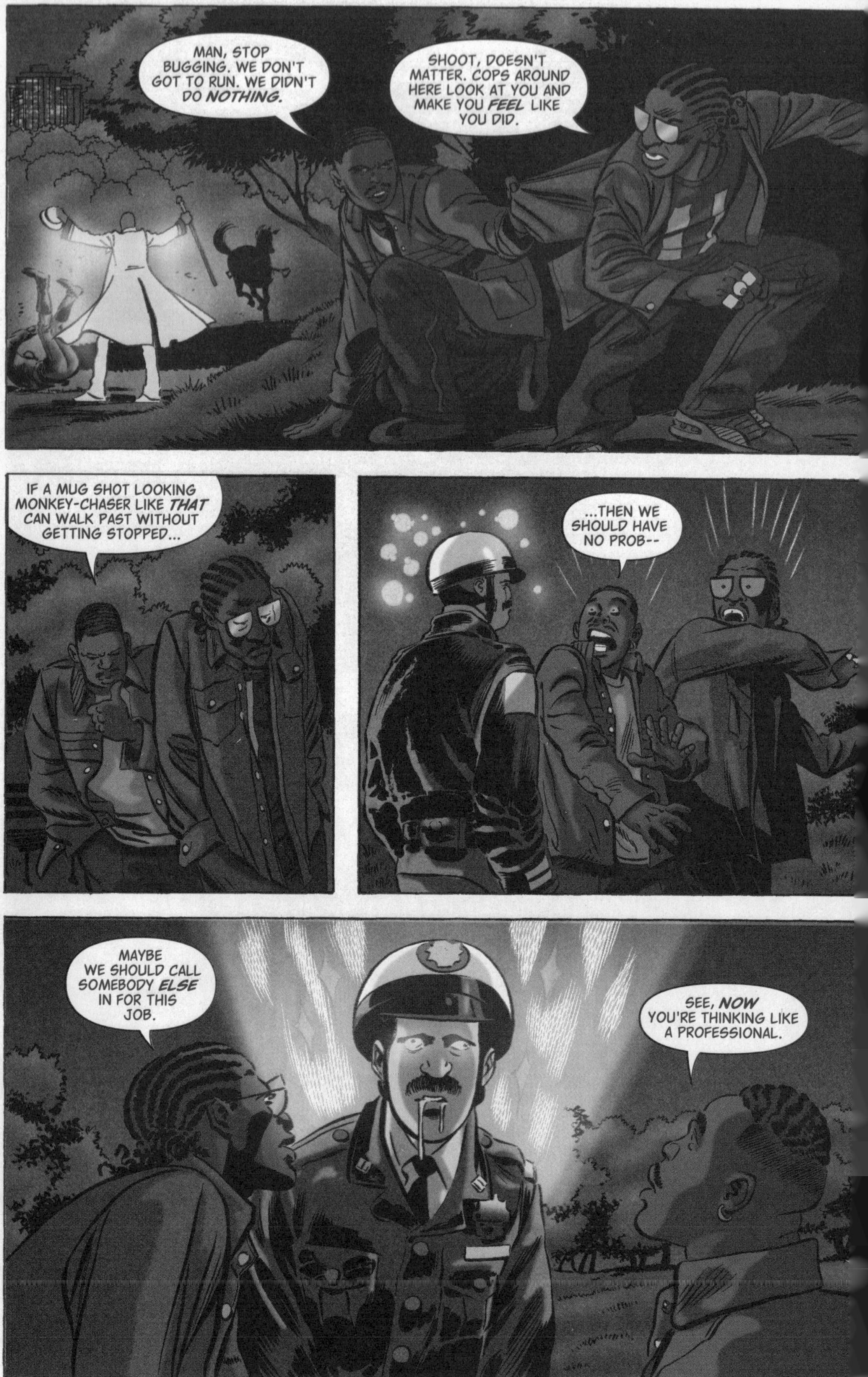
MAN, STOP BUGGING. WE DON'T GOT TO RUN. WE DIDN'T DO NOTHING.
SHOOT, DOESN'T MATTER. COPS AROUND HERE LOOK AT YOU AND MAKE YOU FEEL LIKE YOU DID.
IF A MUG SHOT LOOKING MONKEY-CHASER LIKE THAT CAN WALK PAST WITHOUT GETTING STOPPED...
...THEN WE SHOULD HAVE NO PROB--
MAYBE WE SHOULD CALL SOMEBODY ELSE IN FOR THIS JOB.
SEE, NOW YOU'RE THINKING LIKE A PROFESSIONAL.

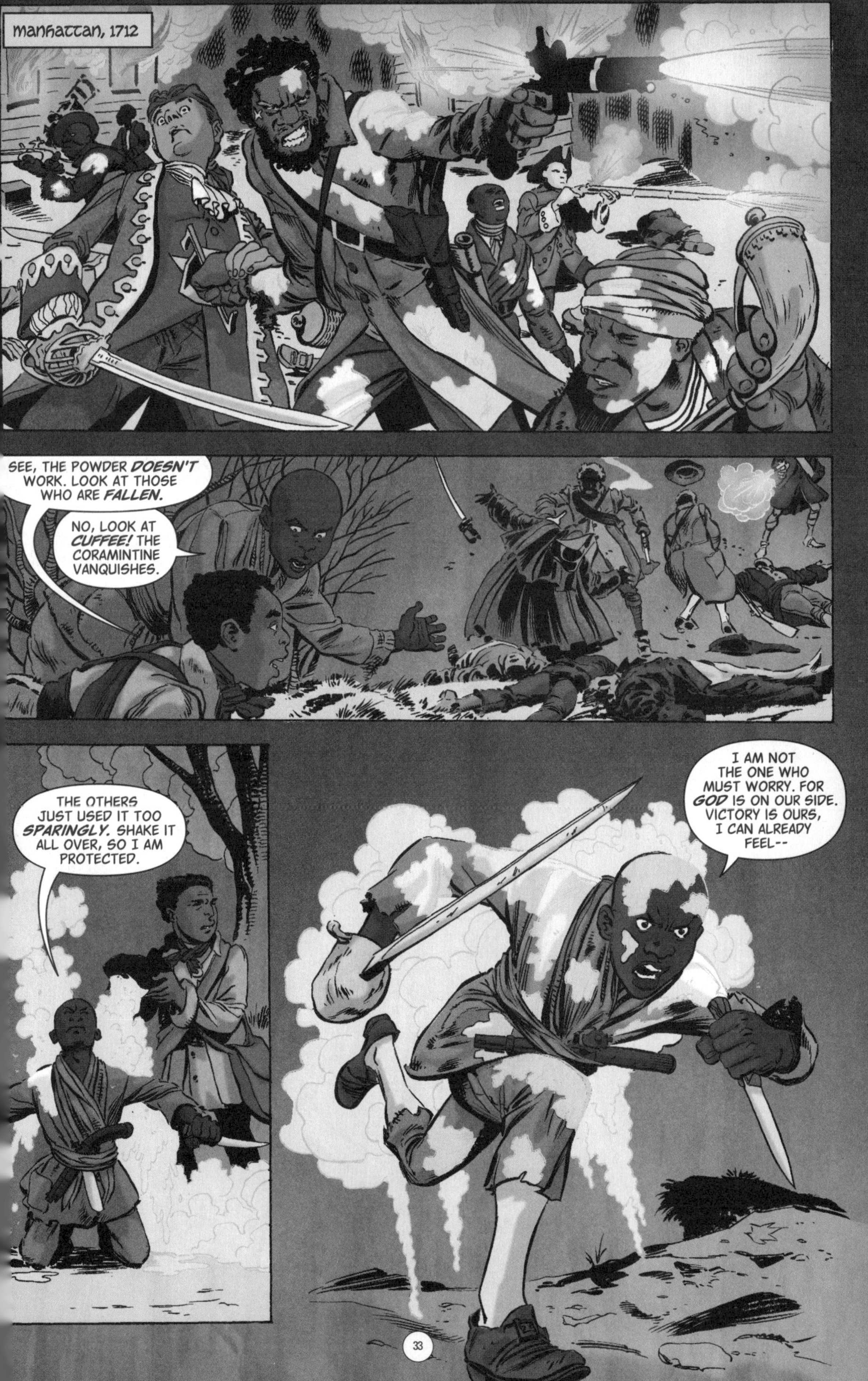
MANHATTAN, 1712
SEE, THE POWDER DOESN'T WORK. LOOK AT THOSE WHO ARE FALLEN.
NO, LOOK AT CUFFEE! THE CORAMINTINE VANQUISHES.
THE OTHERS JUST USED IT TOO SPARINGLY. SHAKE IT ALL OVER, SO I AM PROTECTED.
I AM NOT THE ONE WHO MUST WORRY. FOR GOD IS ON OUR SIDE. VICTORY IS OURS, I CAN ALREADY FEEL--

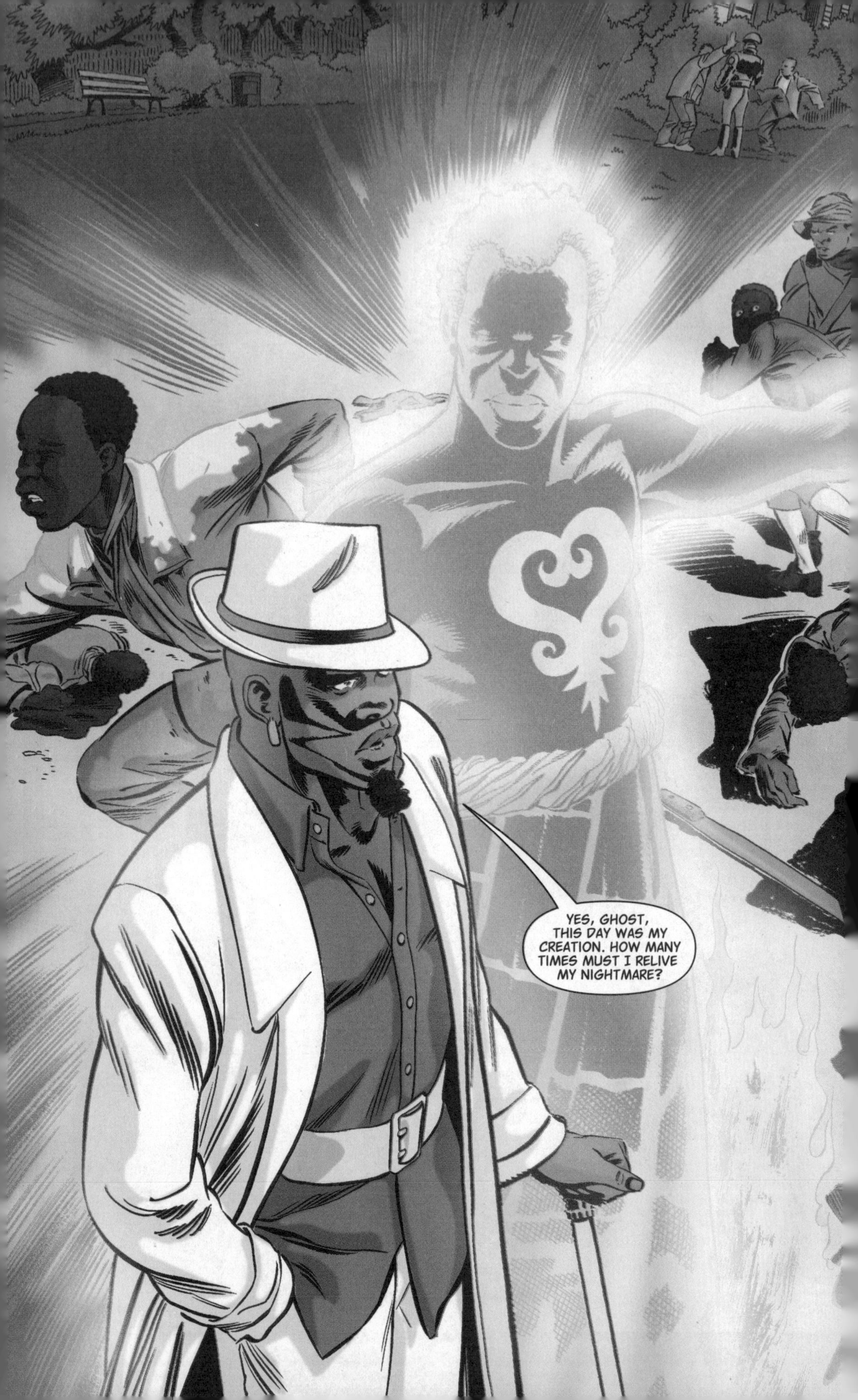
YES, GHOST, THIS DAY WAS MY CREATION. HOW MANY TIMES MUST I RELIVE MY NIGHTMARE?

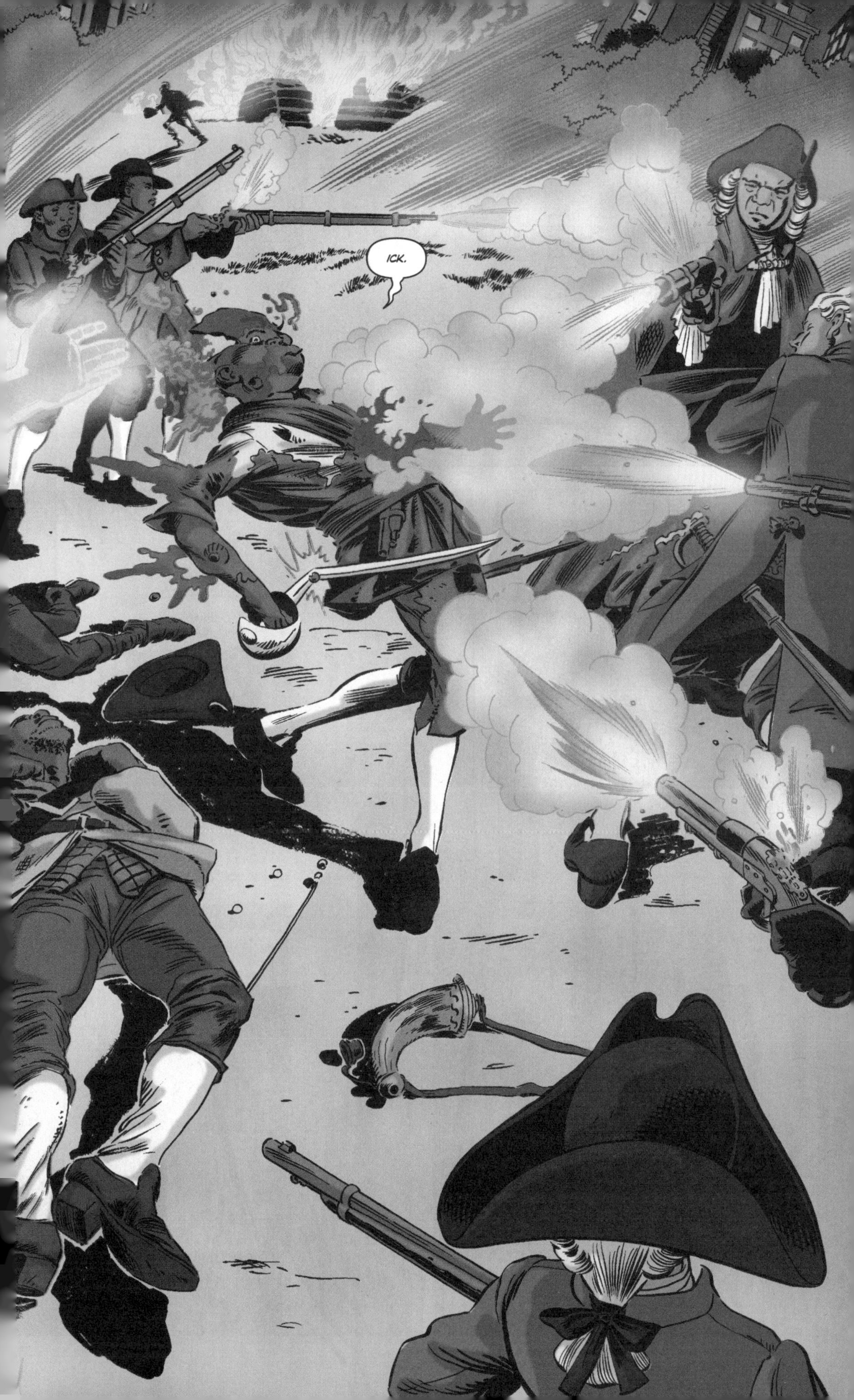
ICK.

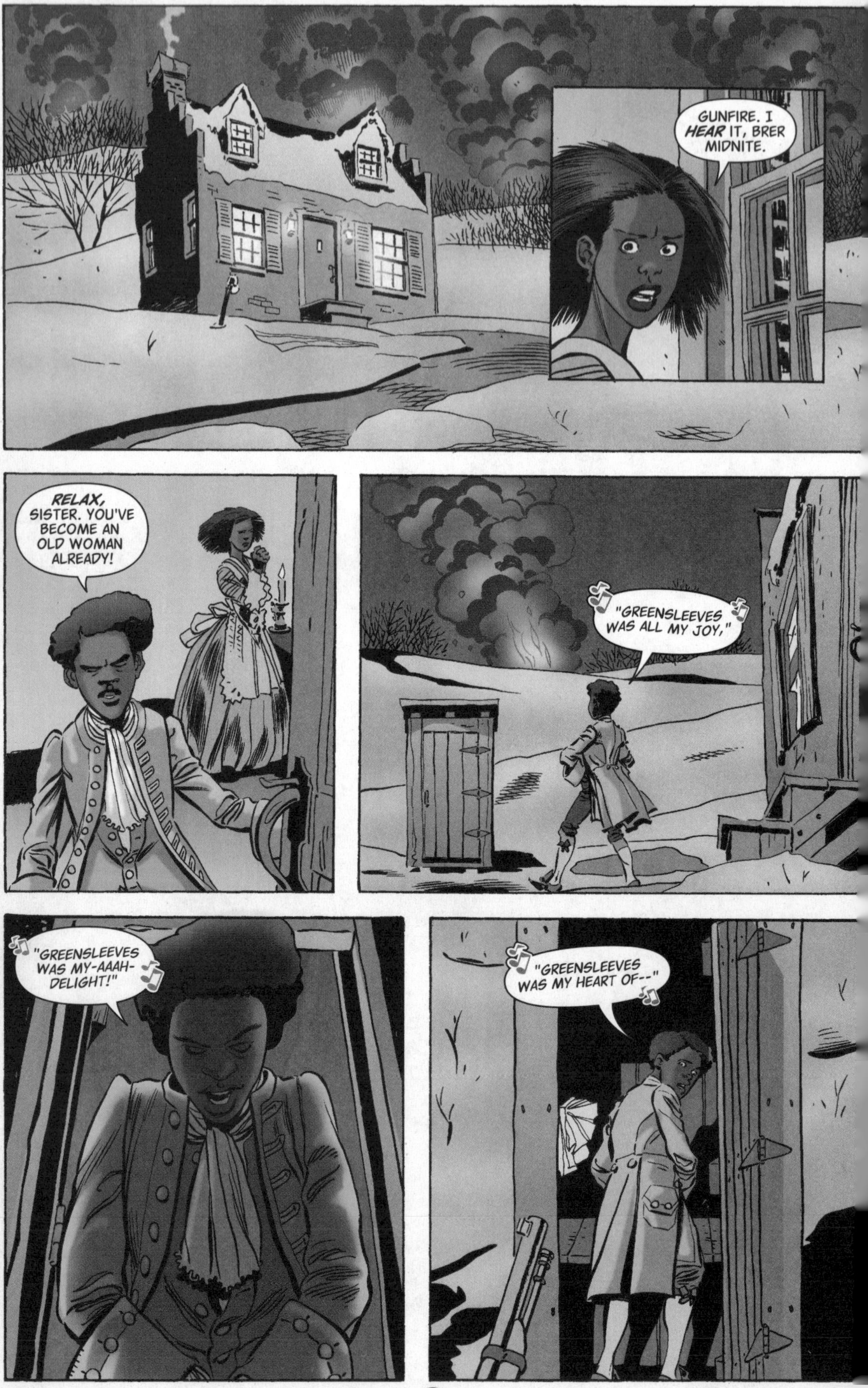
GUNFIRE. I HEAR IT, BRER MIDNITE.
RELAX, SISTER. YOU'VE BECOME AN OLD WOMAN ALREADY!
"GREENSLEEVES WAS ALL MY JOY,"
"GREENSLEEVES WAS MY-AAAH-DELIGHT!"
"GREENSLEEVES WAS MY HEART OF--"

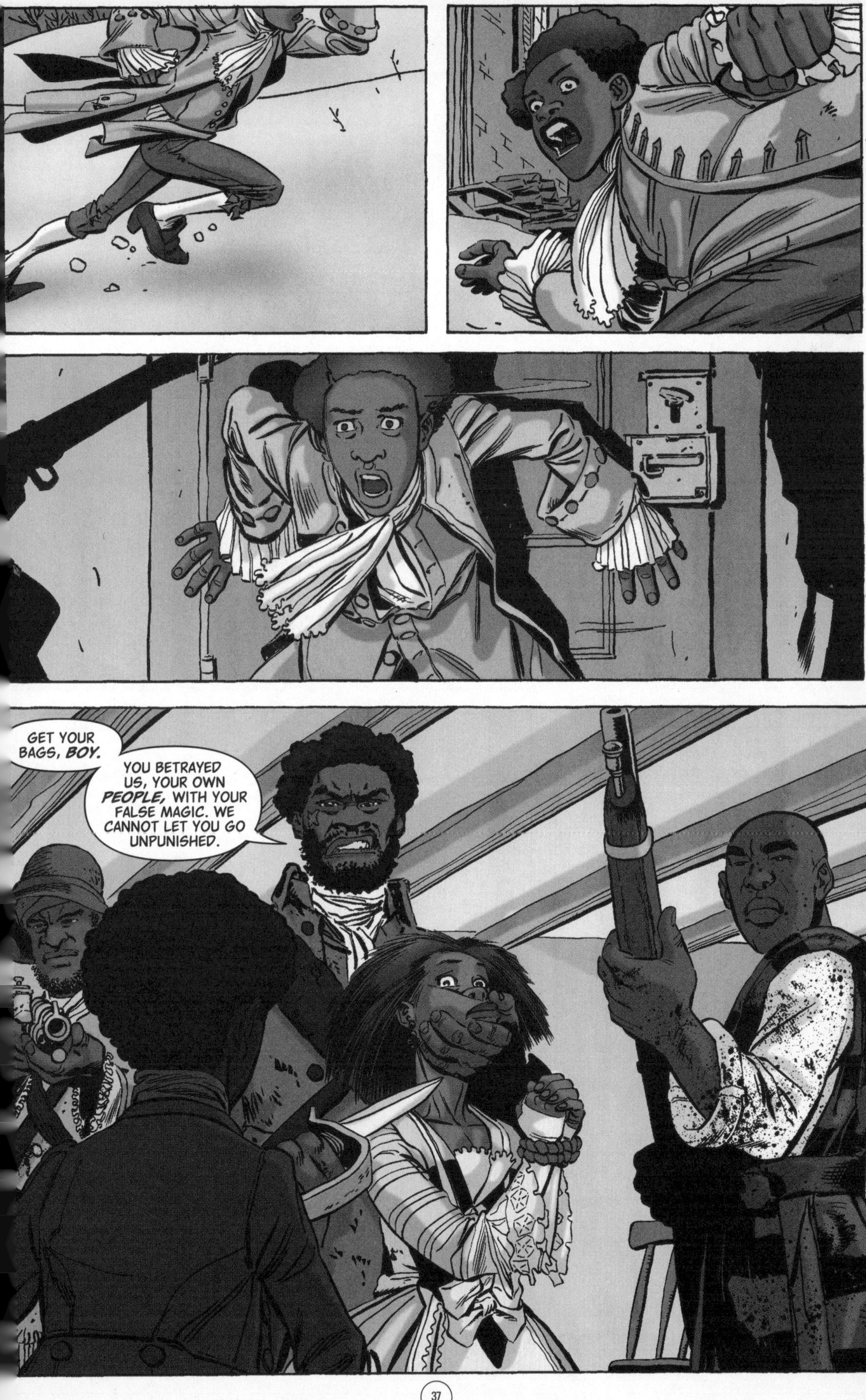
GET YOUR BAGS, BOY.
YOU BETRAYED US, YOUR OWN PEOPLE, WITH YOUR FALSE MAGIC. WE CANNOT LET YOU GO UNPUNISHED.

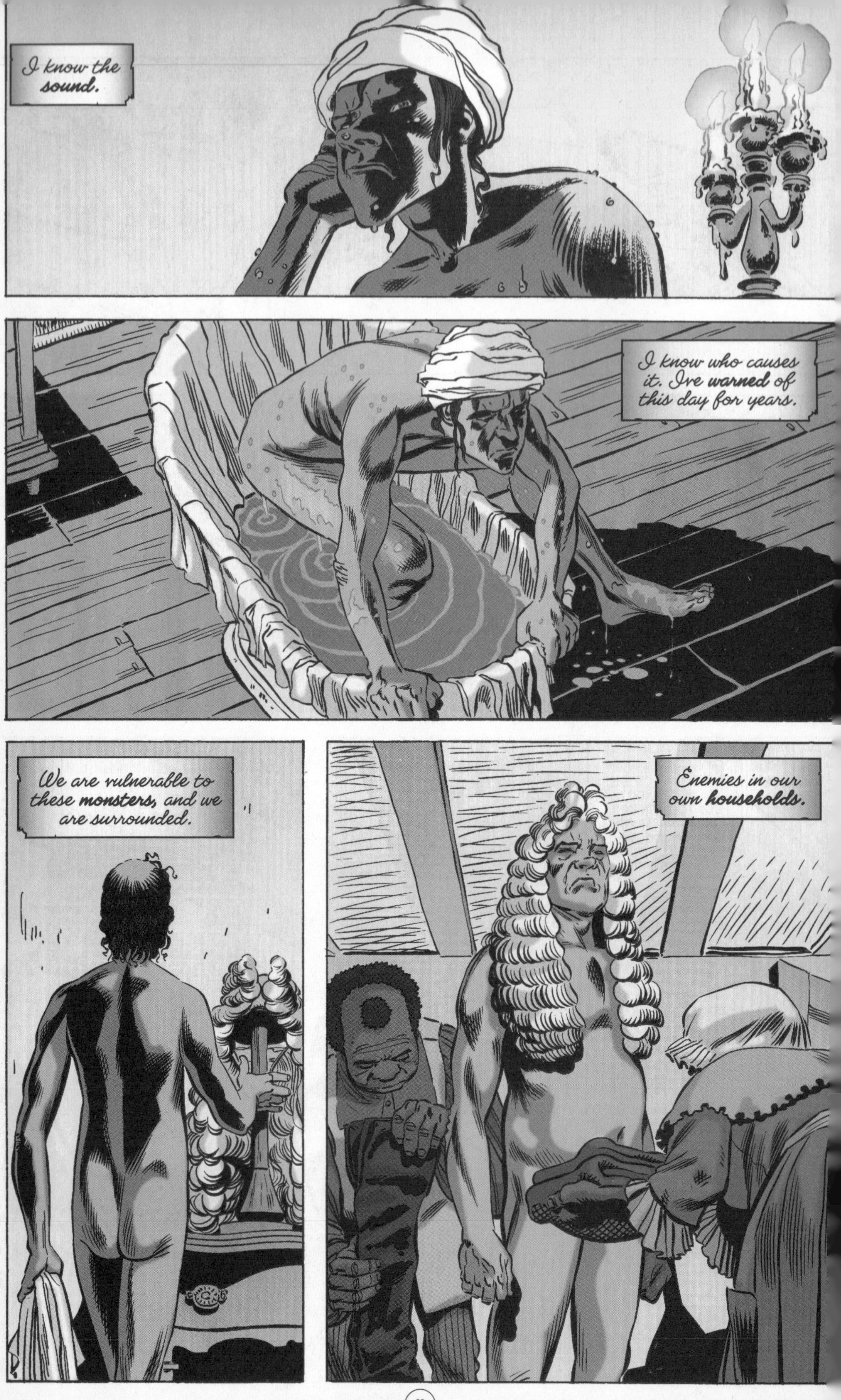
I know the sound.
I know who causes it. I've warned of this day for years.
We are vulnerable to these monsters, and we are surrounded.
Enemies in our own households.

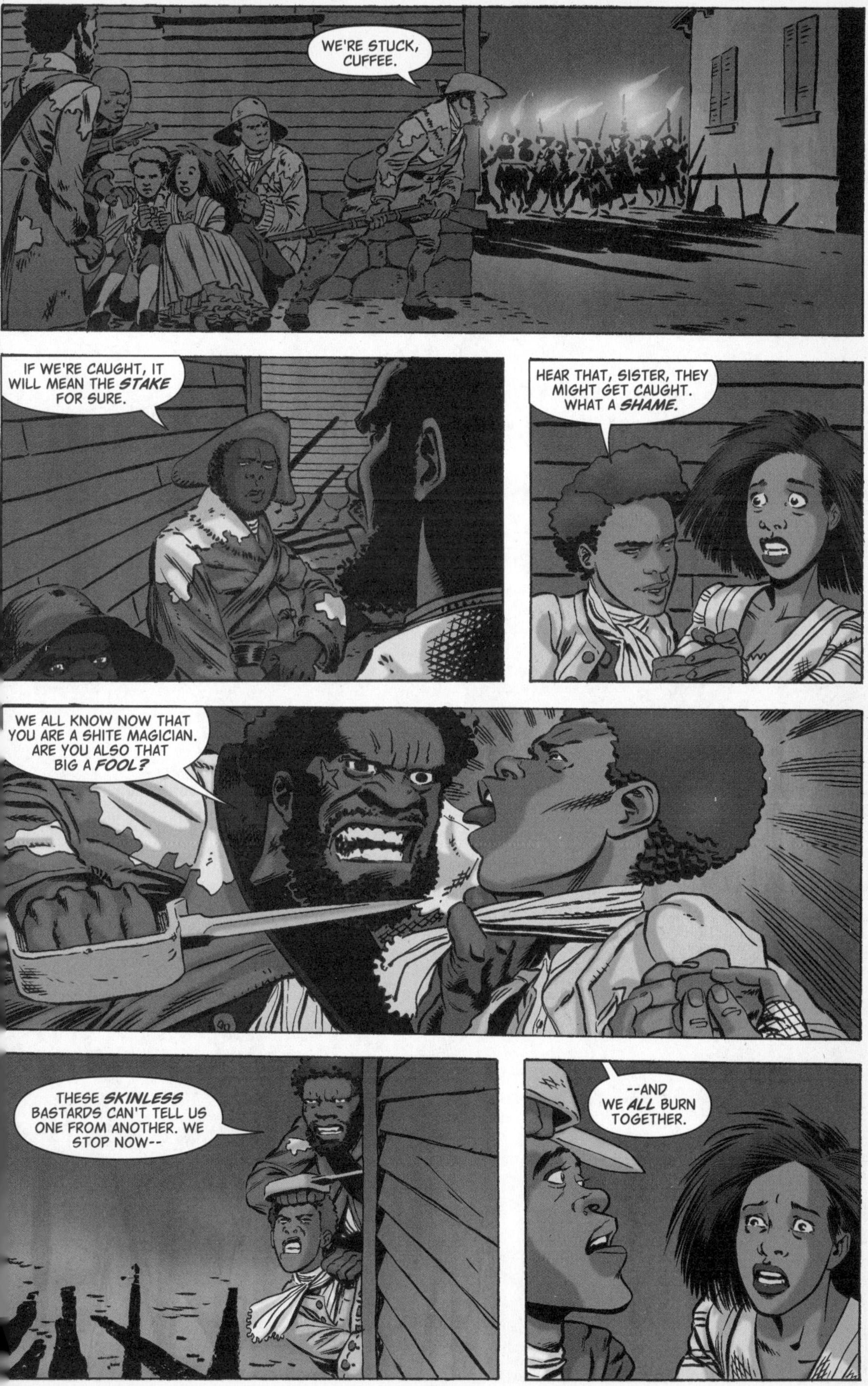
WE'RE STUCK, CUFFEE.
IF WE'RE CAUGHT, IT WILL MEAN THE STAKE FOR SURE.
HEAR THAT, SISTER, THEY MIGHT GET CAUGHT. WHAT A SHAME.
WE ALL KNOW NOW THAT YOU ARE A SHITE MAGICIAN. ARE YOU ALSO THAT BIG A FOOL?
THESE SKINLESS BASTARDS CAN'T TELL US ONE FROM ANOTHER. WE STOP NOW--
--AND WE ALL BURN TOGETHER.

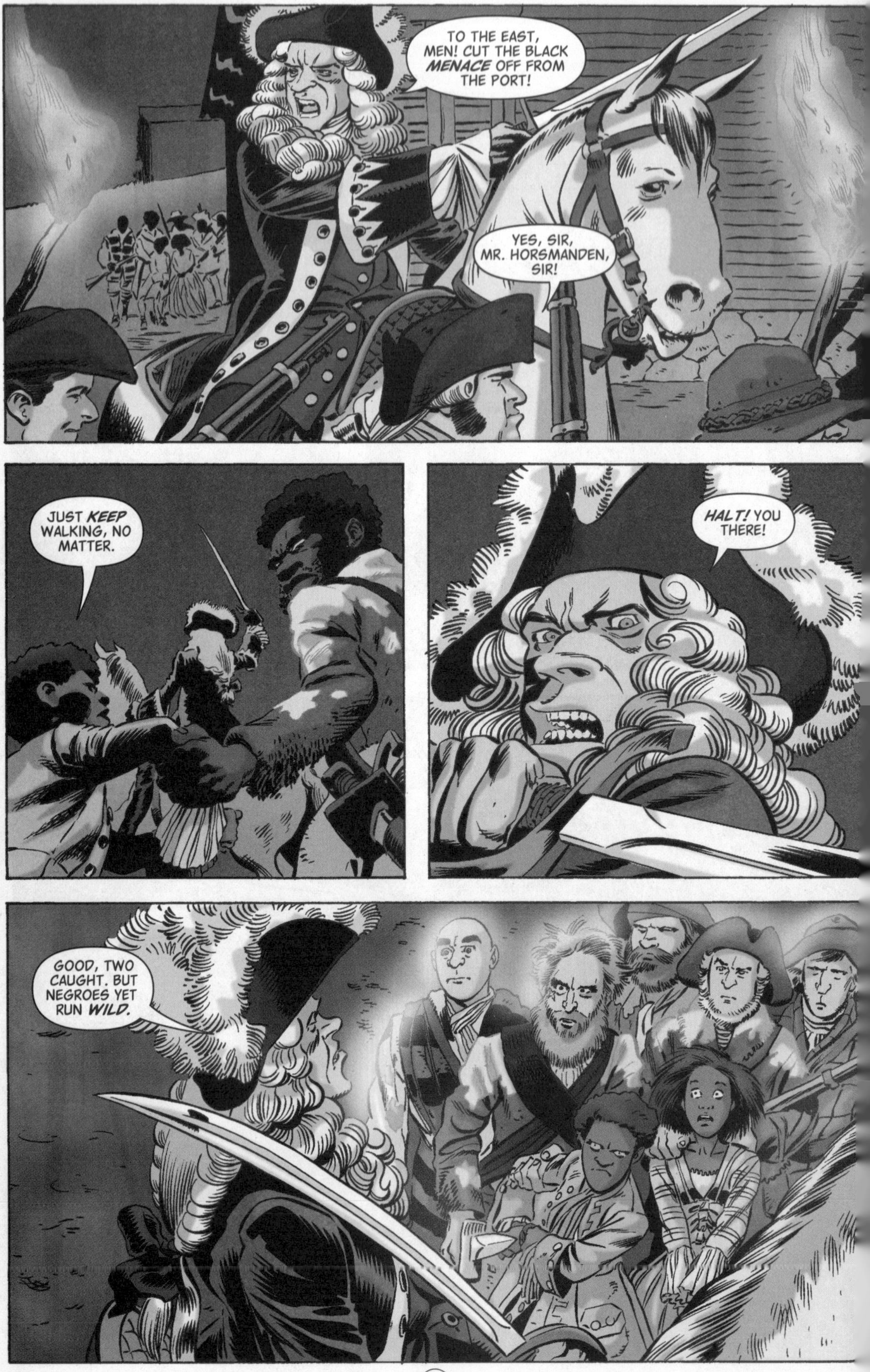

TO THE EAST, MEN! CUT THE BLACK MENACE OFF FROM THE PORT!
YES, SIR, MR. HORSMANDEN, SIR!
JUST KEEP WALKING, NO MATTER.
HALT! YOU THERE!
GOOD, TWO CAUGHT. BUT NEGROES YET RUN WILD.

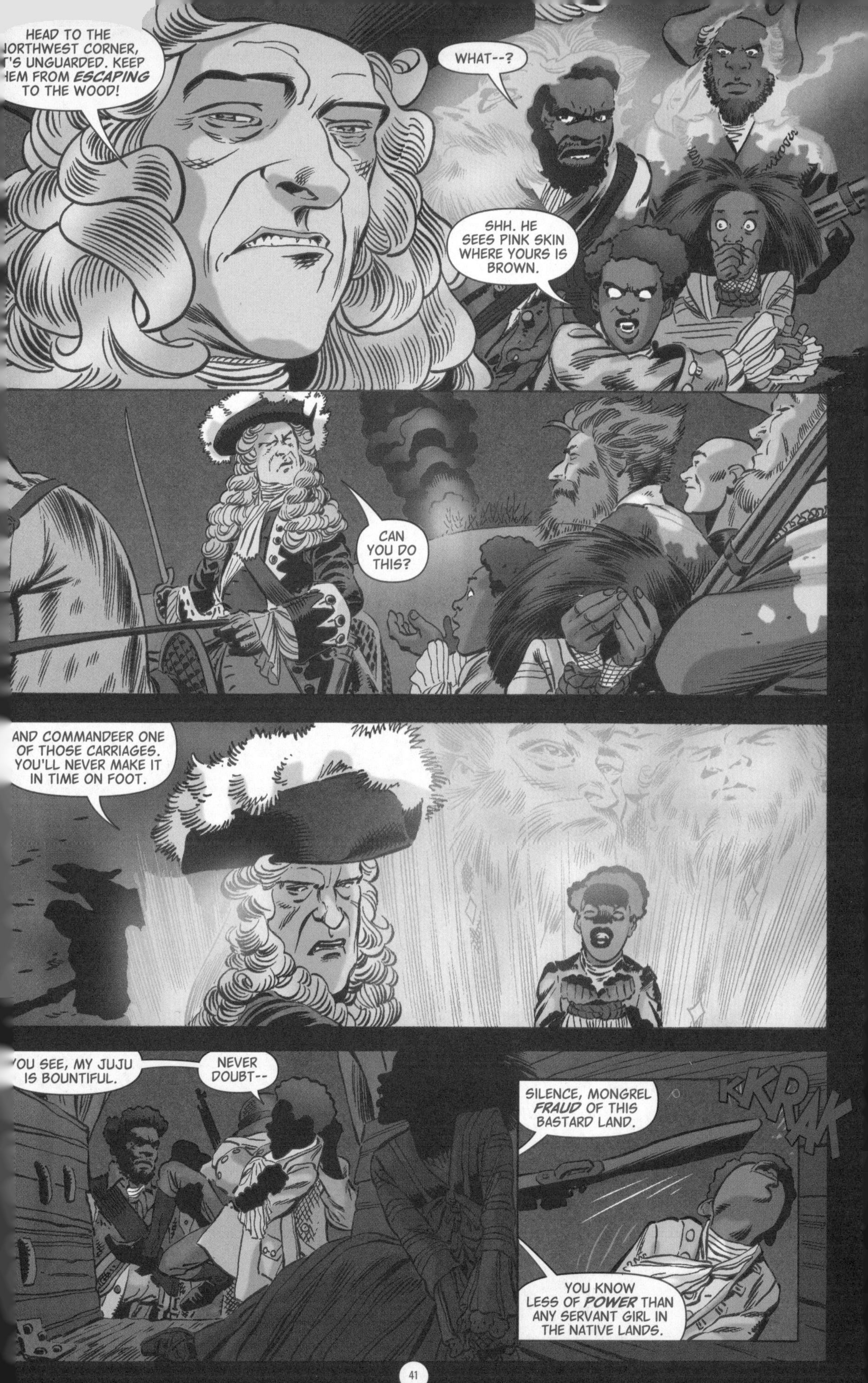
HEAD TO THE NORTHWEST CORNER, IT'S UNGUARDED. KEEP THEM FROM *ESCAPING* TO THE WOOD!
WHAT--?
SHH. HE SEES PINK SKIN WHERE YOURS IS BROWN.
CAN YOU DO THIS?
AND COMMANDEER ONE OF THOSE CARRIAGES. YOU'LL NEVER MAKE IT IN TIME ON FOOT.
YOU SEE, MY JUJU IS BOUNTIFUL.
NEVER DOUBT--
SILENCE, MONGREL *FRAUD* OF THIS BASTARD LAND.
KKRAK
YOU KNOW LESS OF *POWER* THAN ANY SERVANT GIRL IN THE NATIVE LANDS.

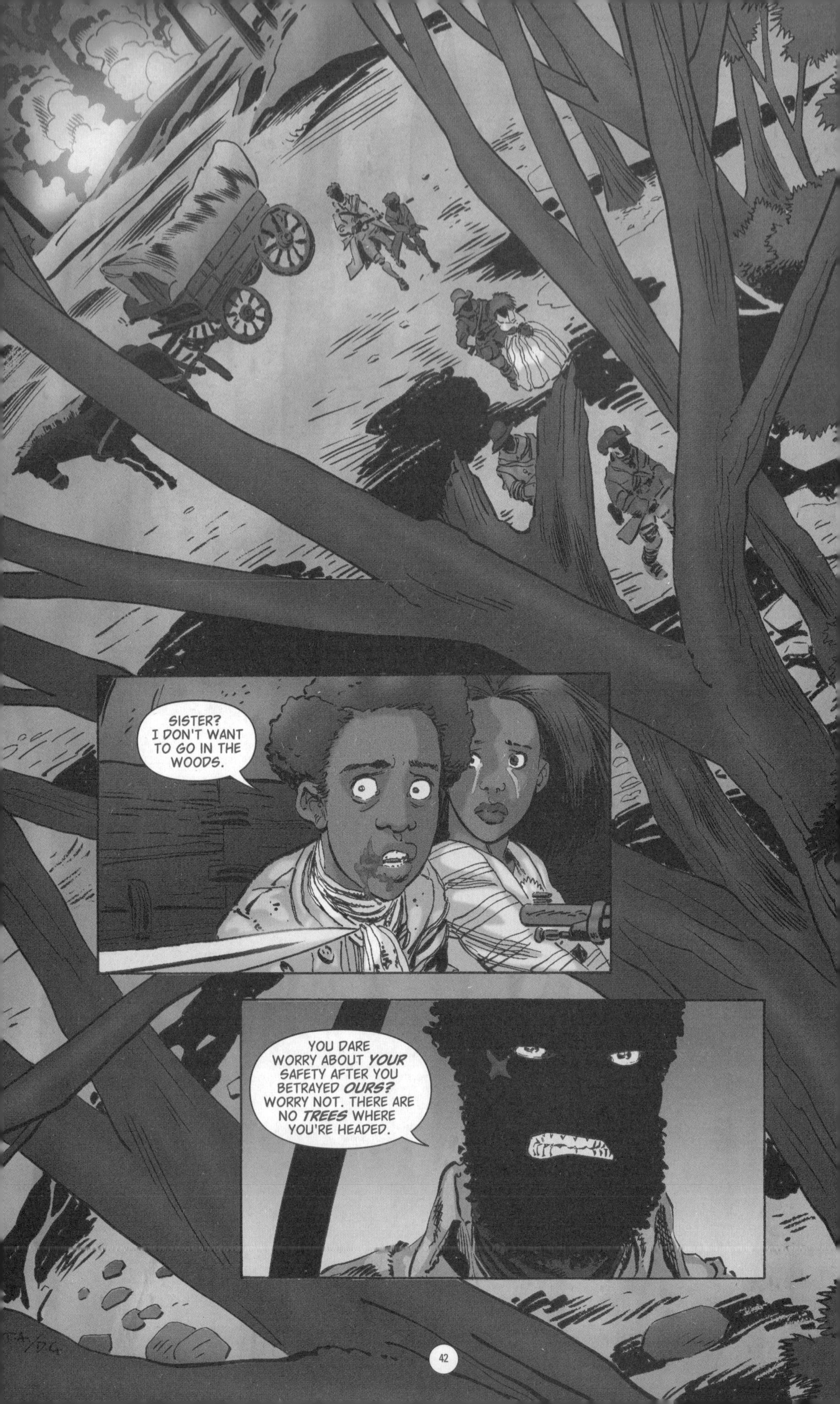
SISTER? I DON'T WANT TO GO IN THE WOODS.
YOU DARE WORRY ABOUT *YOUR* SAFETY AFTER YOU BETRAYED *OURS?* WORRY NOT. THERE ARE NO *TREES* WHERE YOU'RE HEADED.

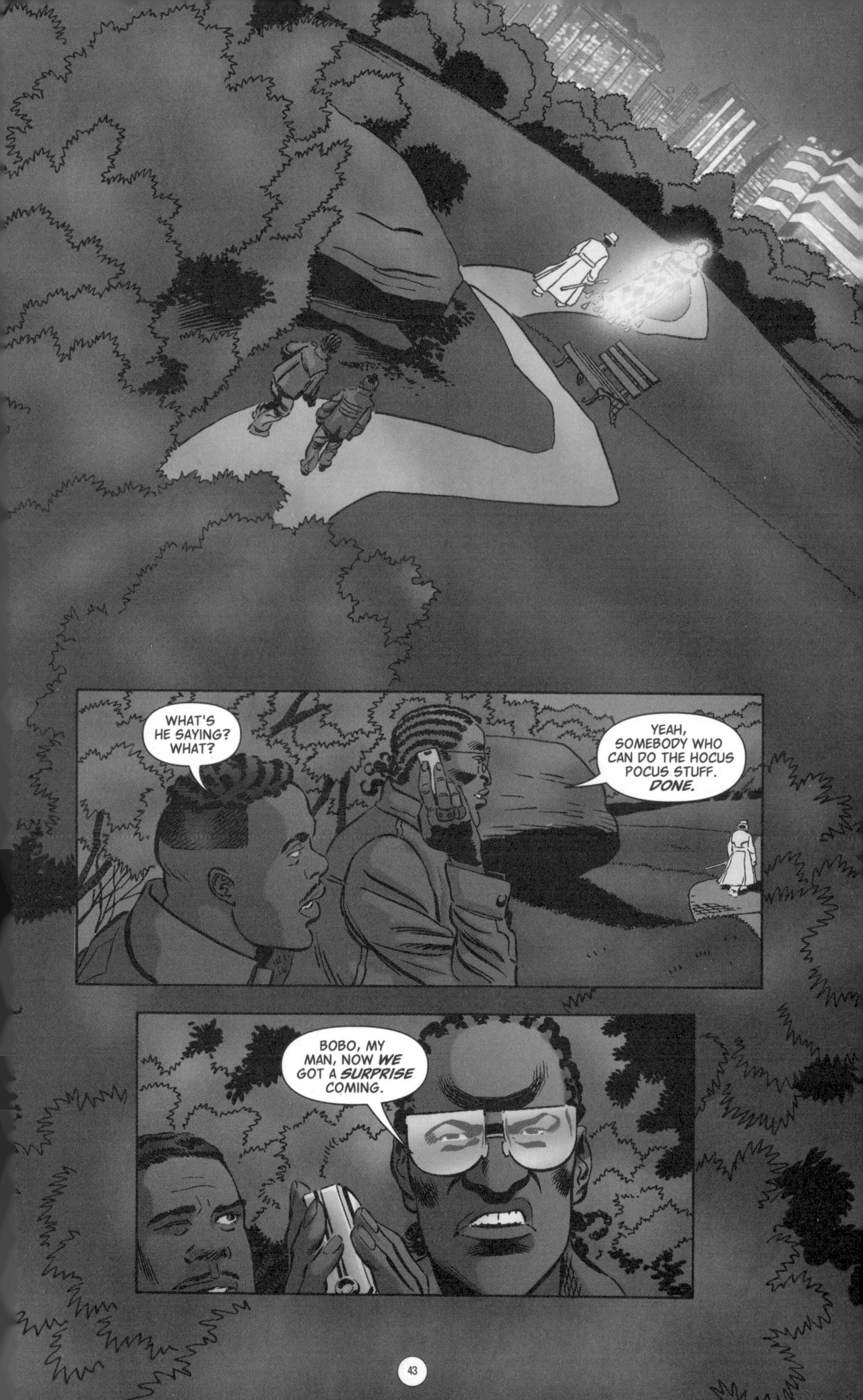
WHAT'S HE SAYING? WHAT?
YEAH, SOMEBODY WHO CAN DO THE HOCUS POCUS STUFF. *DONE.*
BOBO, MY MAN, NOW *WE* GOT A *SURPRISE* COMING.

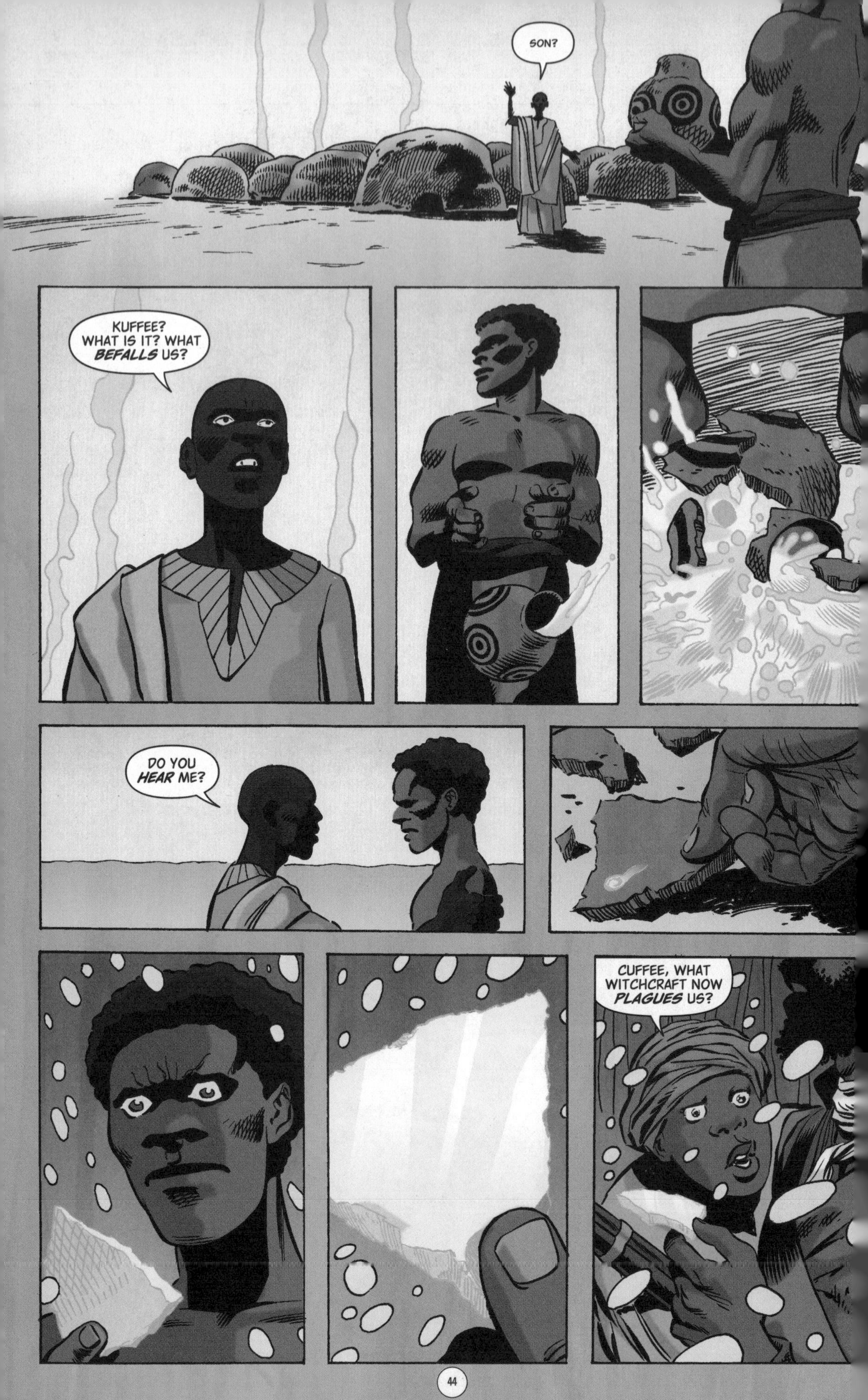
SON?
KUFFEE? WHAT IS IT? WHAT BEFALLS US?
DO YOU HEAR ME?
CUFFEE, WHAT WITCHCRAFT NOW PLAGUES US?

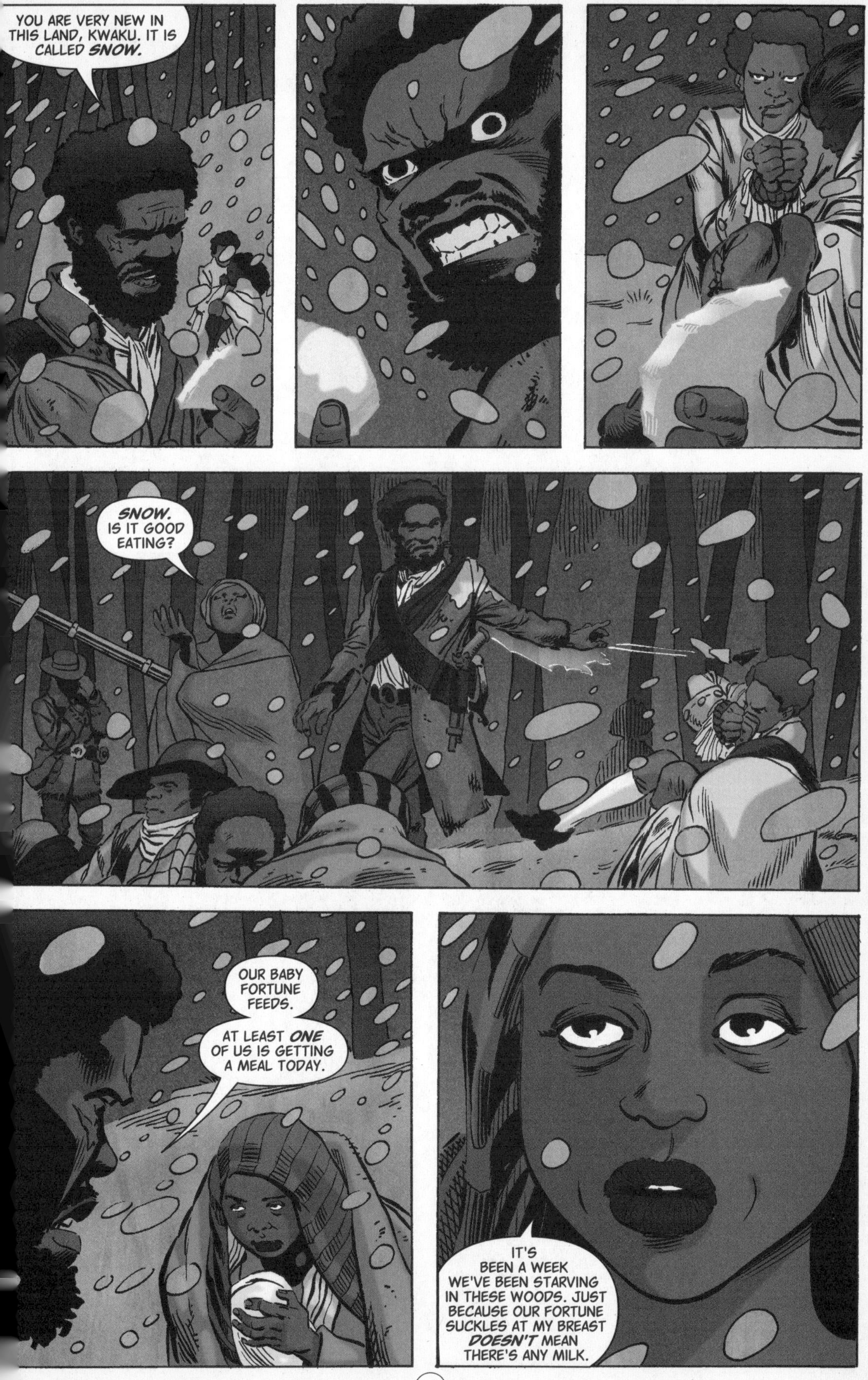
YOU ARE VERY NEW IN THIS LAND, KWAKU. IT IS CALLED SNOW.
SNOW. IS IT GOOD EATING?
OUR BABY FORTUNE FEEDS.
AT LEAST ONE OF US IS GETTING A MEAL TODAY.
IT'S BEEN A WEEK WE'VE BEEN STARVING IN THESE WOODS. JUST BECAUSE OUR FORTUNE SUCKLES AT MY BREAST DOESN'T MEAN THERE'S ANY MILK.

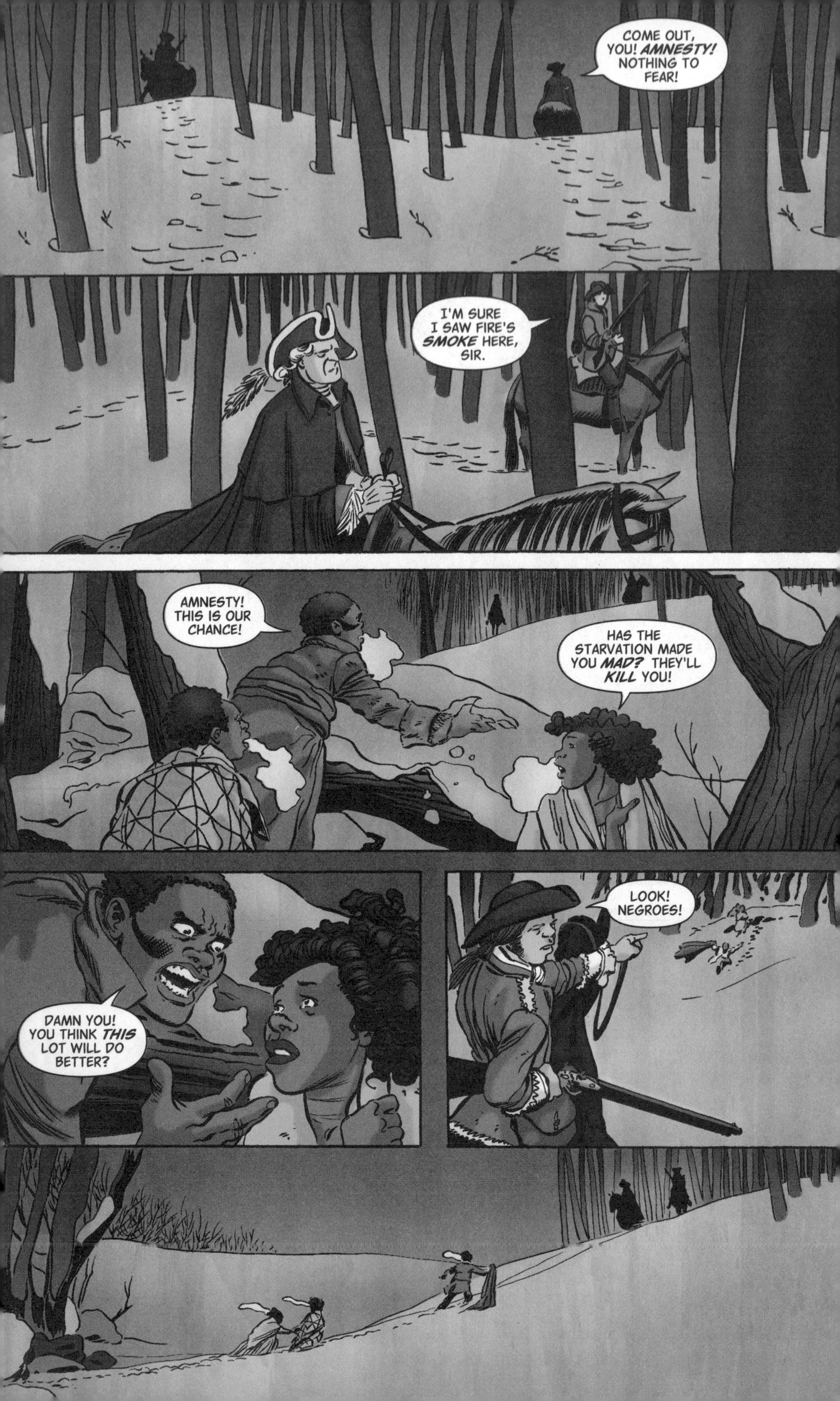
COME OUT, YOU! AMNESTY! NOTHING TO FEAR!
I'M SURE I SAW FIRE'S SMOKE HERE, SIR.
AMNESTY! THIS IS OUR CHANCE!
HAS THE STARVATION MADE YOU MAD? THEY'LL KILL YOU!
DAMN YOU! YOU THINK THIS LOT WILL DO BETTER?
LOOK! NEGROES!

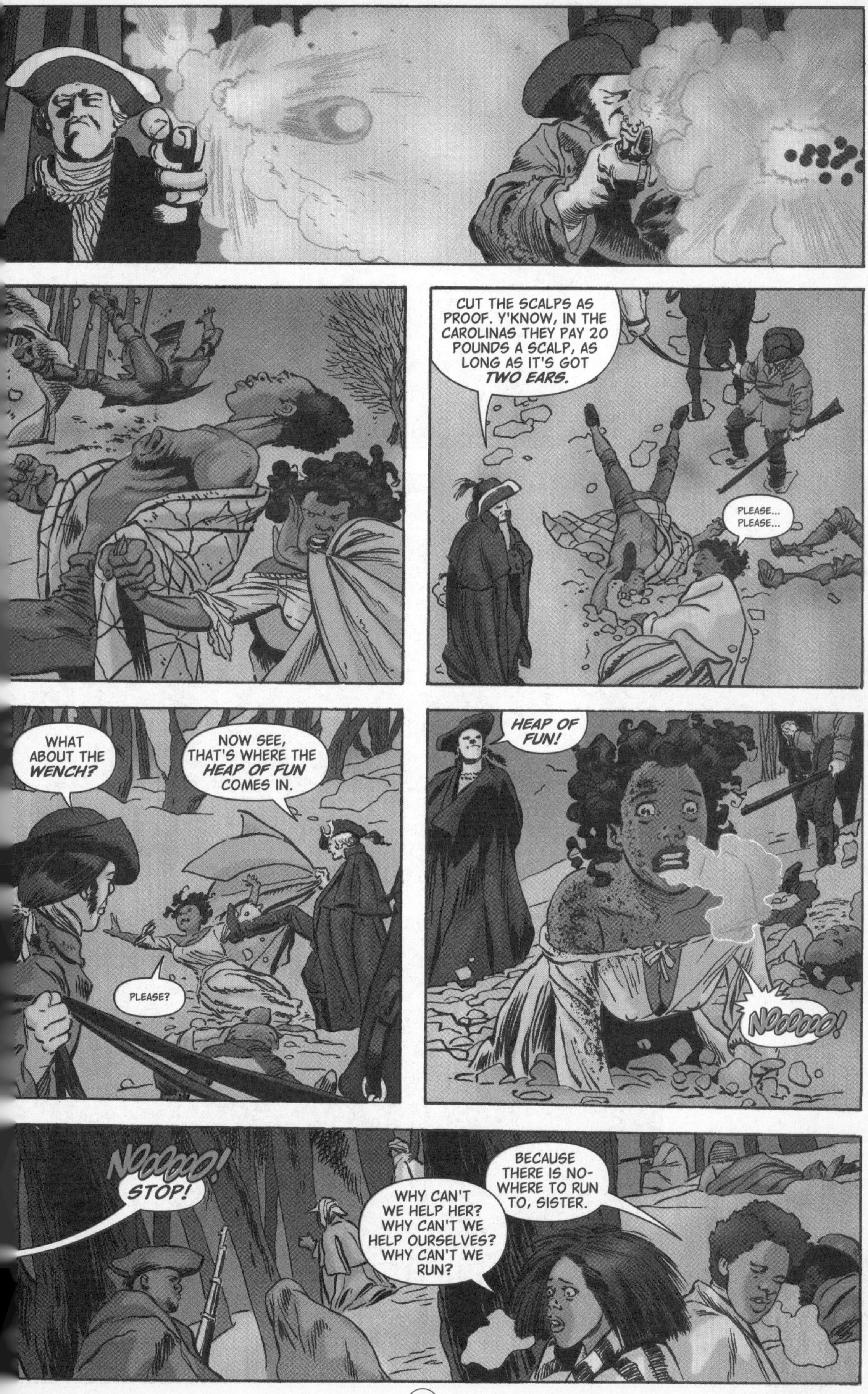
CUT THE SCALPS AS PROOF. Y'KNOW, IN THE CAROLINAS THEY PAY 20 POUNDS A SCALP, AS LONG AS IT'S GOT TWO EARS.
PLEASE... PLEASE...
WHAT ABOUT THE WENCH?
NOW SEE, THAT'S WHERE THE HEAP OF FUN COMES IN.
PLEASE?
HEAP OF FUN!
NOOOOOO!
NOOOOOO! STOP!
WHY CAN'T WE HELP HER? WHY CAN'T WE HELP OURSELVES? WHY CAN'T WE RUN?
BECAUSE THERE IS NO-WHERE TO RUN TO, SISTER.

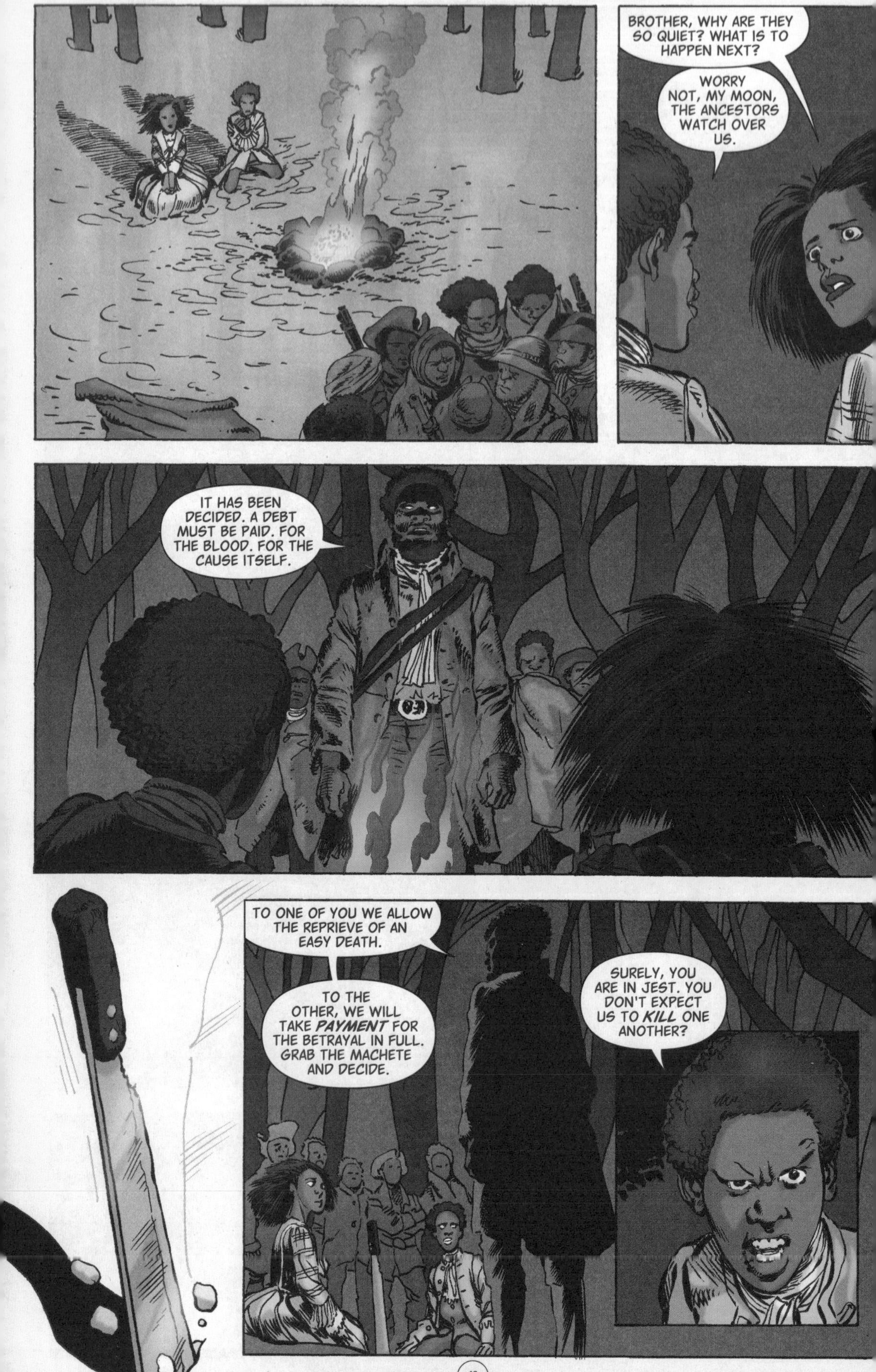
BROTHER, WHY ARE THEY SO QUIET? WHAT IS TO HAPPEN NEXT?
WORRY NOT, MY MOON, THE ANCESTORS WATCH OVER US.
IT HAS BEEN DECIDED. A DEBT MUST BE PAID. FOR THE BLOOD. FOR THE CAUSE ITSELF.
TO ONE OF YOU WE ALLOW THE REPRIEVE OF AN EASY DEATH.
TO THE OTHER, WE WILL TAKE *PAYMENT* FOR THE BETRAYAL IN FULL. GRAB THE MACHETE AND DECIDE.
SURELY, YOU ARE IN JEST. YOU DON'T EXPECT US TO *KILL* ONE ANOTHER?

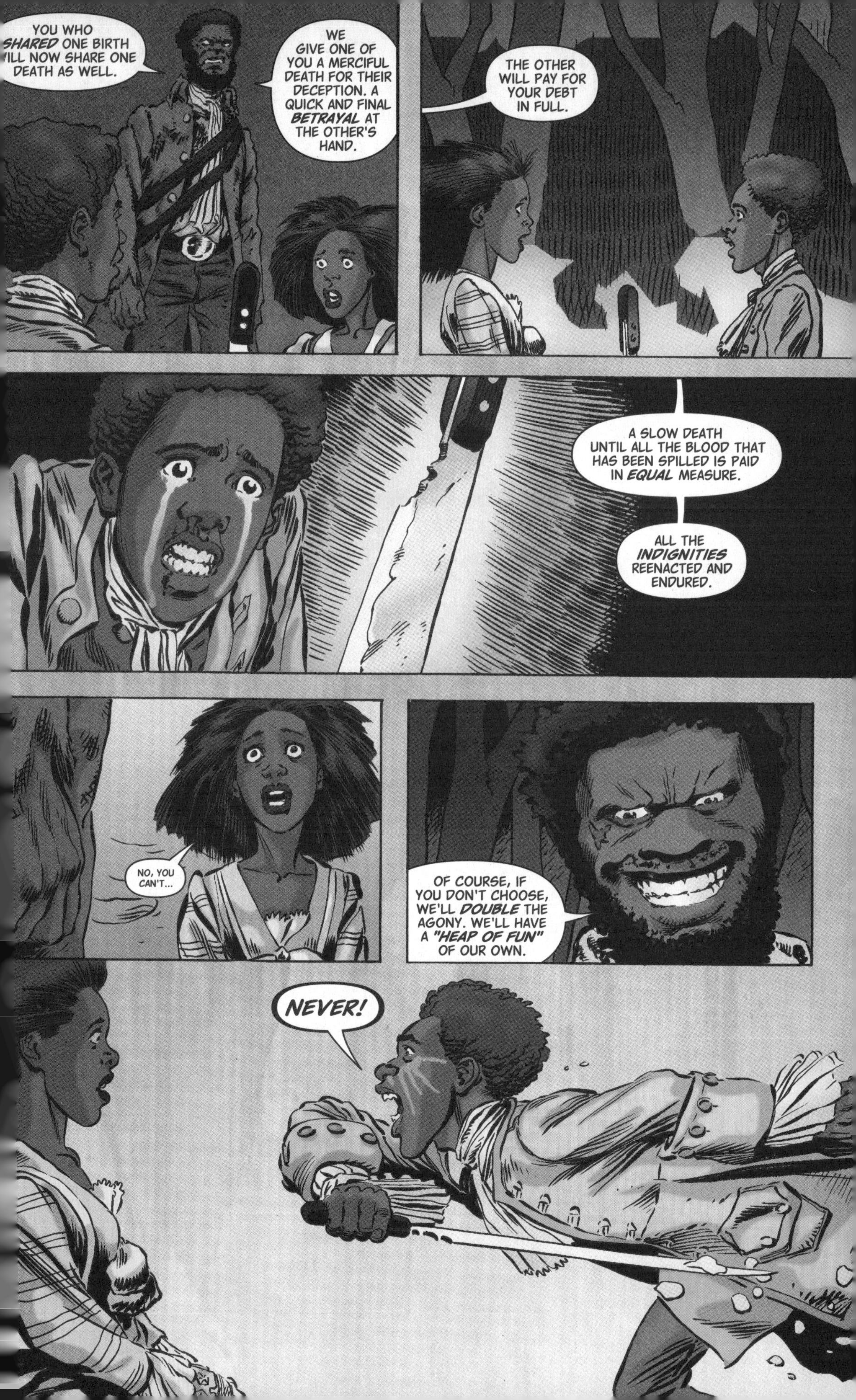
YOU WHO SHARED ONE BIRTH WILL NOW SHARE ONE DEATH AS WELL.
WE GIVE ONE OF YOU A MERCIFUL DEATH FOR THEIR DECEPTION. A QUICK AND FINAL BETRAYAL AT THE OTHER'S HAND.
THE OTHER WILL PAY FOR YOUR DEBT IN FULL.
A SLOW DEATH UNTIL ALL THE BLOOD THAT HAS BEEN SPILLED IS PAID IN EQUAL MEASURE.
ALL THE INDIGNITIES REENACTED AND ENDURED.
NO, YOU CAN'T...
OF COURSE, IF YOU DON'T CHOOSE, WE'LL DOUBLE THE AGONY. WE'LL HAVE A "HEAP OF FUN" OF OUR OWN.
NEVER!

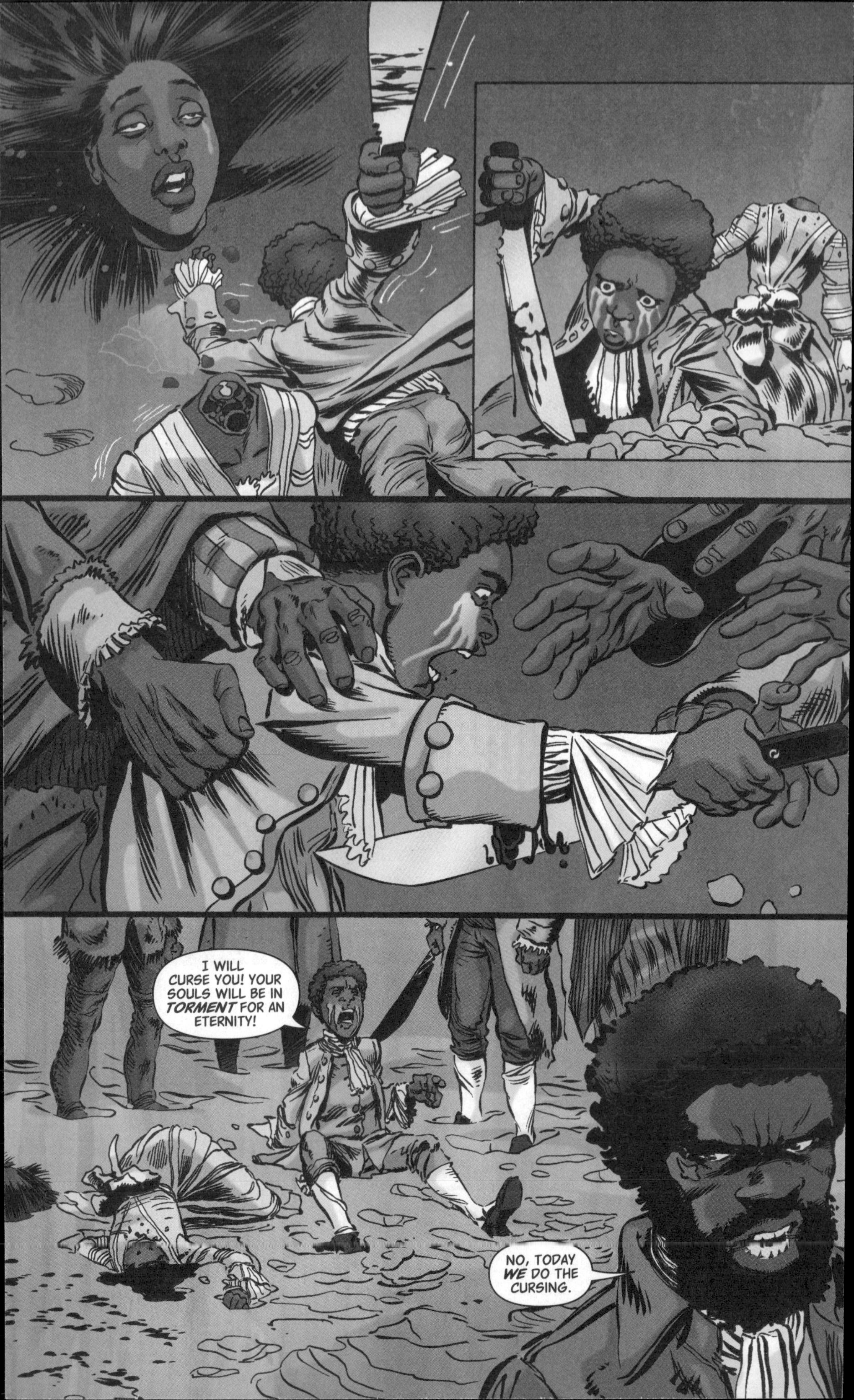
I WILL CURSE YOU! YOUR SOULS WILL BE IN *TORMENT* FOR AN ETERNITY!
NO, TODAY *WE* DO THE CURSING.

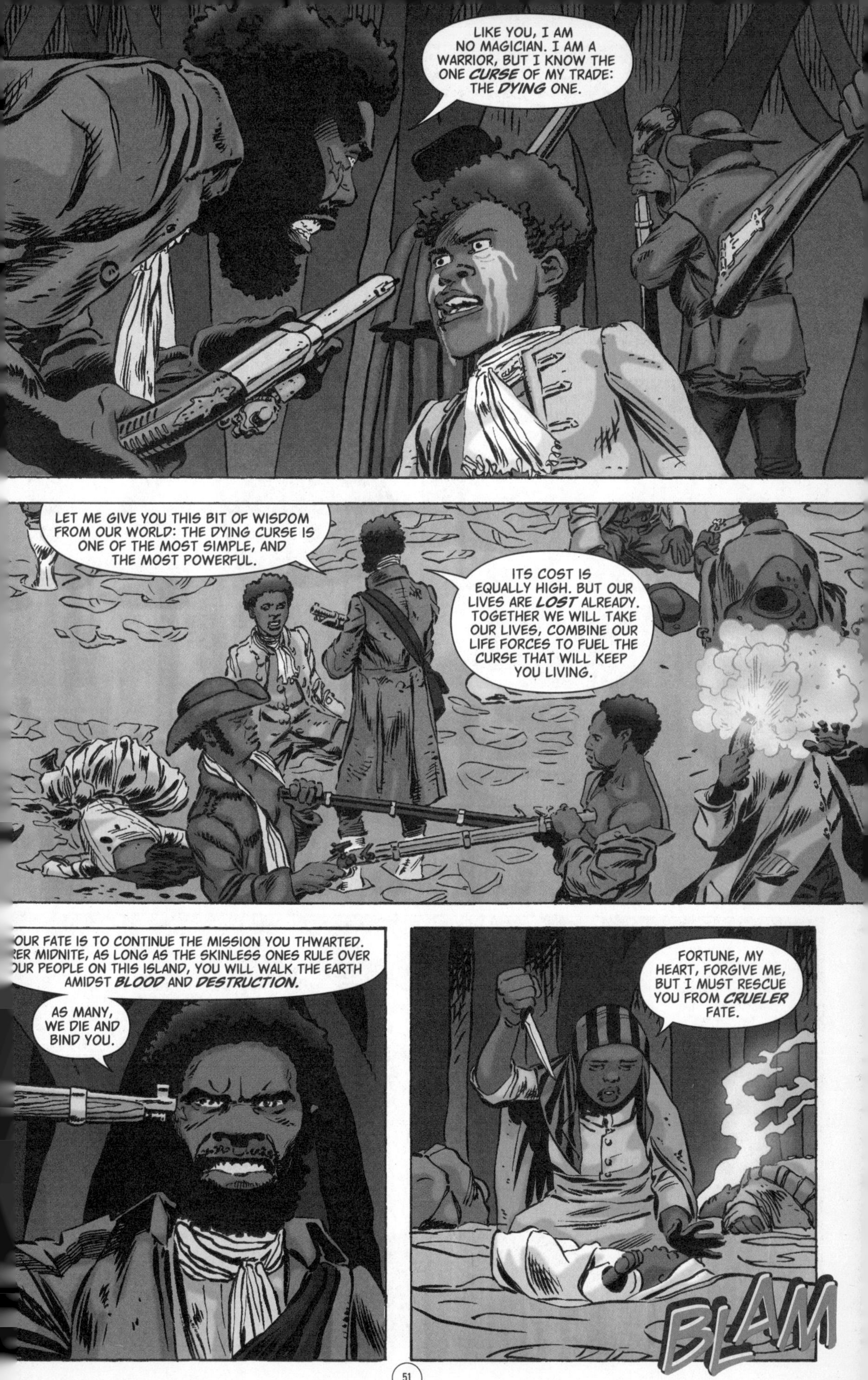
LIKE YOU, I AM NO MAGICIAN. I AM A WARRIOR, BUT I KNOW THE ONE CURSE OF MY TRADE: THE DYING ONE.
LET ME GIVE YOU THIS BIT OF WISDOM FROM OUR WORLD: THE DYING CURSE IS ONE OF THE MOST SIMPLE, AND THE MOST POWERFUL.
ITS COST IS EQUALLY HIGH. BUT OUR LIVES ARE LOST ALREADY. TOGETHER WE WILL TAKE OUR LIVES, COMBINE OUR LIFE FORCES TO FUEL THE CURSE THAT WILL KEEP YOU LIVING.
OUR FATE IS TO CONTINUE THE MISSION YOU THWARTED. ER MIDNITE, AS LONG AS THE SKINLESS ONES RULE OVER OUR PEOPLE ON THIS ISLAND, YOU WILL WALK THE EARTH AMIDST BLOOD AND DESTRUCTION.
AS MANY, WE DIE AND BIND YOU.
FORTUNE, MY HEART, FORGIVE ME, BUT I MUST RESCUE YOU FROM CRUELER FATE.
BLAM

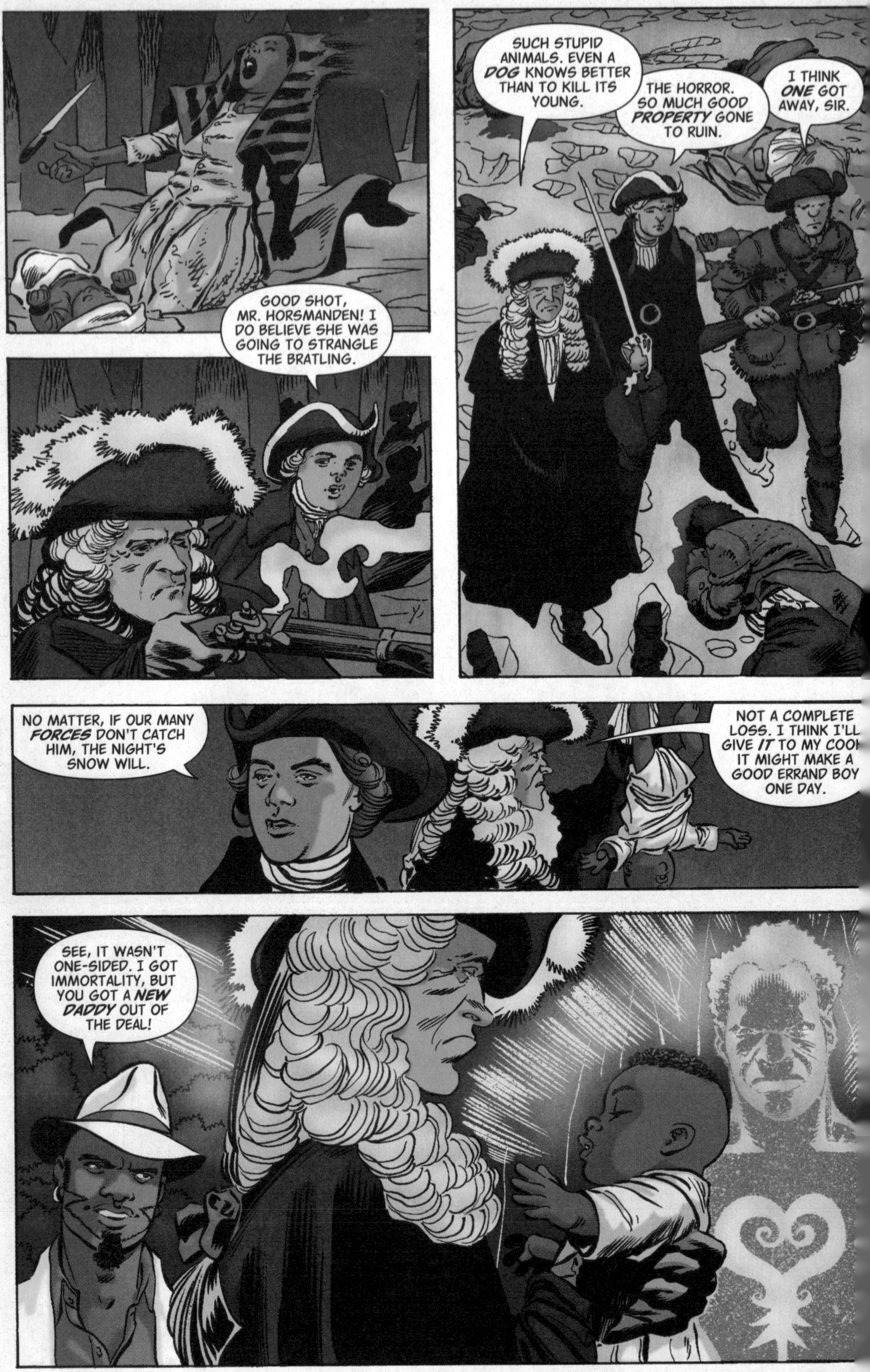
GOOD SHOT, MR. HORSMANDEN! I DO BELIEVE SHE WAS GOING TO STRANGLE THE BRATLING.
SUCH STUPID ANIMALS. EVEN A DOG KNOWS BETTER THAN TO KILL ITS YOUNG.
THE HORROR. SO MUCH GOOD PROPERTY GONE TO RUIN.
I THINK ONE GOT AWAY, SIR.
NO MATTER, IF OUR MANY FORCES DON'T CATCH HIM, THE NIGHT'S SNOW WILL.
NOT A COMPLETE LOSS. I THINK I'LL GIVE IT TO MY COOK. IT MIGHT MAKE A GOOD ERRAND BOY ONE DAY.
SEE, IT WASN'T ONE-SIDED. I GOT IMMORTALITY, BUT YOU GOT A NEW DADDY OUT OF THE DEAL!

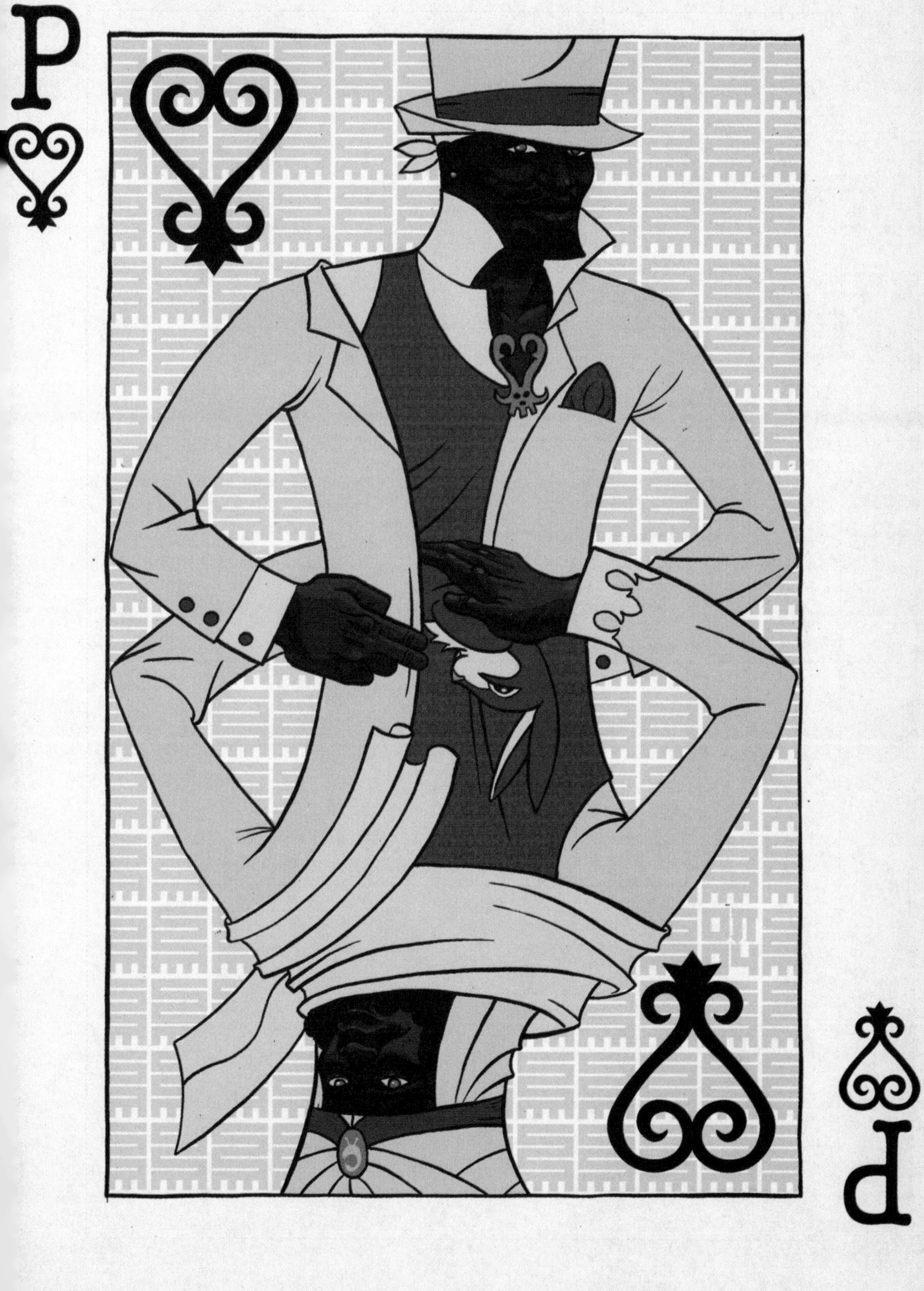
P

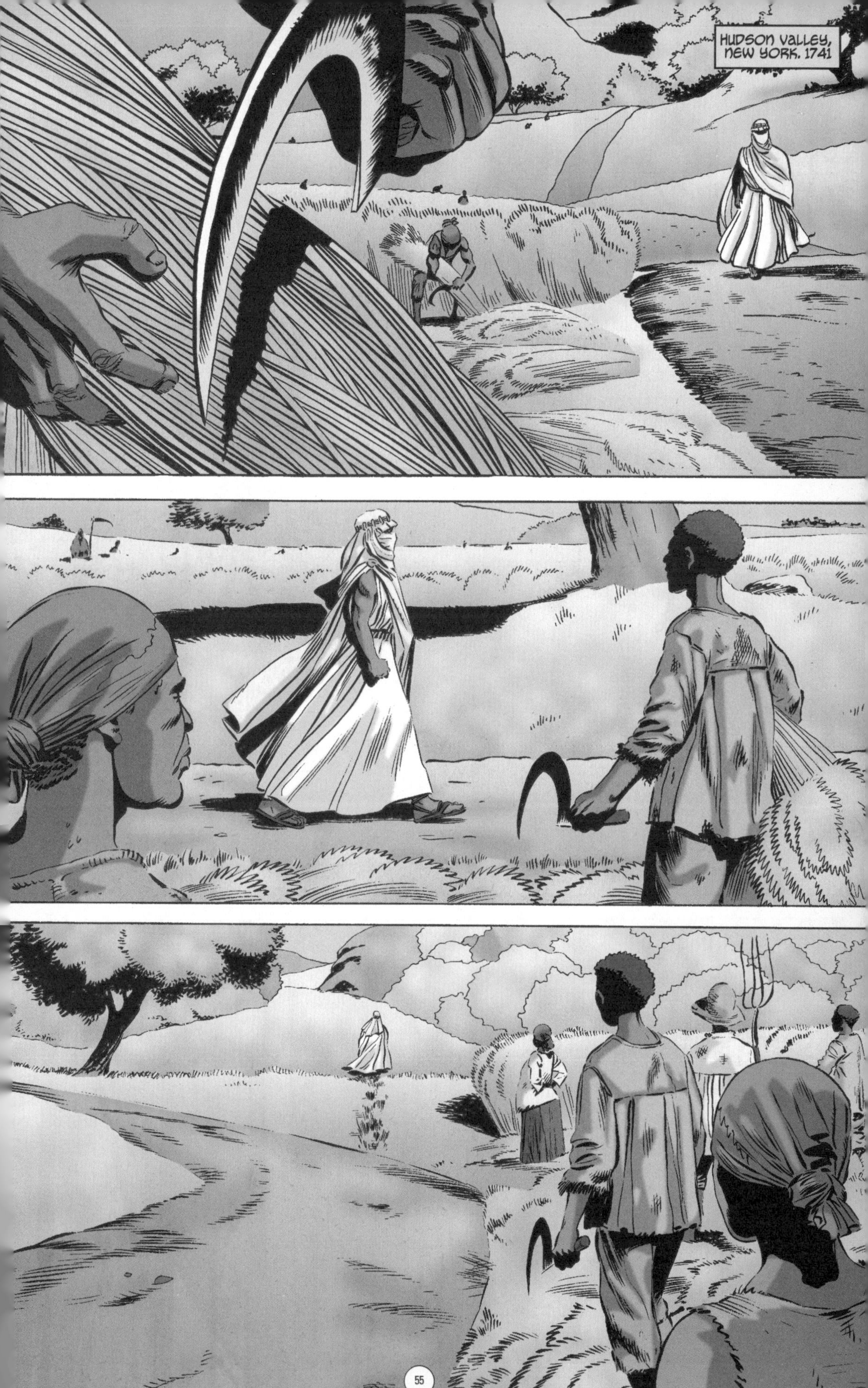
HUDSON VALLEY, NEW YORK. 1741

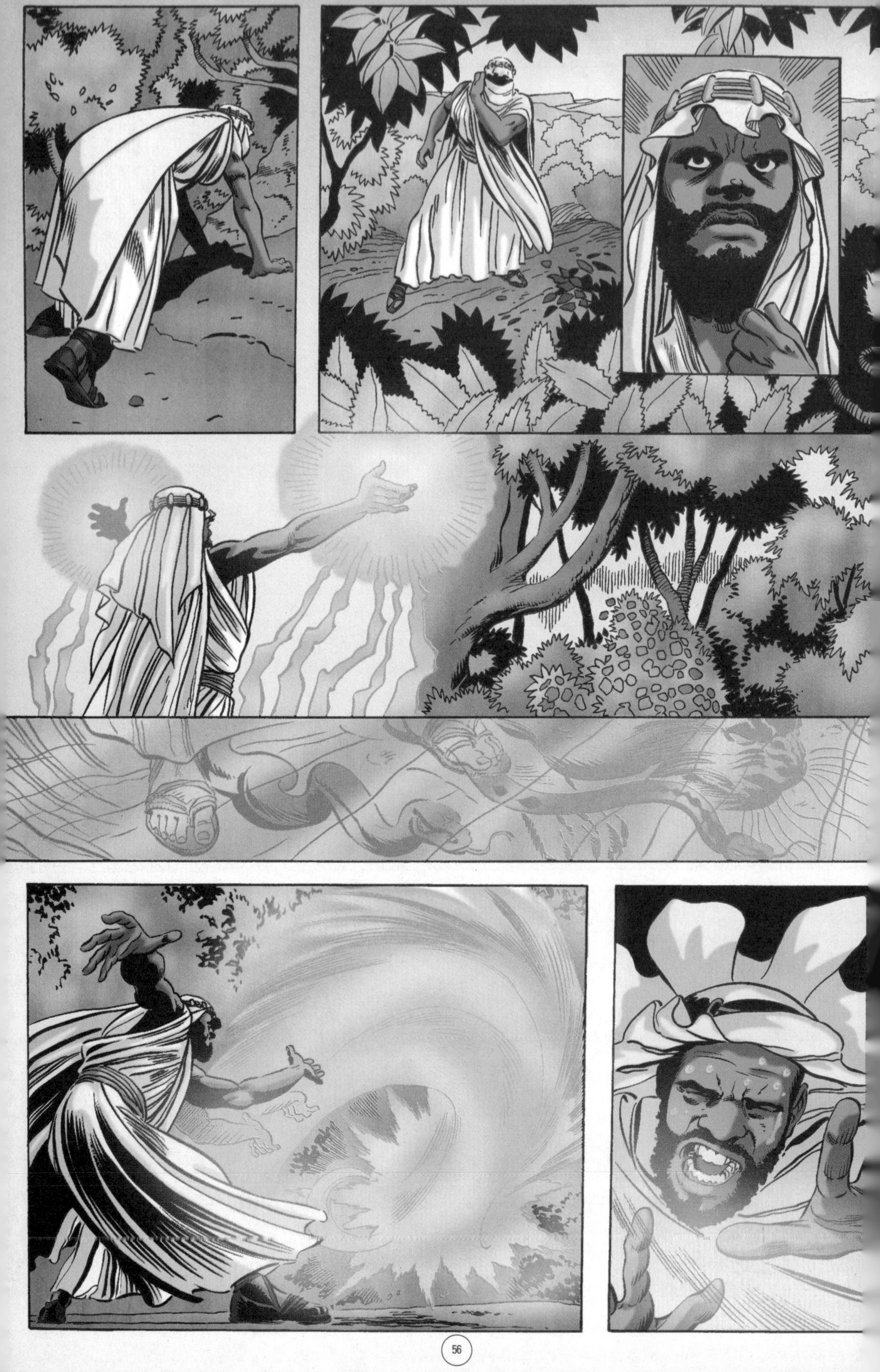

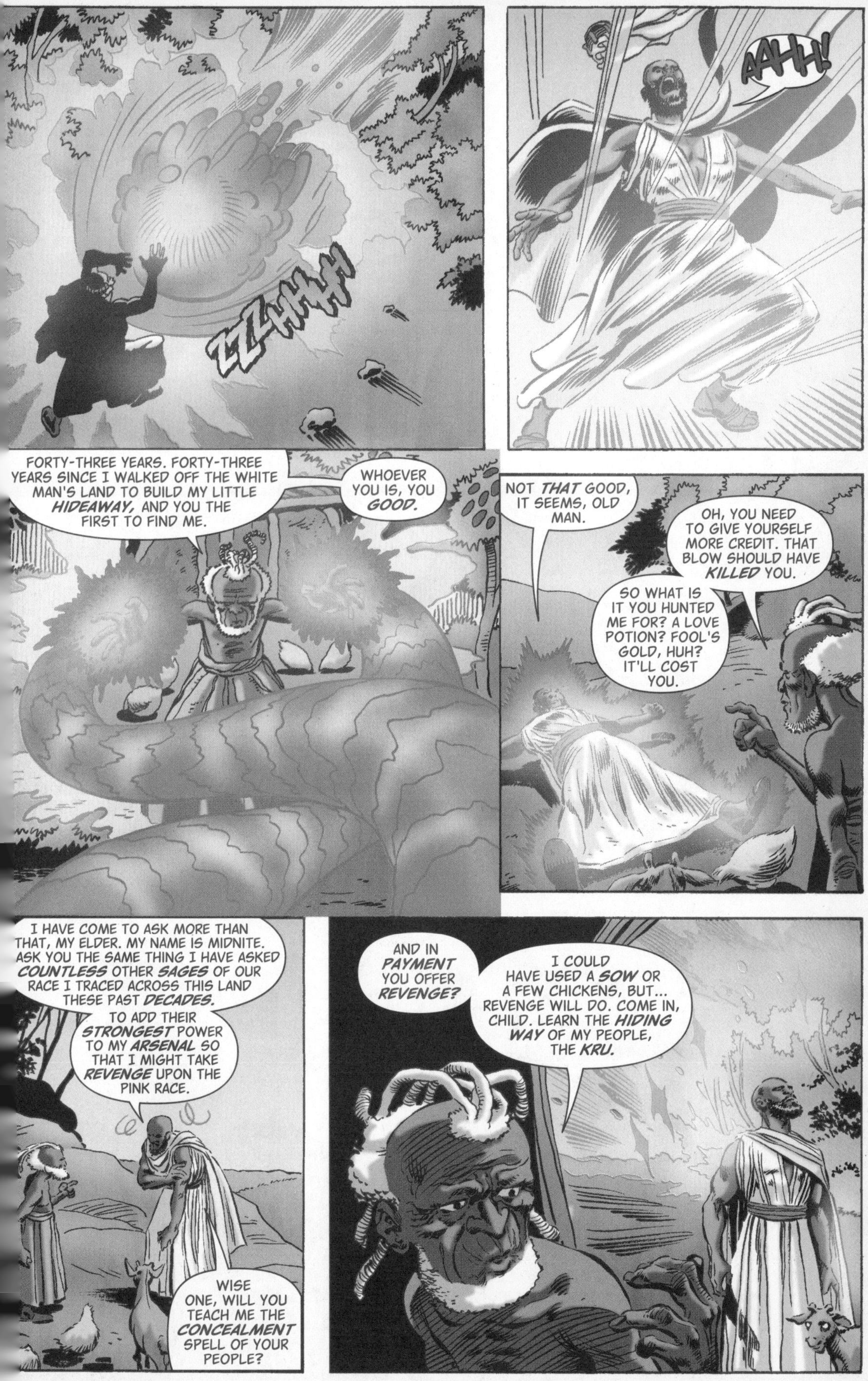
ZZZHHHH
AAHH!
FORTY-THREE YEARS. FORTY-THREE YEARS SINCE I WALKED OFF THE WHITE MAN'S LAND TO BUILD MY LITTLE HIDEAWAY, AND YOU THE FIRST TO FIND ME.
WHOEVER YOU IS, YOU GOOD.
NOT THAT GOOD, IT SEEMS, OLD MAN.
OH, YOU NEED TO GIVE YOURSELF MORE CREDIT. THAT BLOW SHOULD HAVE KILLED YOU.
SO WHAT IS IT YOU HUNTED ME FOR? A LOVE POTION? FOOL'S GOLD, HUH? IT'LL COST YOU.
I HAVE COME TO ASK MORE THAN THAT, MY ELDER. MY NAME IS MIDNITE. ASK YOU THE SAME THING I HAVE ASKED COUNTLESS OTHER SAGES OF OUR RACE I TRACED ACROSS THIS LAND THESE PAST DECADES.
TO ADD THEIR STRONGEST POWER TO MY ARSENAL SO THAT I MIGHT TAKE REVENGE UPON THE PINK RACE.
WISE ONE, WILL YOU TEACH ME THE CONCEALMENT SPELL OF YOUR PEOPLE?
AND IN PAYMENT YOU OFFER REVENGE?
I COULD HAVE USED A SOW OR A FEW CHICKENS, BUT... REVENGE WILL DO. COME IN, CHILD. LEARN THE HIDING WAY OF MY PEOPLE, THE KRU.

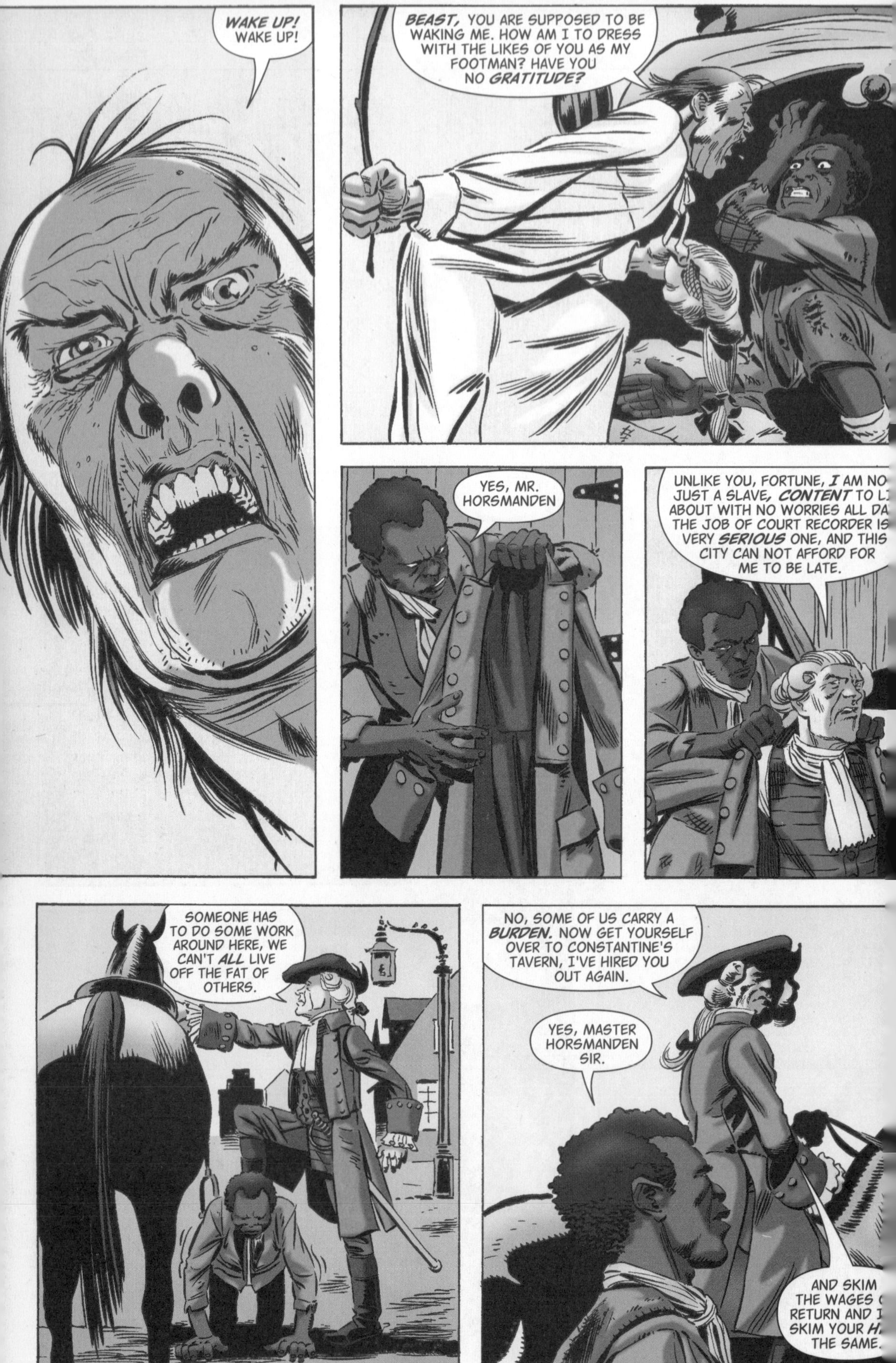

WAKE UP! WAKE UP!
BEAST, YOU ARE SUPPOSED TO BE WAKING ME. HOW AM I TO DRESS WITH THE LIKES OF YOU AS MY FOOTMAN? HAVE YOU NO GRATITUDE?
YES, MR. HORSMANDEN
UNLIKE YOU, FORTUNE, I AM NO JUST A SLAVE, CONTENT TO L ABOUT WITH NO WORRIES ALL DA THE JOB OF COURT RECORDER IS VERY SERIOUS ONE, AND THIS CITY CAN NOT AFFORD FOR ME TO BE LATE.
SOMEONE HAS TO DO SOME WORK AROUND HERE, WE CAN'T ALL LIVE OFF THE FAT OF OTHERS.
NO, SOME OF US CARRY A BURDEN. NOW GET YOURSELF OVER TO CONSTANTINE'S TAVERN, I'VE HIRED YOU OUT AGAIN.
YES, MASTER HORSMANDEN SIR.
AND SKIM THE WAGES RETURN AND I SKIM YOUR THE SAME.

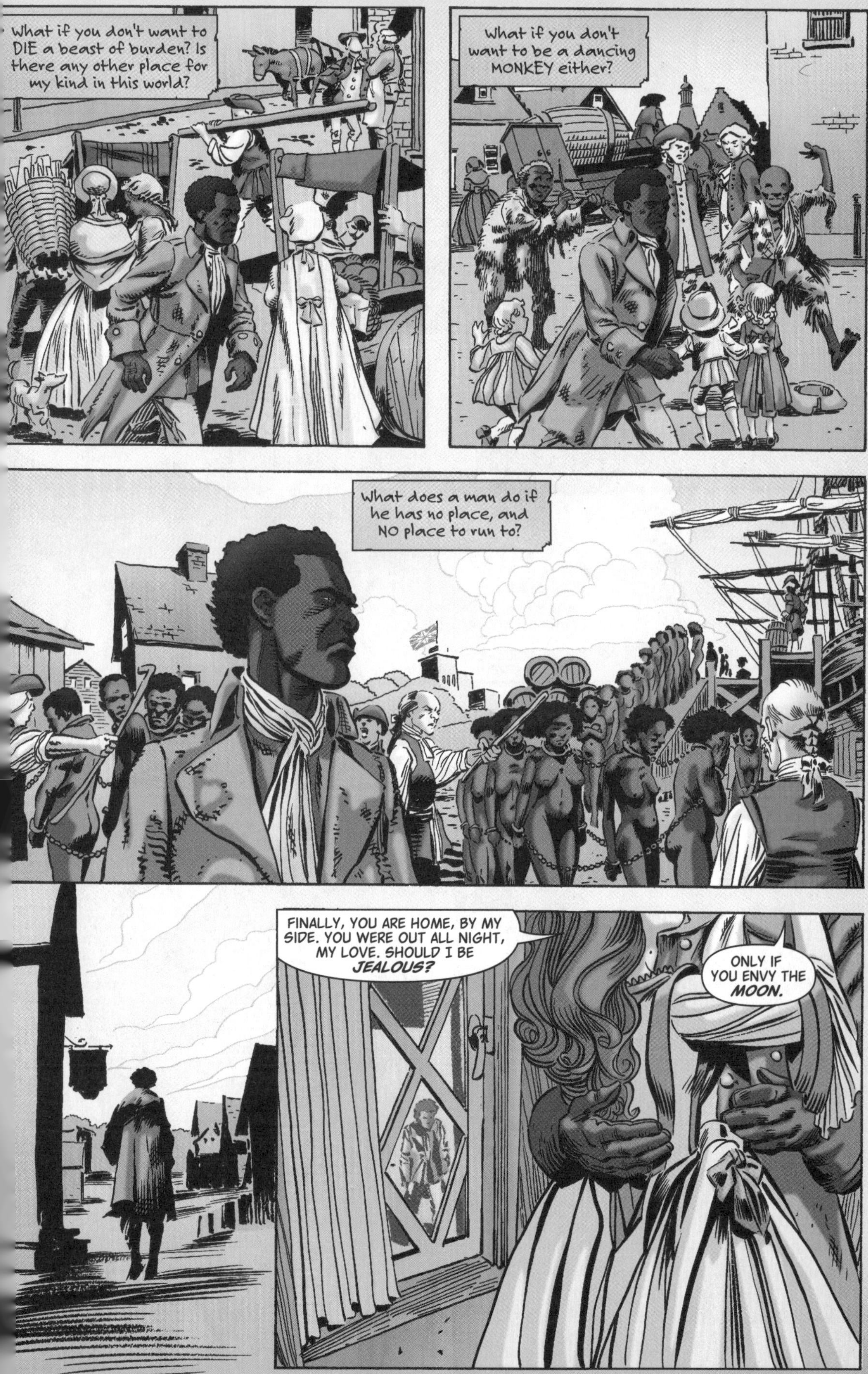
What if you don't want to DIE a beast of burden? Is there any other place for my kind in this world?
What if you don't want to be a dancing MONKEY either?
What does a man do if he has no place, and NO place to run to?
FINALLY, YOU ARE HOME, BY MY SIDE. YOU WERE OUT ALL NIGHT, MY LOVE. SHOULD I BE JEALOUS?
ONLY IF YOU ENVY THE MOON.

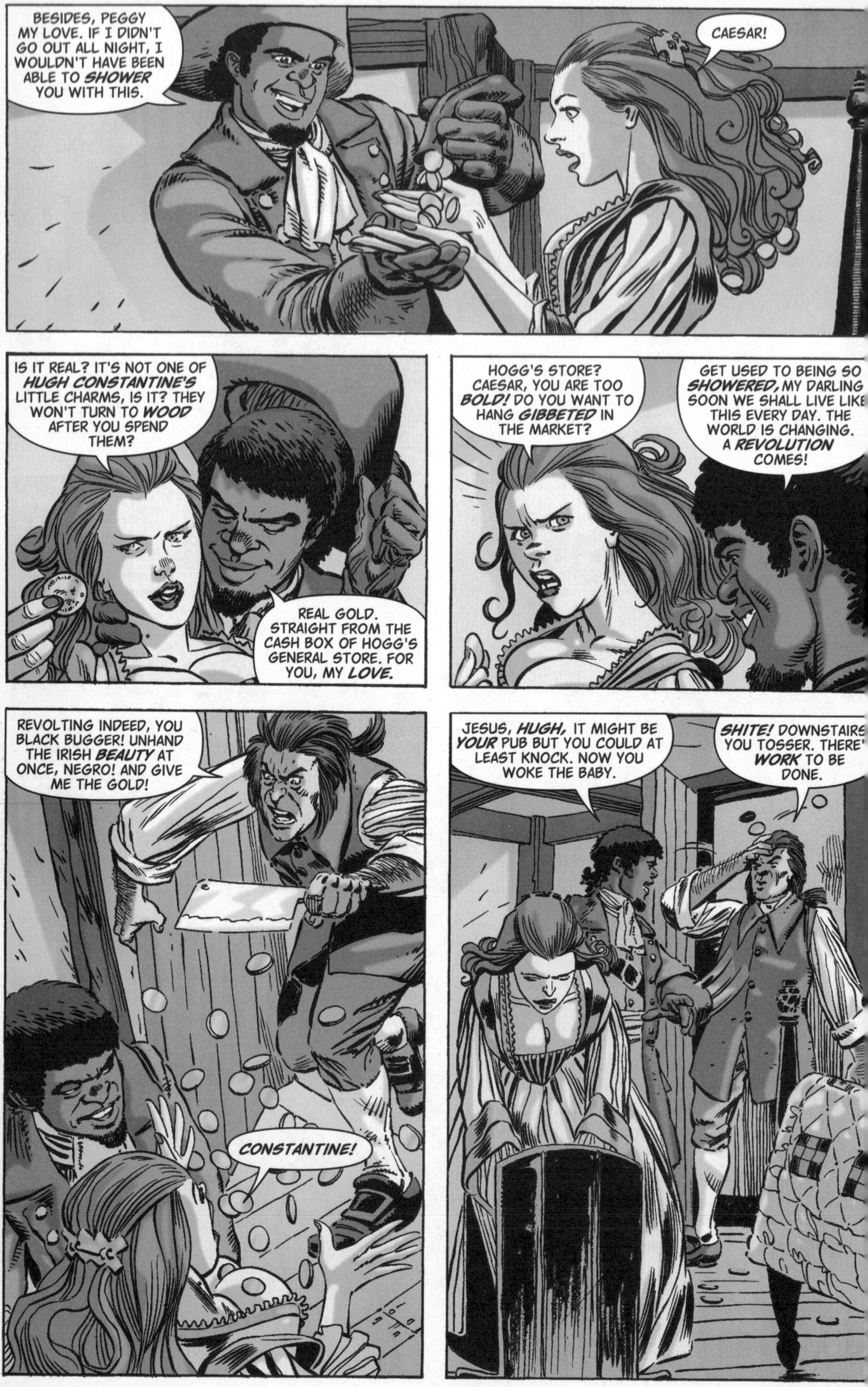
BESIDES, PEGGY MY LOVE. IF I DIDN'T GO OUT ALL NIGHT, I WOULDN'T HAVE BEEN ABLE TO SHOWER YOU WITH THIS.
CAESAR!
IS IT REAL? IT'S NOT ONE OF HUGH CONSTANTINE'S LITTLE CHARMS, IS IT? THEY WON'T TURN TO WOOD AFTER YOU SPEND THEM?
REAL GOLD. STRAIGHT FROM THE CASH BOX OF HOGG'S GENERAL STORE. FOR YOU, MY LOVE.
HOGG'S STORE? CAESAR, YOU ARE TOO BOLD! DO YOU WANT TO HANG GIBBETED IN THE MARKET?
GET USED TO BEING SO SHOWERED, MY DARLING SOON WE SHALL LIVE LIKE THIS EVERY DAY. THE WORLD IS CHANGING. A REVOLUTION COMES!
REVOLTING INDEED, YOU BLACK BUGGER! UNHAND THE IRISH BEAUTY AT ONCE, NEGRO! AND GIVE ME THE GOLD!
CONSTANTINE!
JESUS, HUGH, IT MIGHT BE YOUR PUB BUT YOU COULD AT LEAST KNOCK. NOW YOU WOKE THE BABY.
SHITE! DOWNSTAIRS YOU TOSSER. THERE' WORK TO BE DONE.

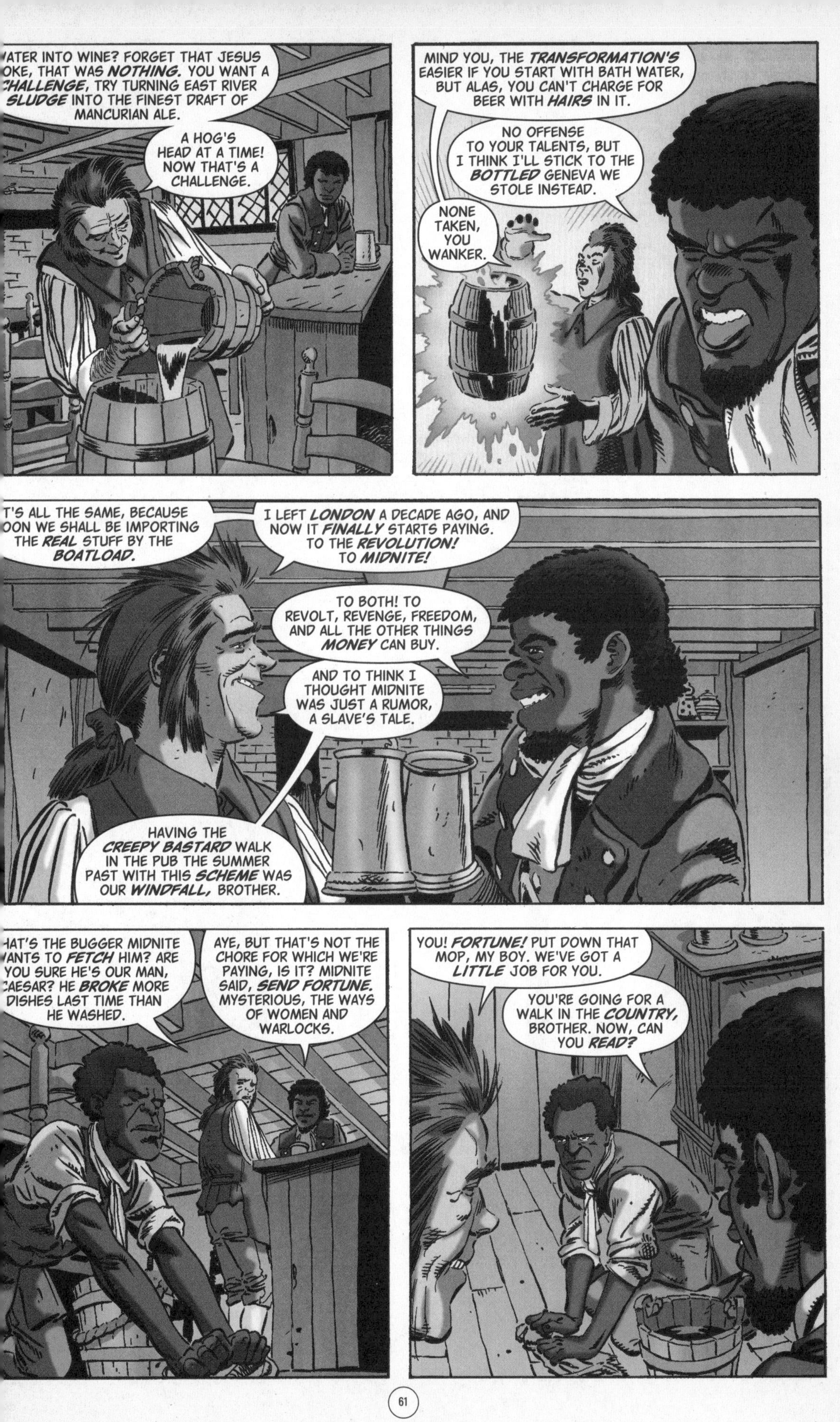

WATER INTO WINE? FORGET THAT JESUS JOKE, THAT WAS NOTHING. YOU WANT A CHALLENGE, TRY TURNING EAST RIVER SLUDGE INTO THE FINEST DRAFT OF MANCURIAN ALE.
A HOG'S HEAD AT A TIME! NOW THAT'S A CHALLENGE.
MIND YOU, THE TRANSFORMATION'S EASIER IF YOU START WITH BATH WATER, BUT ALAS, YOU CAN'T CHARGE FOR BEER WITH HAIRS IN IT.
NO OFFENSE TO YOUR TALENTS, BUT I THINK I'LL STICK TO THE BOTTLED GENEVA WE STOLE INSTEAD.
NONE TAKEN, YOU WANKER.
IT'S ALL THE SAME, BECAUSE SOON WE SHALL BE IMPORTING THE REAL STUFF BY THE BOATLOAD.
I LEFT LONDON A DECADE AGO, AND NOW IT FINALLY STARTS PAYING. TO THE REVOLUTION! TO MIDNITE!
TO BOTH! TO REVOLT, REVENGE, FREEDOM, AND ALL THE OTHER THINGS MONEY CAN BUY.
AND TO THINK I THOUGHT MIDNITE WAS JUST A RUMOR, A SLAVE'S TALE.
HAVING THE CREEPY BASTARD WALK IN THE PUB THE SUMMER PAST WITH THIS SCHEME WAS OUR WINDFALL, BROTHER.
THAT'S THE BUGGER MIDNITE WANTS TO FETCH HIM? ARE YOU SURE HE'S OUR MAN, CAESAR? HE BROKE MORE DISHES LAST TIME THAN HE WASHED.
AYE, BUT THAT'S NOT THE CHORE FOR WHICH WE'RE PAYING, IS IT? MIDNITE SAID, SEND FORTUNE. MYSTERIOUS, THE WAYS OF WOMEN AND WARLOCKS.
YOU! FORTUNE! PUT DOWN THAT MOP, MY BOY. WE'VE GOT A LITTLE JOB FOR YOU.
YOU'RE GOING FOR A WALK IN THE COUNTRY, BROTHER. NOW, CAN YOU READ?

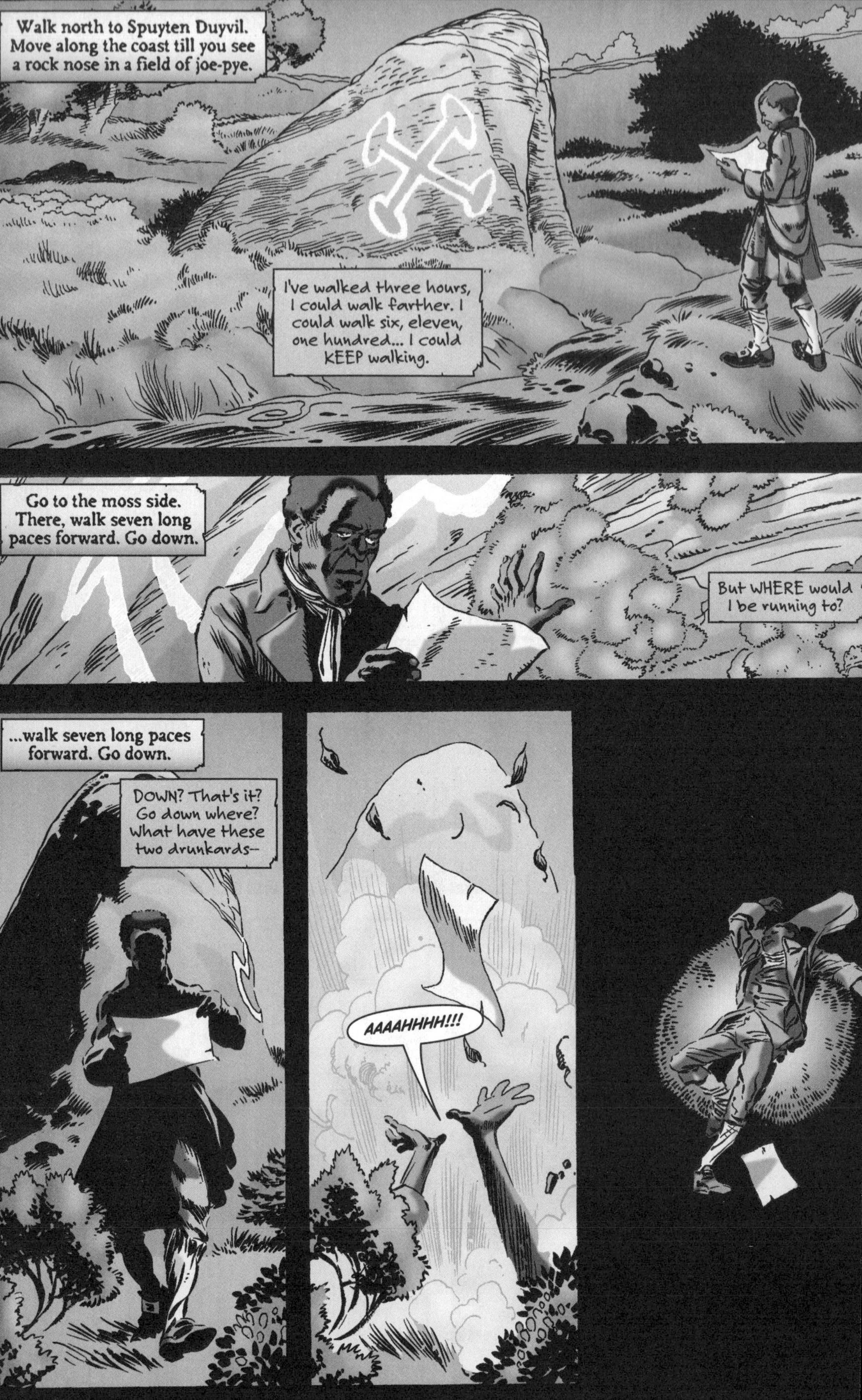
Walk north to Spuyten Duyvil. Move along the coast till you see a rock nose in a field of joe-pye.
I've walked three hours, I could walk farther. I could walk six, eleven, one hundred... I could KEEP walking.
Go to the moss side. There, walk seven long paces forward. Go down.
But WHERE would I be running to?
...walk seven long paces forward. Go down.
DOWN? That's it? Go down where? What have these two drunkards-
AAAAHHHH!!!

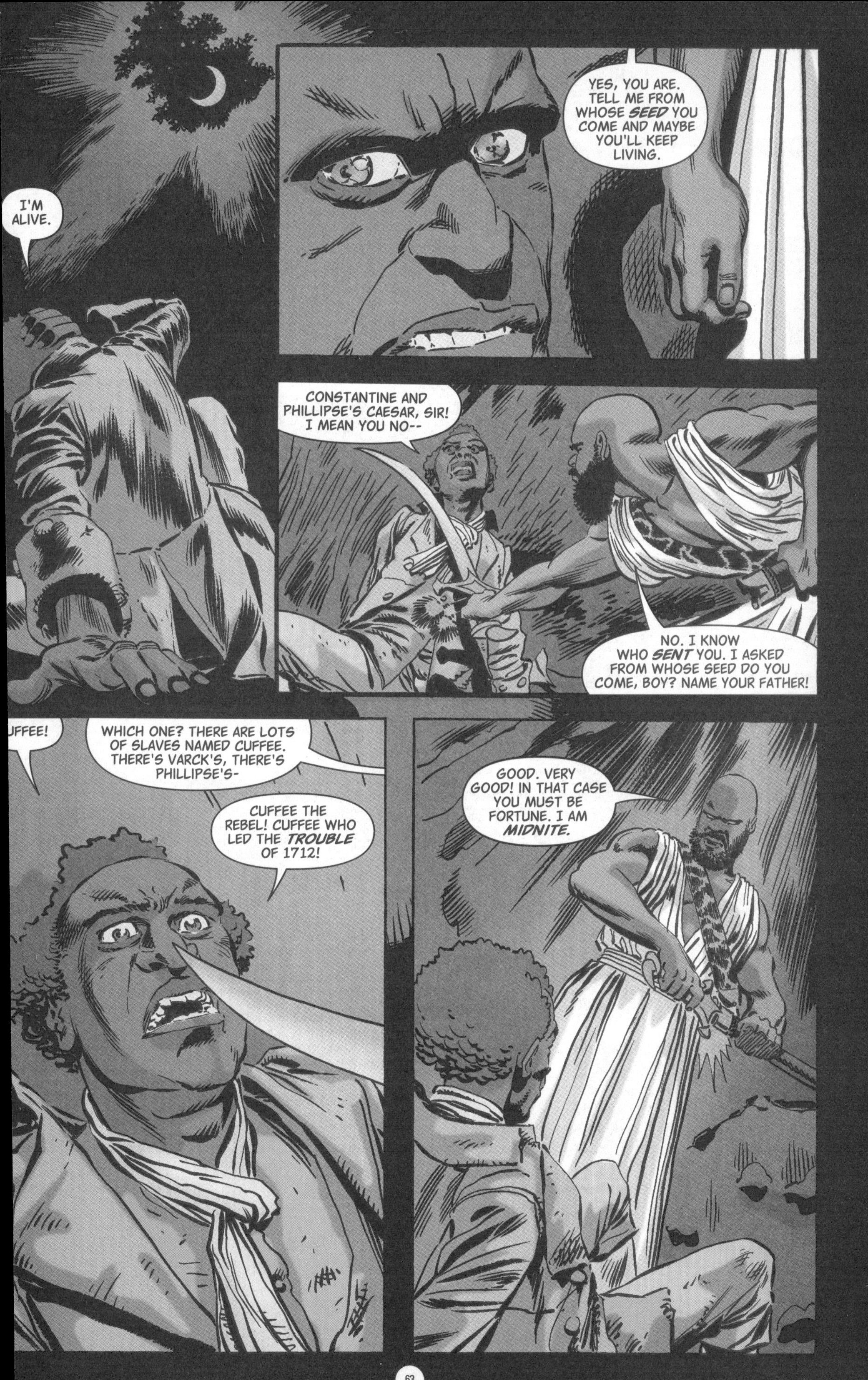
I'M ALIVE.
YES, YOU ARE. TELL ME FROM WHOSE SEED YOU COME AND MAYBE YOU'LL KEEP LIVING.
CONSTANTINE AND PHILLIPSE'S CAESAR, SIR! I MEAN YOU NO--
NO. I KNOW WHO SENT YOU. I ASKED FROM WHOSE SEED DO YOU COME, BOY? NAME YOUR FATHER!
UFFEE!
WHICH ONE? THERE ARE LOTS OF SLAVES NAMED CUFFEE. THERE'S VARCK'S, THERE'S PHILLIPSE'S-
CUFFEE THE REBEL! CUFFEE WHO LED THE TROUBLE OF 1712!
GOOD. VERY GOOD! IN THAT CASE YOU MUST BE FORTUNE. I AM MIDNITE.

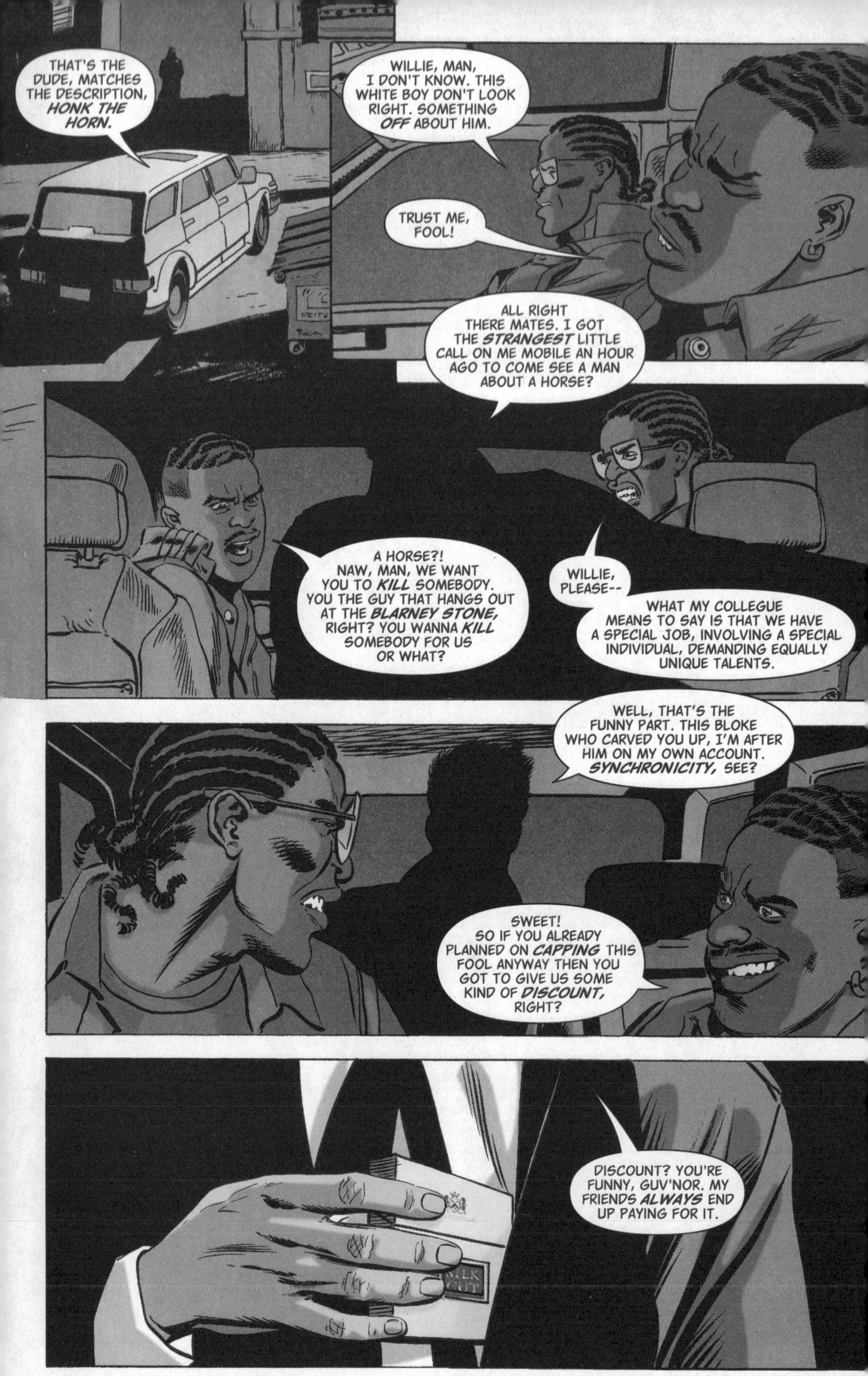
THAT'S THE DUDE, MATCHES THE DESCRIPTION, HONK THE HORN.
WILLIE, MAN, I DON'T KNOW. THIS WHITE BOY DON'T LOOK RIGHT. SOMETHING OFF ABOUT HIM.
TRUST ME, FOOL!
ALL RIGHT THERE MATES. I GOT THE STRANGEST LITTLE CALL ON ME MOBILE AN HOUR AGO TO COME SEE A MAN ABOUT A HORSE?
A HORSE?! NAW, MAN, WE WANT YOU TO KILL SOMEBODY. YOU THE GUY THAT HANGS OUT AT THE BLARNEY STONE, RIGHT? YOU WANNA KILL SOMEBODY FOR US OR WHAT?
WILLIE, PLEASE--
WHAT MY COLLEGUE MEANS TO SAY IS THAT WE HAVE A SPECIAL JOB, INVOLVING A SPECIAL INDIVIDUAL, DEMANDING EQUALLY UNIQUE TALENTS.
WELL, THAT'S THE FUNNY PART. THIS BLOKE WHO CARVED YOU UP, I'M AFTER HIM ON MY OWN ACCOUNT. SYNCHRONICITY, SEE?
SWEET! SO IF YOU ALREADY PLANNED ON CAPPING THIS FOOL ANYWAY THEN YOU GOT TO GIVE US SOME KIND OF DISCOUNT, RIGHT?
DISCOUNT? YOU'RE FUNNY, GUV'NOR. MY FRIENDS ALWAYS END UP PAYING FOR IT.

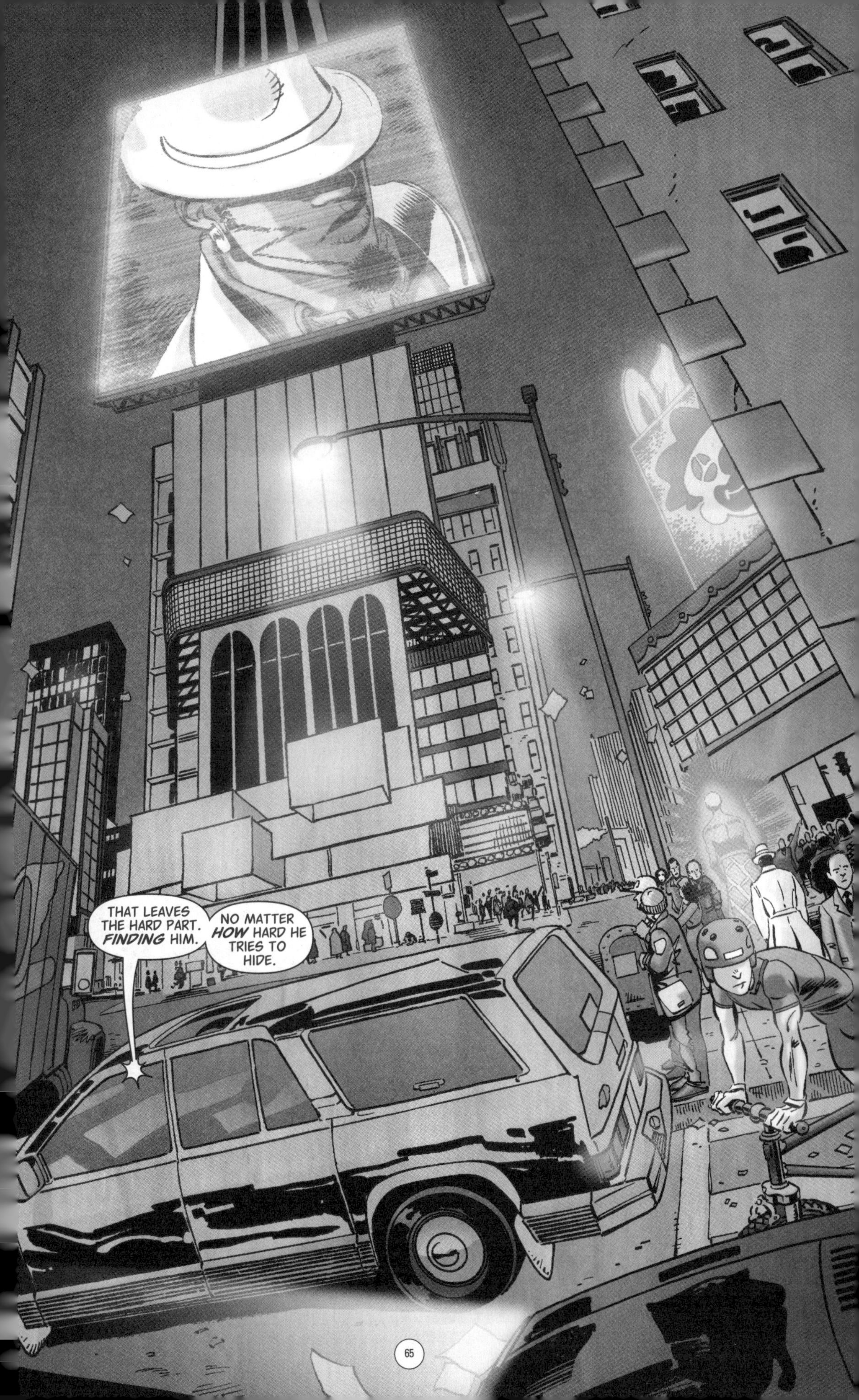
THAT LEAVES THE HARD PART. FINDING HIM.
NO MATTER HOW HARD HE TRIES TO HIDE.

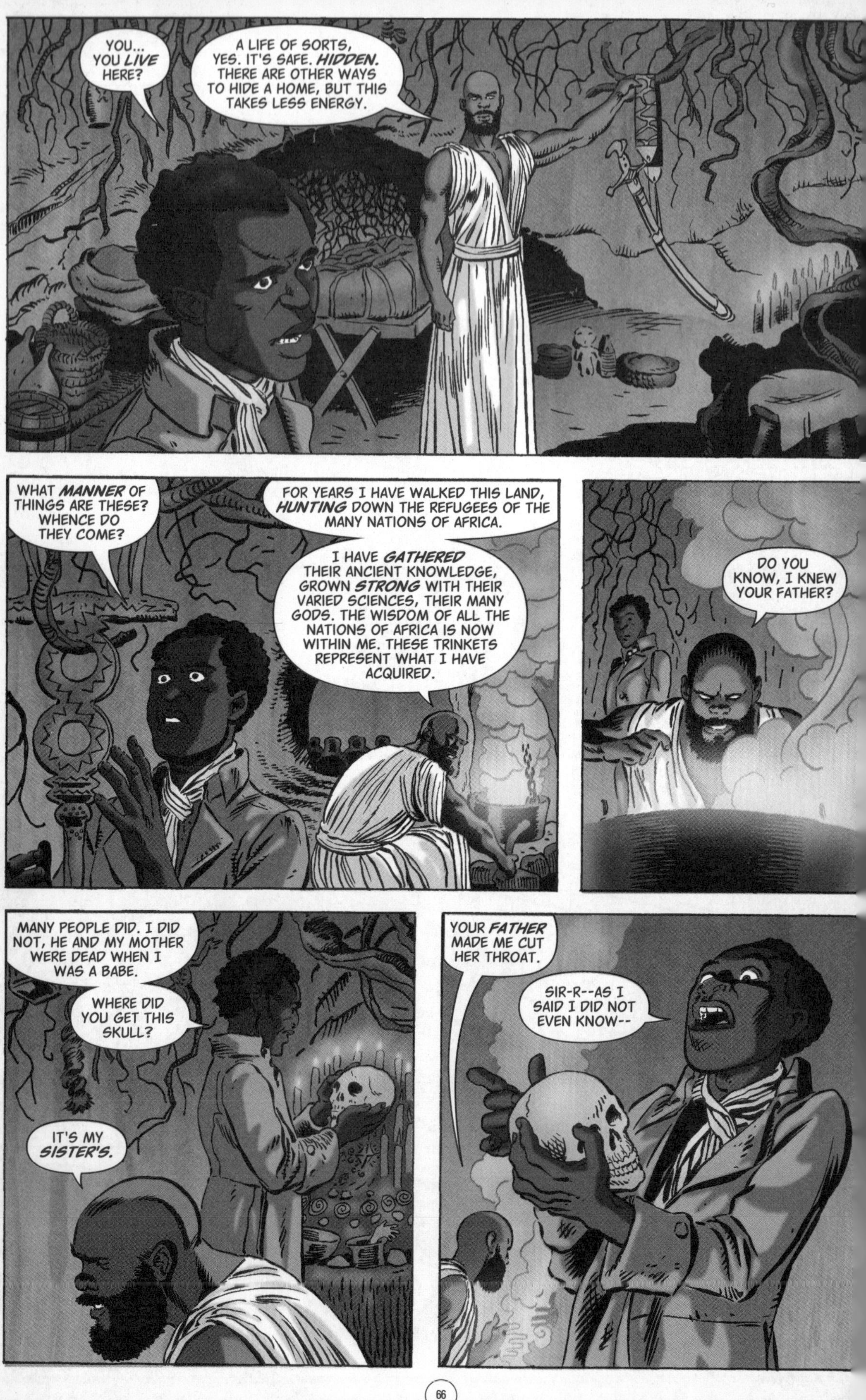
YOU... YOU LIVE HERE?
A LIFE OF SORTS, YES. IT'S SAFE. HIDDEN. THERE ARE OTHER WAYS TO HIDE A HOME, BUT THIS TAKES LESS ENERGY.
WHAT MANNER OF THINGS ARE THESE? WHENCE DO THEY COME?
FOR YEARS I HAVE WALKED THIS LAND, HUNTING DOWN THE REFUGEES OF THE MANY NATIONS OF AFRICA.
I HAVE GATHERED THEIR ANCIENT KNOWLEDGE, GROWN STRONG WITH THEIR VARIED SCIENCES, THEIR MANY GODS. THE WISDOM OF ALL THE NATIONS OF AFRICA IS NOW WITHIN ME. THESE TRINKETS REPRESENT WHAT I HAVE ACQUIRED.
DO YOU KNOW, I KNEW YOUR FATHER?
MANY PEOPLE DID. I DID NOT, HE AND MY MOTHER WERE DEAD WHEN I WAS A BABE.
WHERE DID YOU GET THIS SKULL?
IT'S MY SISTER'S.
YOUR FATHER MADE ME CUT HER THROAT.
SIR-R--AS I SAID I DID NOT EVEN KNOW--

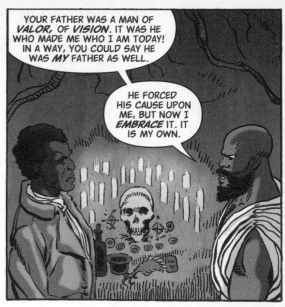

STOP. I DO NOT HATE HIM FOR IT. I *DID*, FOR MANY YEARS, BUT THAT'S GONE. NOW I HATE THE FATE *I* CAUSED. IT WAS THE REVOLT. YOUR FATHER...HE WAS A GREAT MAN.

I WAS NOT EVEN A *DECENT* BOY.

YOUR FATHER WAS A MAN OF *VALOR*, OF *VISION*. IT WAS HE WHO MADE ME WHO I AM TODAY! IN A WAY, YOU COULD SAY HE WAS *MY* FATHER AS WELL.

HE FORCED HIS CAUSE UPON ME, BUT NOW I *EMBRACE* IT. IT IS MY OWN.

AND WHAT WAS HIS CAUSE? MASS *SUICIDE*?

THE END OF OUR PEOPLE'S SERVITUDE! THE *DESTRUCTION* OF THIS WORLD!

WHAT IS THE USE? THIS WORLD IS OUR *ONLY* HOME.

ISN'T THAT RIGHT, MY SISTER?

SO WE SHALL MAKE A *NEW* WORLD IN OUR *OWN* IMAGE.

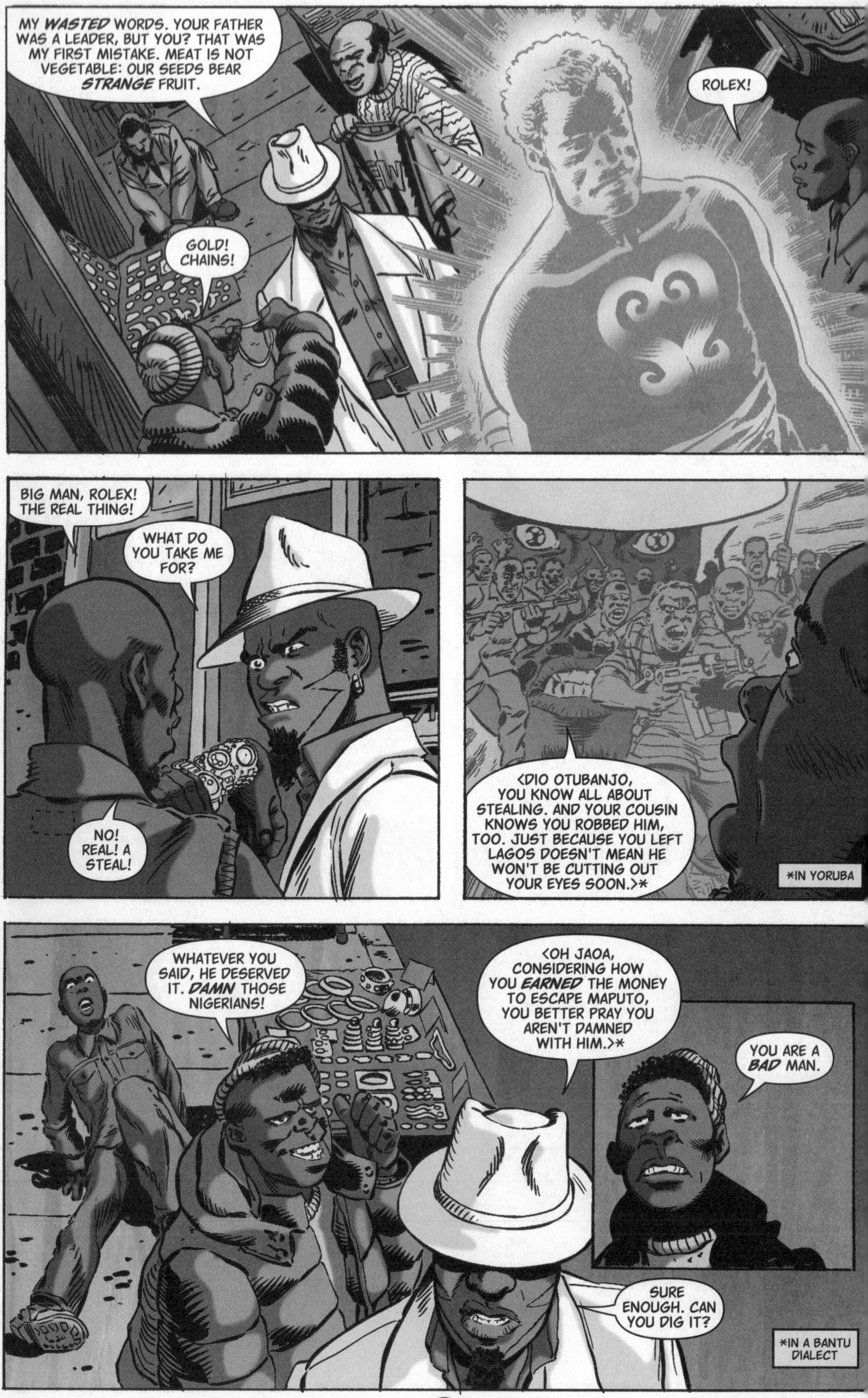

MY WASTED WORDS. YOUR FATHER WAS A LEADER, BUT YOU? THAT WAS MY FIRST MISTAKE. MEAT IS NOT VEGETABLE: OUR SEEDS BEAR STRANGE FRUIT.
ROLEX!
GOLD! CHAINS!
BIG MAN, ROLEX! THE REAL THING!
WHAT DO YOU TAKE ME FOR?
NO! REAL! A STEAL!
<DIO OTUBANJO, YOU KNOW ALL ABOUT STEALING. AND YOUR COUSIN KNOWS YOU ROBBED HIM, TOO. JUST BECAUSE YOU LEFT LAGOS DOESN'T MEAN HE WON'T BE CUTTING OUT YOUR EYES SOON.>*
*IN YORUBA
WHATEVER YOU SAID, HE DESERVED IT. DAMN THOSE NIGERIANS!
<OH JAOA, CONSIDERING HOW YOU EARNED THE MONEY TO ESCAPE MAPUTO, YOU BETTER PRAY YOU AREN'T DAMNED WITH HIM.>*
YOU ARE A BAD MAN.
SURE ENOUGH. CAN YOU DIG IT?
*IN A BANTU DIALECT

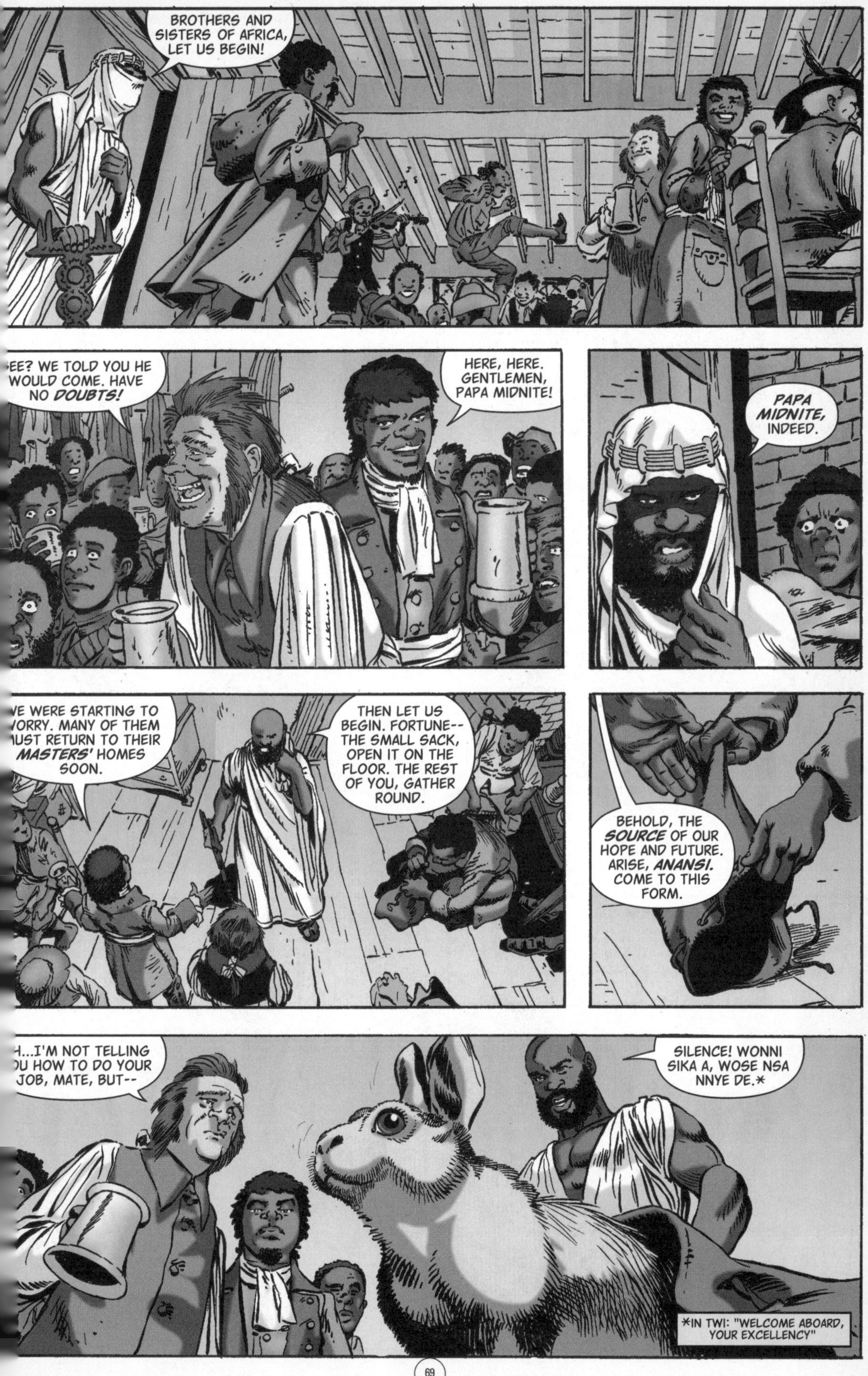
BROTHERS AND SISTERS OF AFRICA, LET US BEGIN!
EE? WE TOLD YOU HE WOULD COME. HAVE NO DOUBTS!
HERE, HERE. GENTLEMEN, PAPA MIDNITE!
PAPA MIDNITE, INDEED.
E WERE STARTING TO ORRY. MANY OF THEM UST RETURN TO THEIR MASTERS' HOMES SOON.
THEN LET US BEGIN. FORTUNE-- THE SMALL SACK, OPEN IT ON THE FLOOR. THE REST OF YOU, GATHER ROUND.
BEHOLD, THE SOURCE OF OUR HOPE AND FUTURE. ARISE, ANANSI. COME TO THIS FORM.
H...I'M NOT TELLING U HOW TO DO YOUR JOB, MATE, BUT--
SILENCE! WONNI SIKA A, WOSE NSA NNYE DE.*
*IN TWI: "WELCOME ABOARD, YOUR EXCELLENCY"

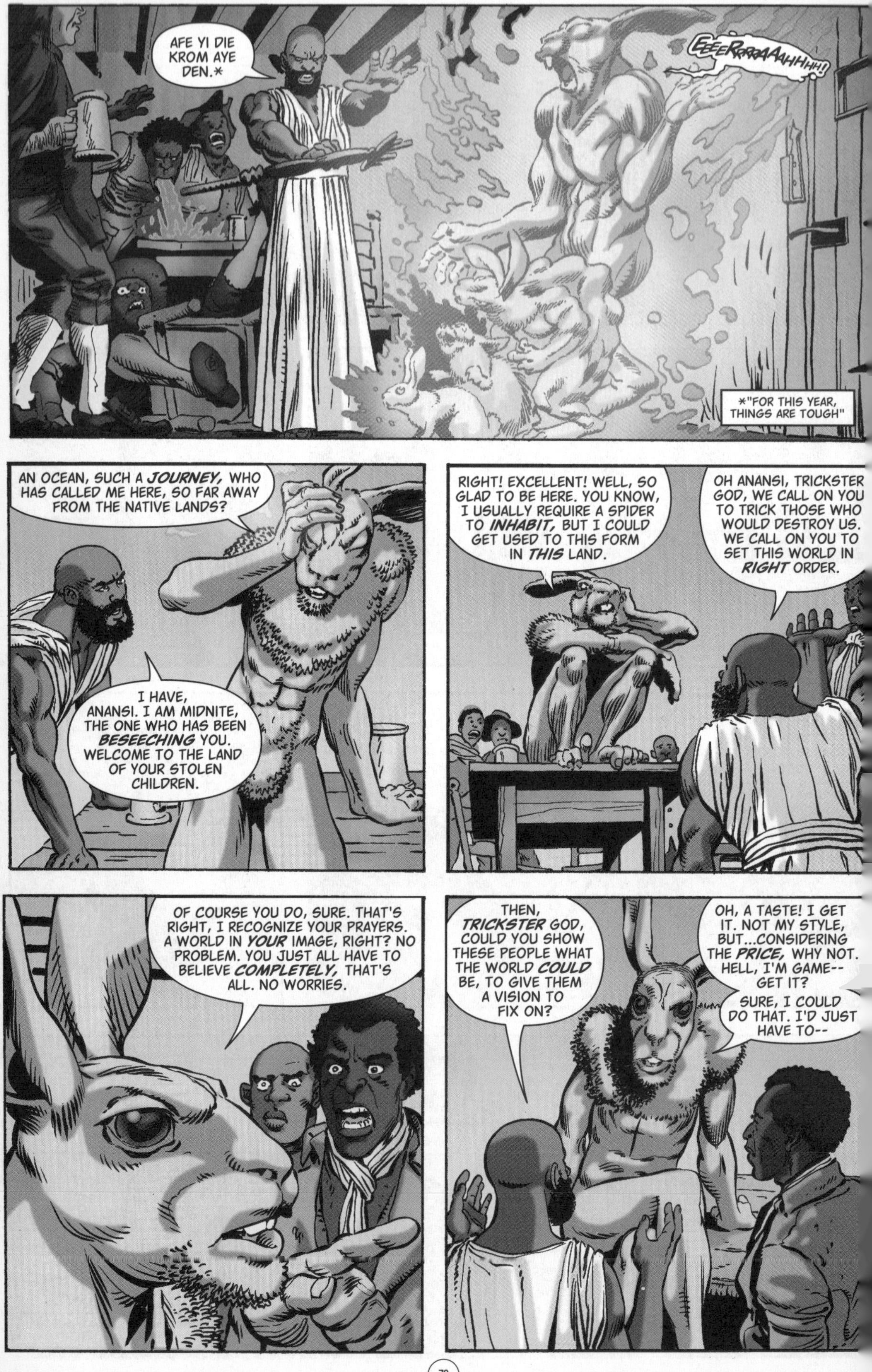
AFE YI DIE KROM AYE DEN.*
EEEERRRRAAAHHHH!
*"FOR THIS YEAR, THINGS ARE TOUGH"
AN OCEAN, SUCH A JOURNEY, WHO HAS CALLED ME HERE, SO FAR AWAY FROM THE NATIVE LANDS?
I HAVE, ANANSI. I AM MIDNITE, THE ONE WHO HAS BEEN BESEECHING YOU. WELCOME TO THE LAND OF YOUR STOLEN CHILDREN.
RIGHT! EXCELLENT! WELL, SO GLAD TO BE HERE. YOU KNOW, I USUALLY REQUIRE A SPIDER TO INHABIT, BUT I COULD GET USED TO THIS FORM IN THIS LAND.
OH ANANSI, TRICKSTER GOD, WE CALL ON YOU TO TRICK THOSE WHO WOULD DESTROY US. WE CALL ON YOU TO SET THIS WORLD IN RIGHT ORDER.
OF COURSE YOU DO, SURE. THAT'S RIGHT, I RECOGNIZE YOUR PRAYERS. A WORLD IN YOUR IMAGE, RIGHT? NO PROBLEM. YOU JUST ALL HAVE TO BELIEVE COMPLETELY, THAT'S ALL. NO WORRIES.
THEN, TRICKSTER GOD, COULD YOU SHOW THESE PEOPLE WHAT THE WORLD COULD BE, TO GIVE THEM A VISION TO FIX ON?
OH, A TASTE! I GET IT. NOT MY STYLE, BUT...CONSIDERING THE PRICE, WHY NOT. HELL, I'M GAME-- GET IT?
SURE, I COULD DO THAT. I'D JUST HAVE TO--

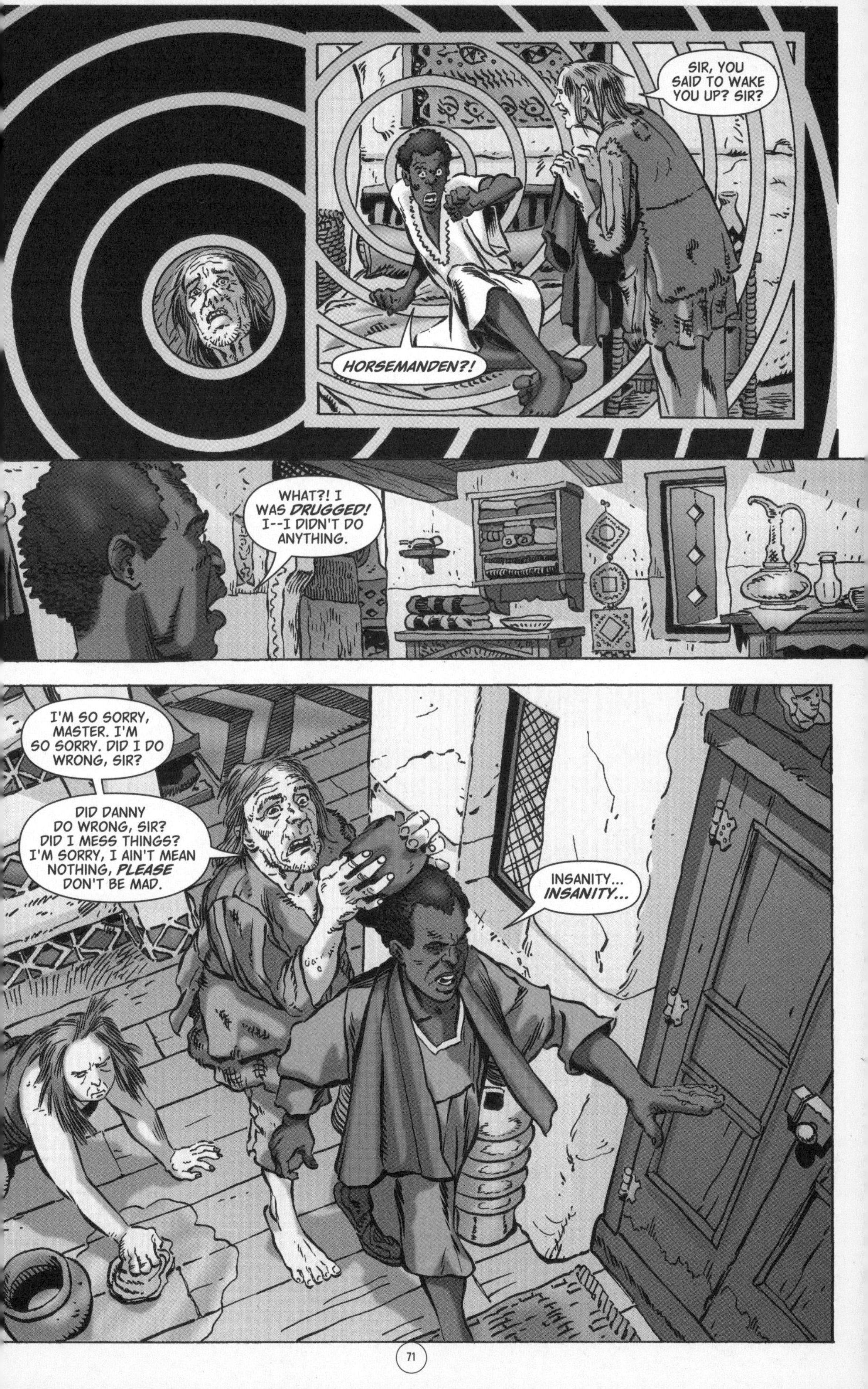

SIR, YOU SAID TO WAKE YOU UP? SIR?
HORSEMANDEN?!
WHAT?! I WAS DRUGGED! I--I DIDN'T DO ANYTHING.
I'M SO SORRY, MASTER. I'M SO SORRY. DID I DO WRONG, SIR?
DID DANNY DO WRONG, SIR? DID I MESS THINGS? I'M SORRY, I AIN'T MEAN NOTHING, PLEASE DON'T BE MAD.
INSANITY... INSANITY...

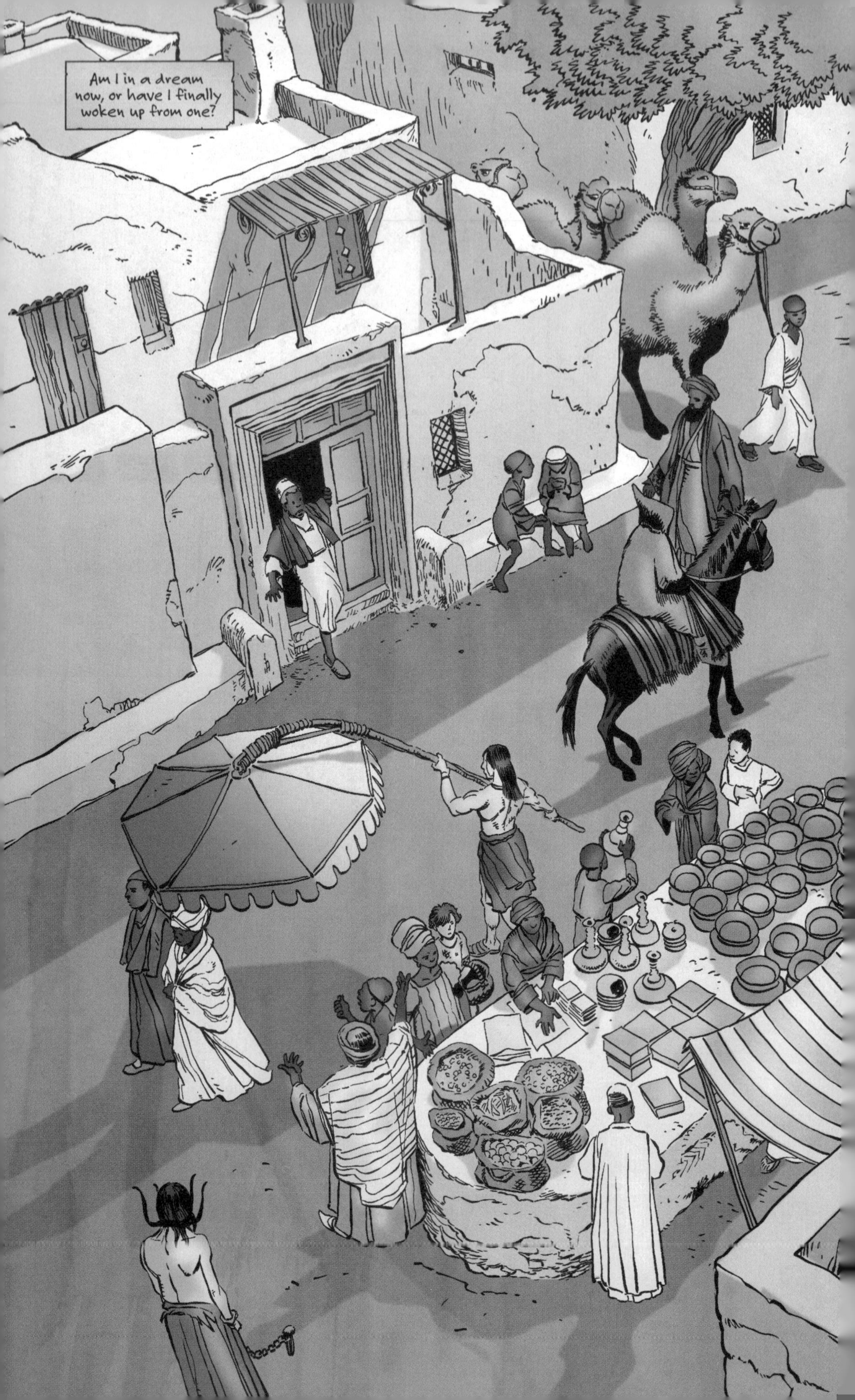
Am I in a dream now, or have I finally woken up from one?

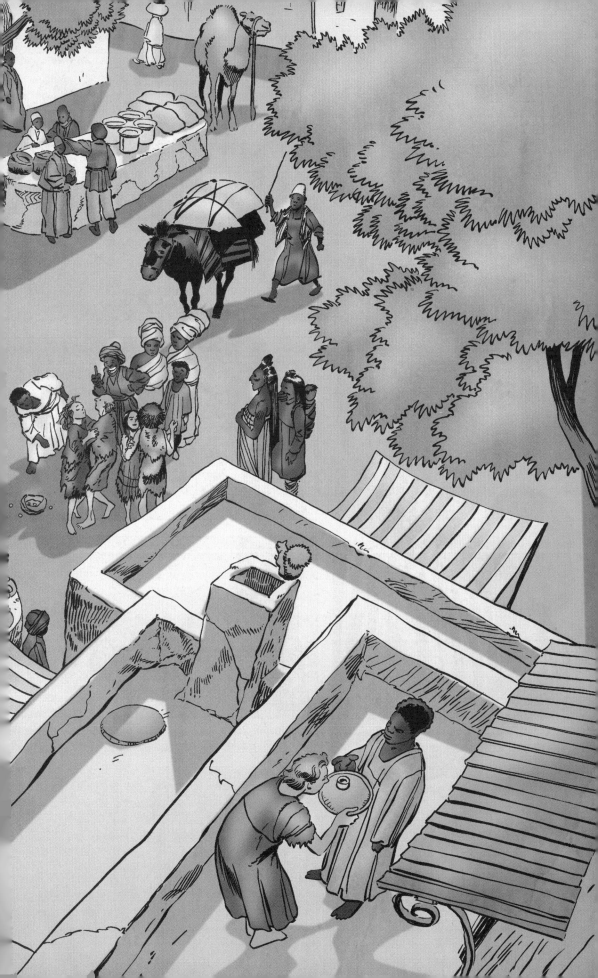

FORTUNE, DO YOU LIKE THIS WORLD? YOU *CAN* MAKE IT HAPPEN, BUT TAKE CARE.

HOW DO YOU KNOW MY NAME? WHO *ARE* YOU? IS THIS REAL?

IT CAN BE. IF YOU SUCCEED. BUT IF YOU FAIL...*BE WARY.*

MY *BROTHER,* HE HAS GREAT VISIONS, BUT HE DOESN'T ALWAYS SEE.

YOU ARE-- MIDNITE SAID YOU WERE DEAD. WHAT--

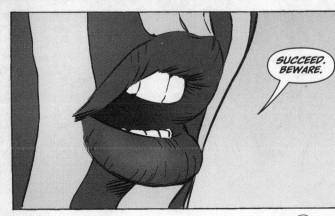

SUCCEED. BEWARE.

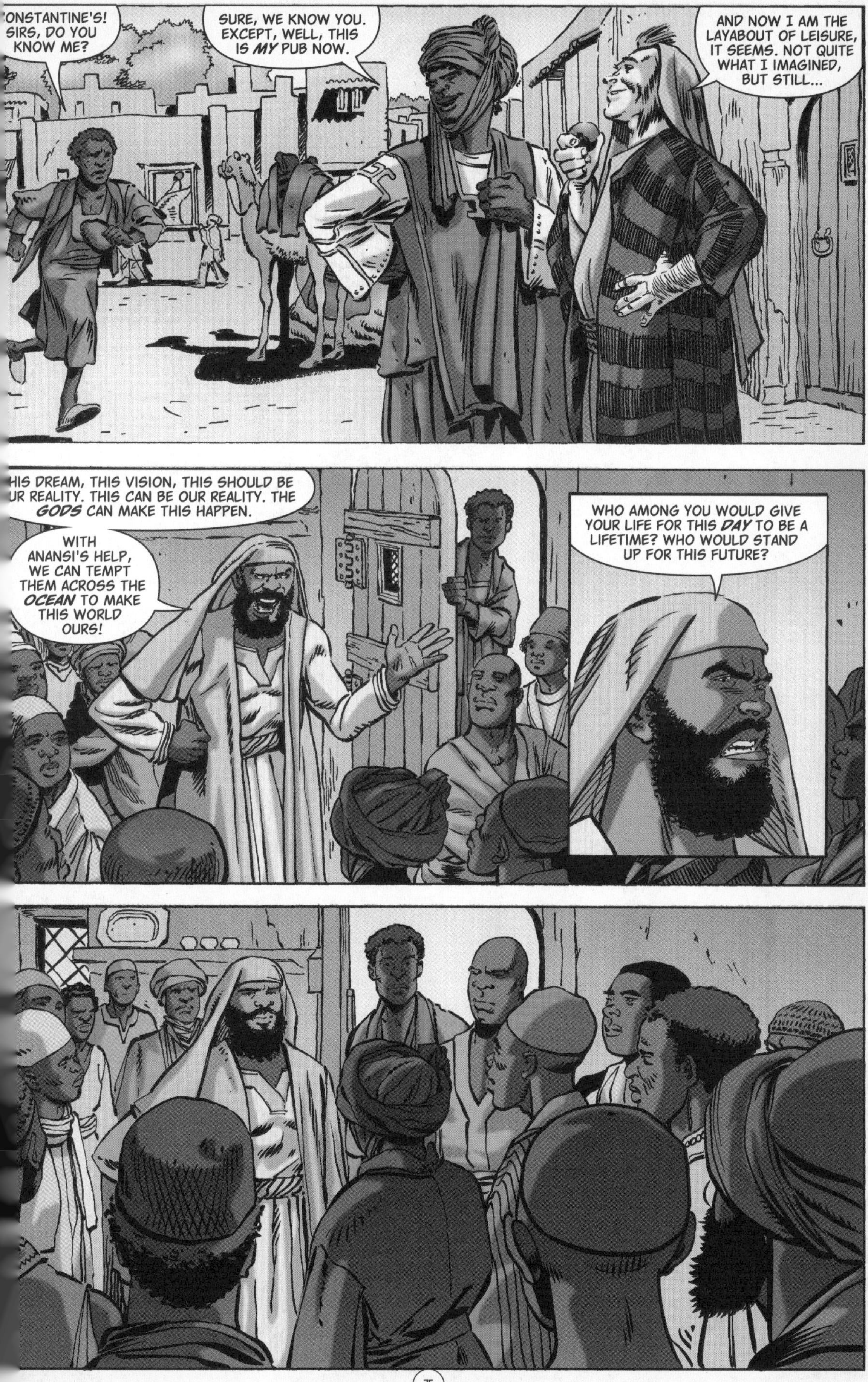
CONSTANTINE'S! SIRS, DO YOU KNOW ME?
SURE, WE KNOW YOU. EXCEPT, WELL, THIS IS *MY* PUB NOW.
AND NOW I AM THE LAYABOUT OF LEISURE, IT SEEMS. NOT QUITE WHAT I IMAGINED, BUT STILL...
HIS DREAM, THIS VISION, THIS SHOULD BE UR REALITY. THIS CAN BE OUR REALITY. THE *GODS* CAN MAKE THIS HAPPEN.
WITH ANANSI'S HELP, WE CAN TEMPT THEM ACROSS THE *OCEAN* TO MAKE THIS WORLD OURS!
WHO AMONG YOU WOULD GIVE YOUR LIFE FOR THIS *DAY* TO BE A LIFETIME? WHO WOULD STAND UP FOR THIS FUTURE?

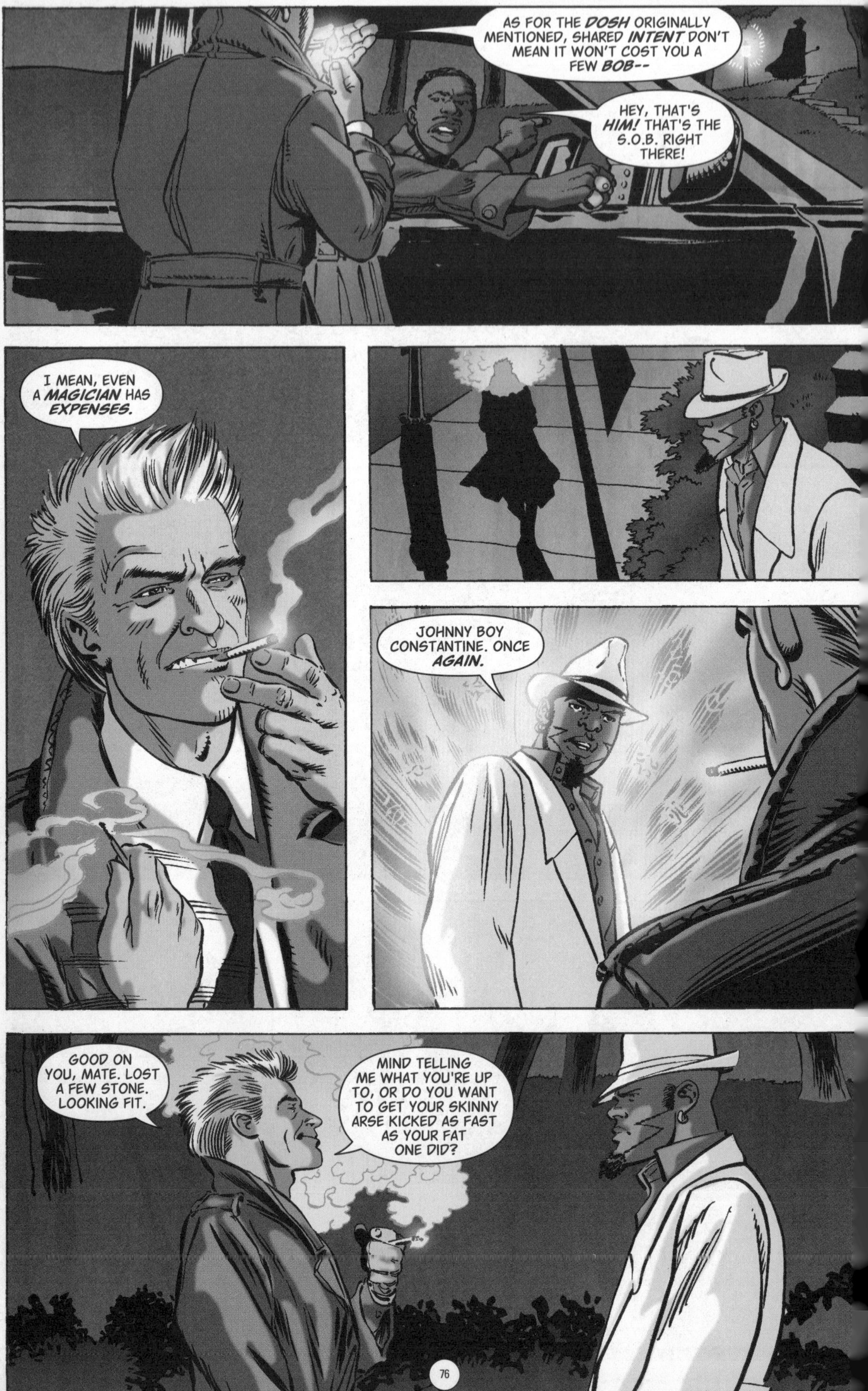
AS FOR THE *DOSH* ORIGINALLY MENTIONED, SHARED *INTENT* DON'T MEAN IT WON'T COST YOU A FEW *BOB*--
HEY, THAT'S *HIM!* THAT'S THE S.O.B. RIGHT THERE!
I MEAN, EVEN A *MAGICIAN* HAS *EXPENSES.*
JOHNNY BOY CONSTANTINE. ONCE *AGAIN.*
GOOD ON YOU, MATE. LOST A FEW STONE. LOOKING FIT.
MIND TELLING ME WHAT YOU'RE UP TO, OR DO YOU WANT TO GET YOUR SKINNY ARSE KICKED AS FAST AS YOUR FAT ONE DID?

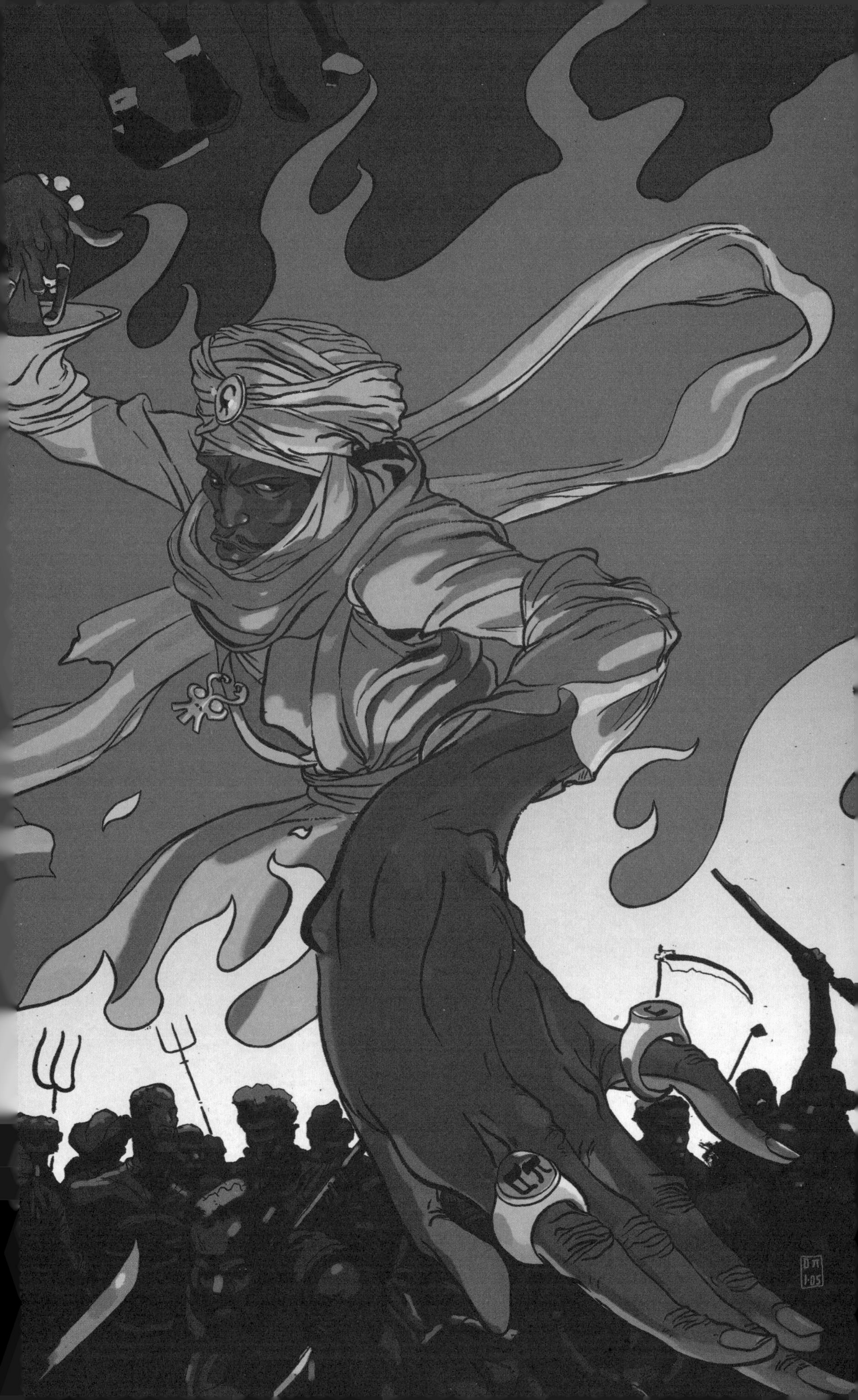

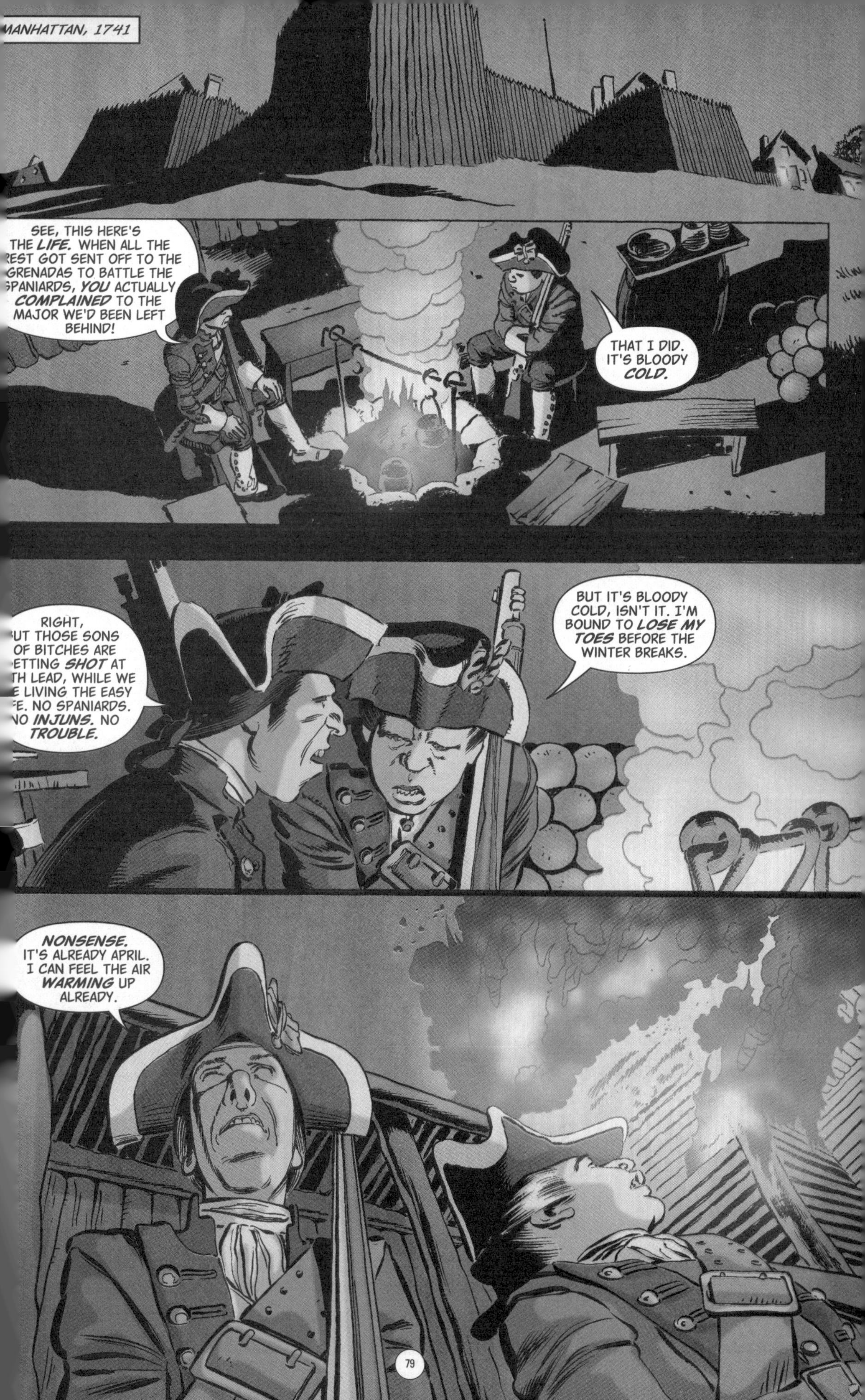
MANHATTAN, 1741
SEE, THIS HERE'S THE LIFE. WHEN ALL THE REST GOT SENT OFF TO THE GRENADAS TO BATTLE THE SPANIARDS, YOU ACTUALLY COMPLAINED TO THE MAJOR WE'D BEEN LEFT BEHIND!
THAT I DID. IT'S BLOODY COLD.
RIGHT, UT THOSE SONS OF BITCHES ARE ETTING SHOT AT TH LEAD, WHILE WE E LIVING THE EASY FE. NO SPANIARDS. NO INJUNS. NO TROUBLE.
BUT IT'S BLOODY COLD, ISN'T IT. I'M BOUND TO LOSE MY TOES BEFORE THE WINTER BREAKS.
NONSENSE. IT'S ALREADY APRIL. I CAN FEEL THE AIR WARMING UP ALREADY.

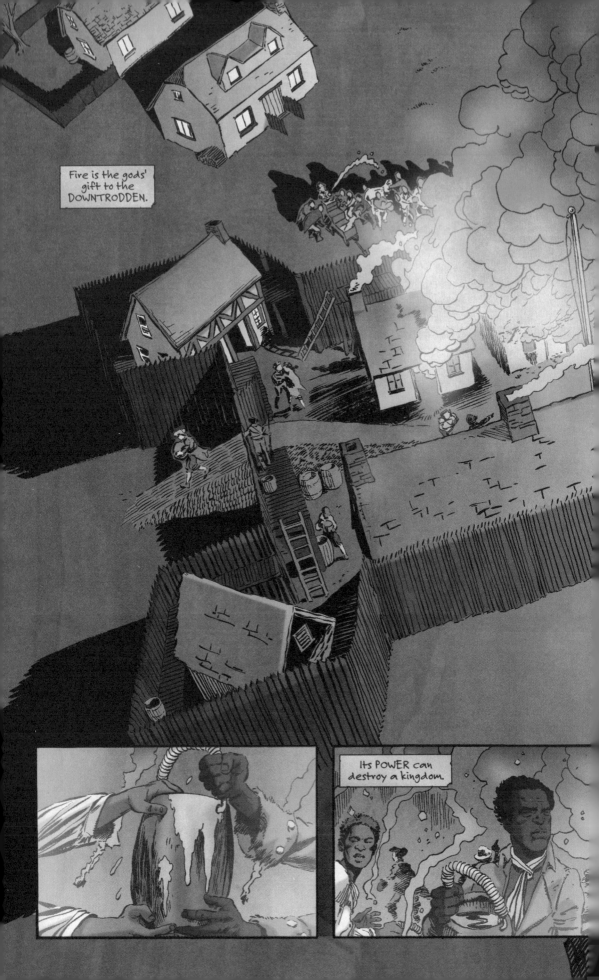

Fire is the gods' gift to the DOWNTRODDEN.

Its POWER can destroy a kingdom.

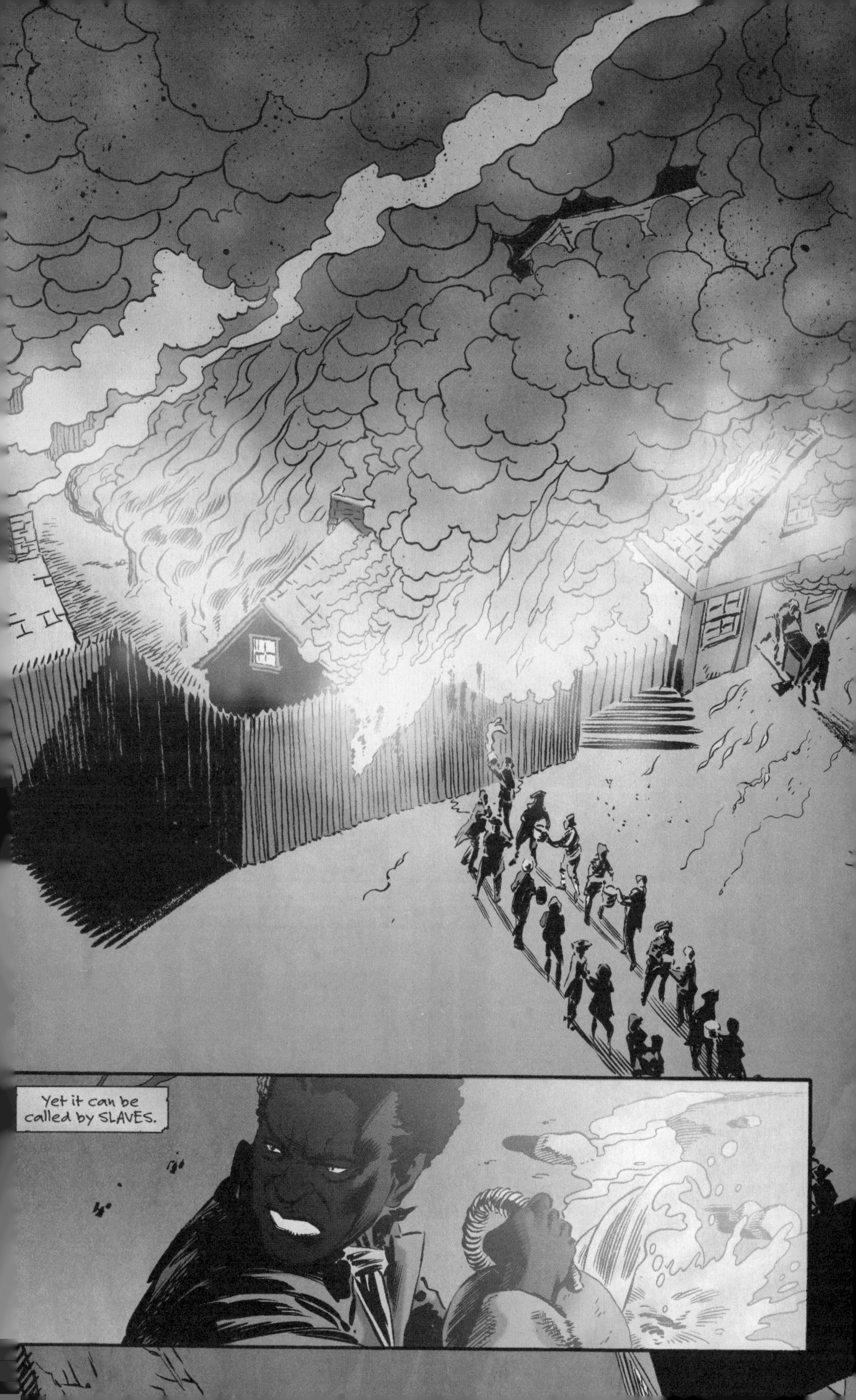
Yet it can be called by SLAVES.

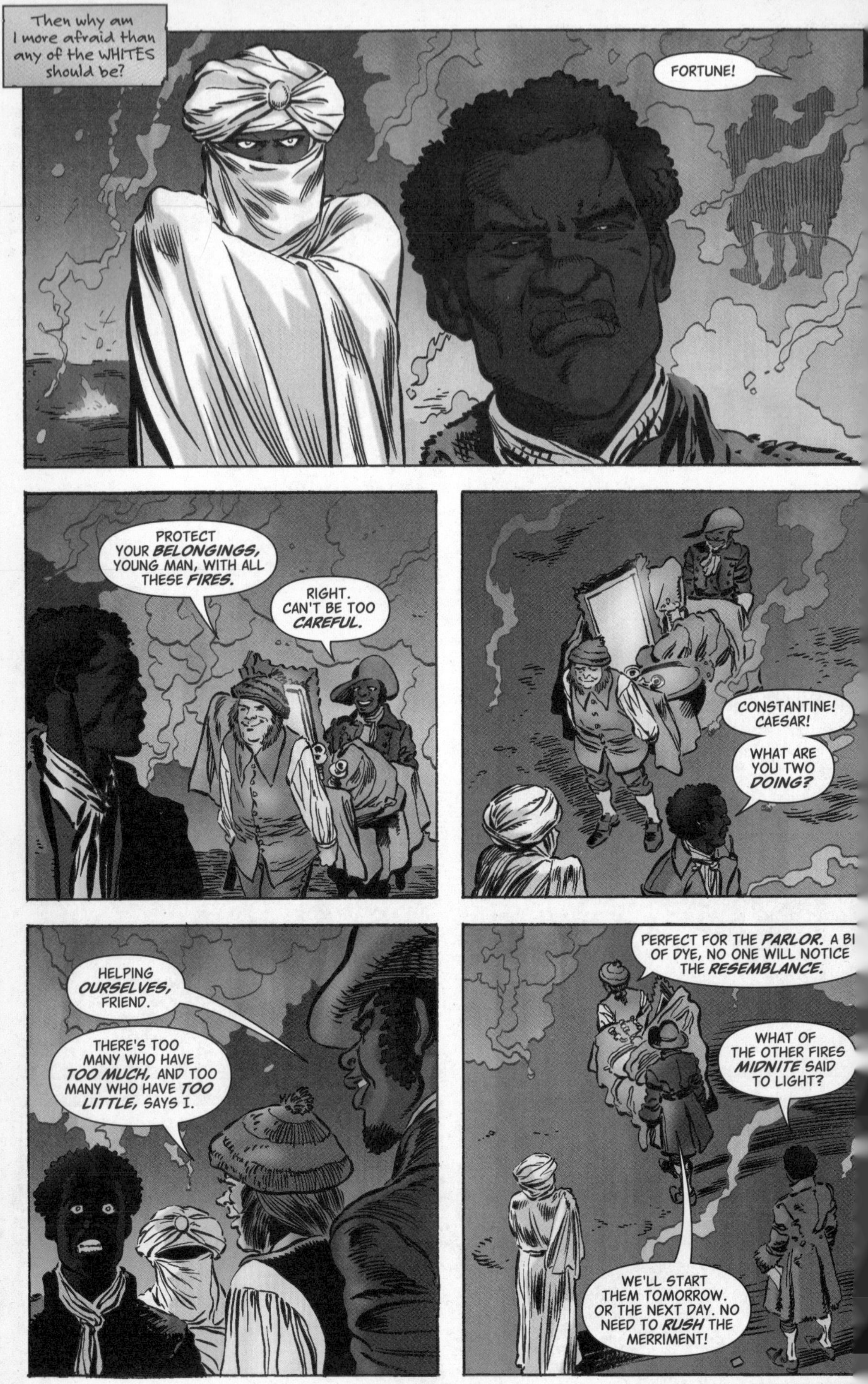
Then why am I more afraid than any of the WHITES should be?
FORTUNE!
PROTECT YOUR BELONGINGS, YOUNG MAN, WITH ALL THESE FIRES.
RIGHT. CAN'T BE TOO CAREFUL.
CONSTANTINE! CAESAR!
WHAT ARE YOU TWO DOING?
HELPING OURSELVES, FRIEND.
THERE'S TOO MANY WHO HAVE TOO MUCH, AND TOO MANY WHO HAVE TOO LITTLE, SAYS I.
PERFECT FOR THE PARLOR. A BI
OF DYE, NO ONE WILL NOTICE THE RESEMBLANCE.
WHAT OF THE OTHER FIRES MIDNITE SAID TO LIGHT?
WE'LL START THEM TOMORROW. OR THE NEXT DAY. NO NEED TO RUSH THE MERRIMENT!

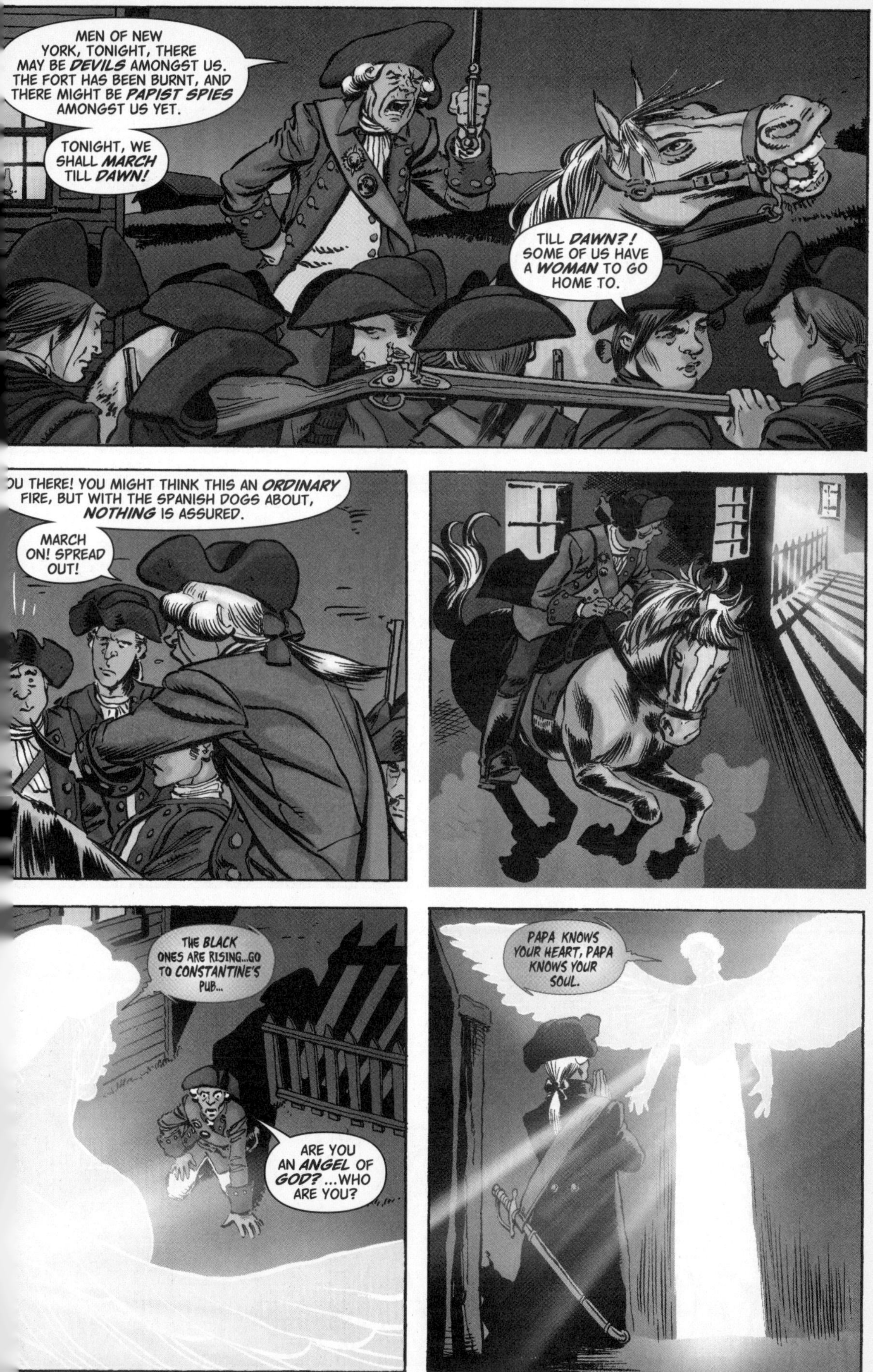
MEN OF NEW YORK, TONIGHT, THERE MAY BE DEVILS AMONGST US. THE FORT HAS BEEN BURNT, AND THERE MIGHT BE PAPIST SPIES AMONGST US YET.
TONIGHT, WE SHALL MARCH TILL DAWN!
TILL DAWN?! SOME OF US HAVE A WOMAN TO GO HOME TO.
OU THERE! YOU MIGHT THINK THIS AN ORDINARY FIRE, BUT WITH THE SPANISH DOGS ABOUT, NOTHING IS ASSURED.
MARCH ON! SPREAD OUT!
THE BLACK ONES ARE RISING...GO TO CONSTANTINE'S PUB...
ARE YOU AN ANGEL OF GOD? ...WHO ARE YOU?
PAPA KNOWS YOUR HEART, PAPA KNOWS YOUR SOUL.

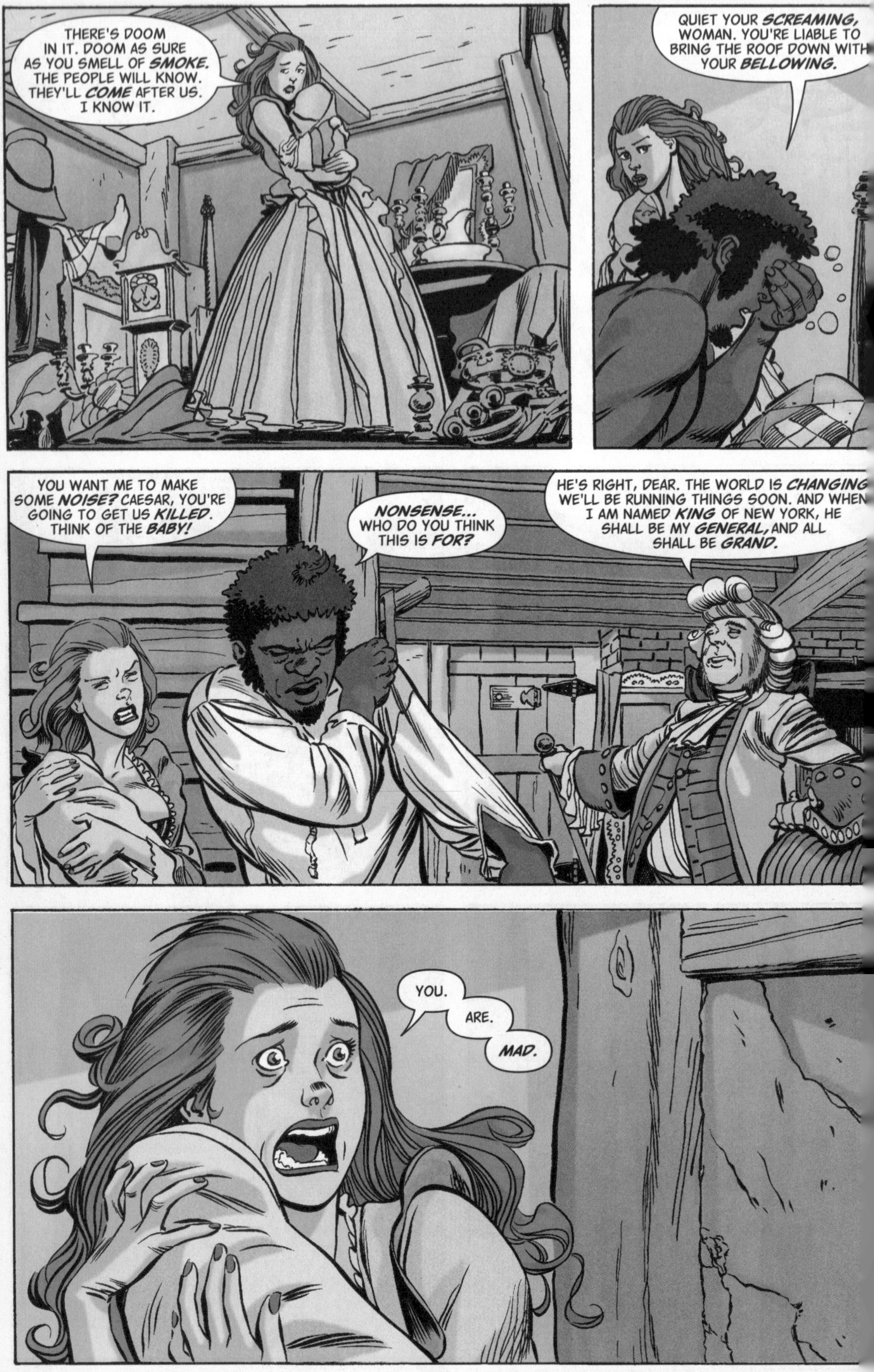
THERE'S DOOM IN IT. DOOM AS SURE AS YOU SMELL OF *SMOKE.* THE PEOPLE WILL KNOW. THEY'LL *COME* AFTER US. I KNOW IT.
QUIET YOUR *SCREAMING,* WOMAN. YOU'RE LIABLE TO BRING THE ROOF DOWN WITH YOUR *BELLOWING.*
YOU WANT ME TO MAKE SOME *NOISE?* CAESAR, YOU'RE GOING TO GET US *KILLED.* THINK OF THE *BABY!*
NONSENSE... WHO DO YOU THINK THIS IS *FOR?*
HE'S RIGHT, DEAR. THE WORLD IS *CHANGING.* WE'LL BE RUNNING THINGS SOON. AND WHEN I AM NAMED *KING* OF NEW YORK, HE SHALL BE MY *GENERAL,* AND ALL SHALL BE *GRAND.*
YOU.
ARE.
MAD.

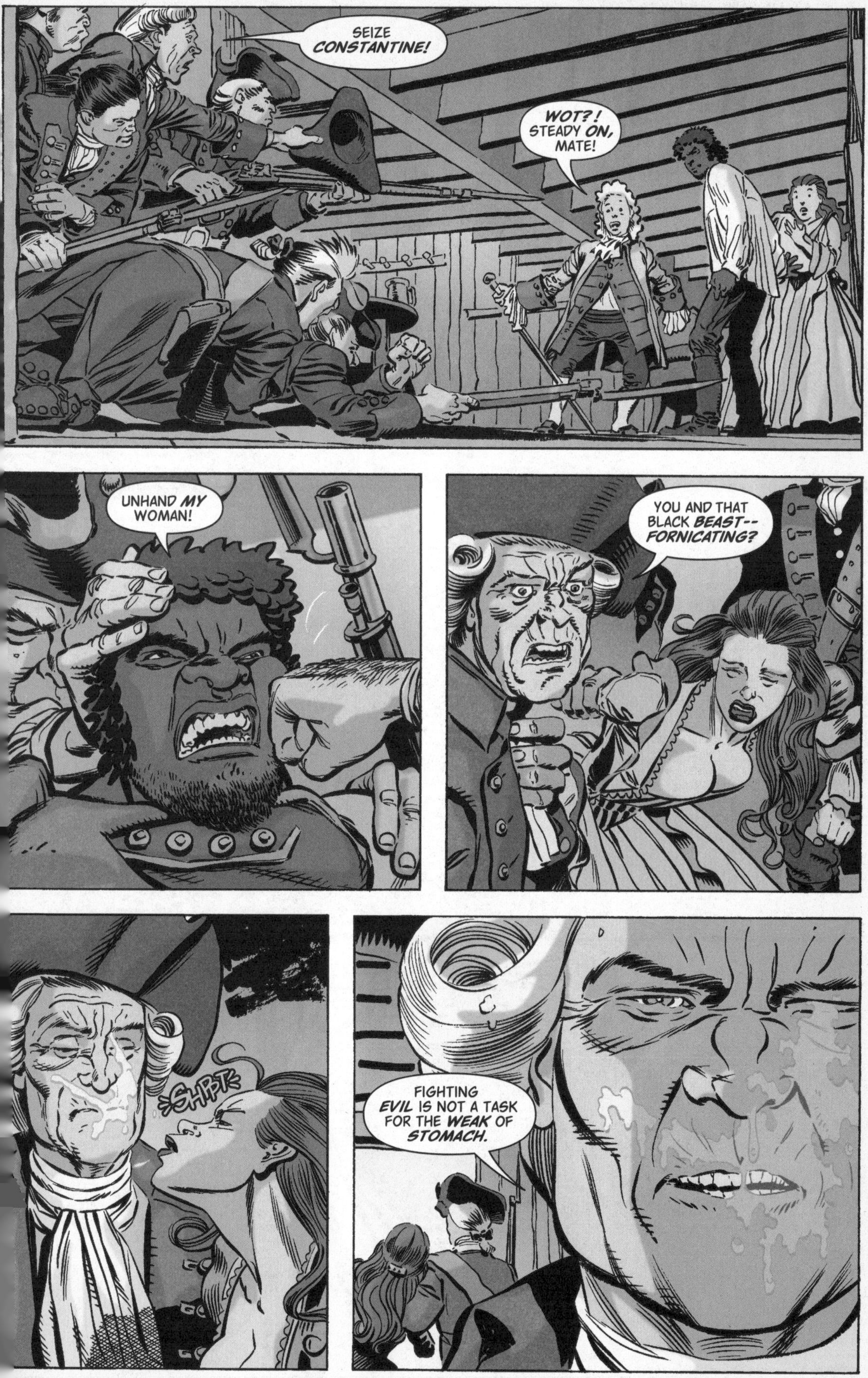
SEIZE CONSTANTINE!
WOT?! STEADY ON, MATE!
UNHAND MY WOMAN!
YOU AND THAT BLACK BEAST--FORNICATING?
SHPT!
FIGHTING EVIL IS NOT A TASK FOR THE WEAK OF STOMACH.

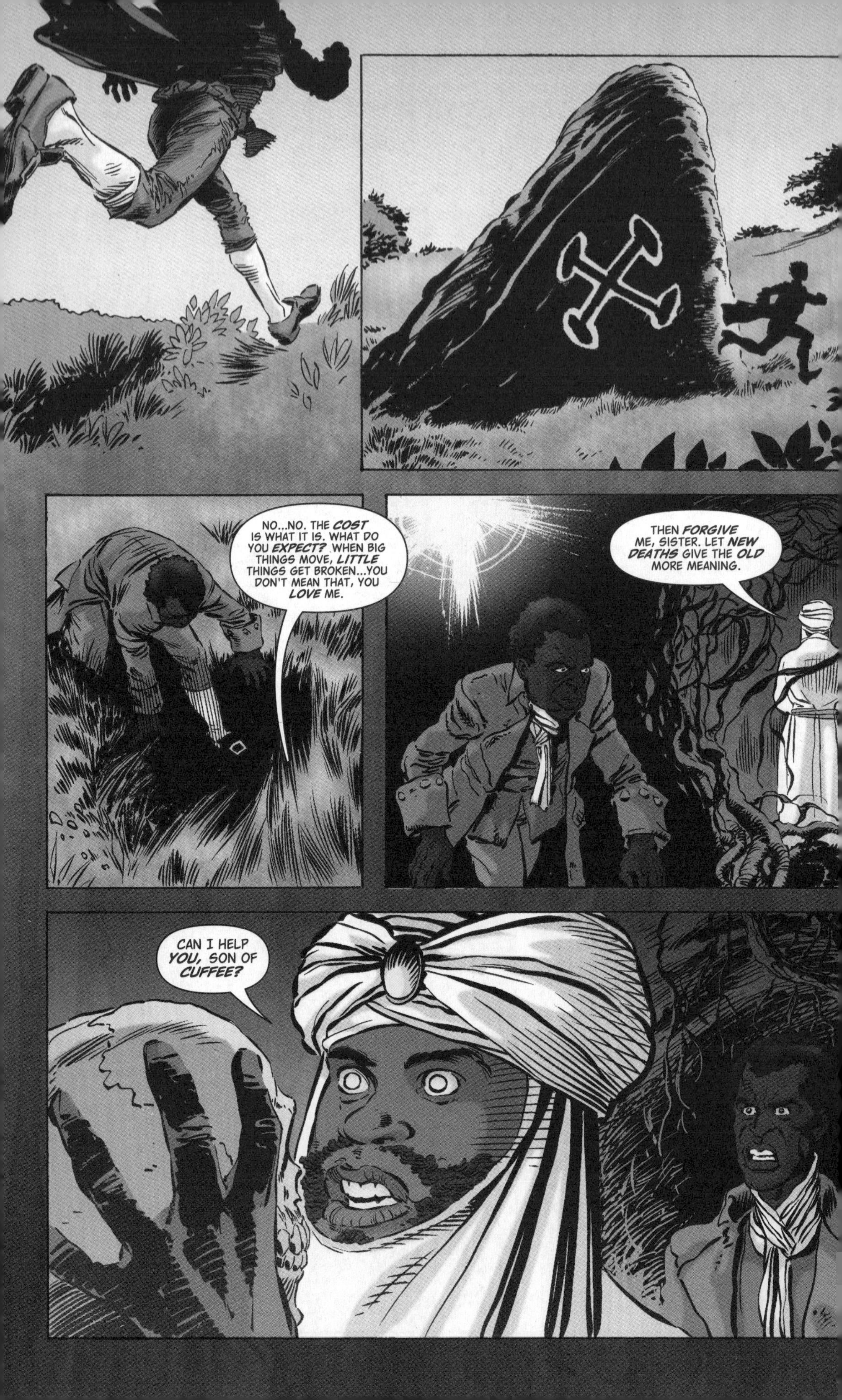
NO...NO. THE COST IS WHAT IT IS. WHAT DO YOU EXPECT? WHEN BIG THINGS MOVE, LITTLE THINGS GET BROKEN...YOU DON'T MEAN THAT, YOU LOVE ME.
THEN FORGIVE ME, SISTER. LET NEW DEATHS GIVE THE OLD MORE MEANING.
CAN I HELP YOU, SON OF CUFFEE?

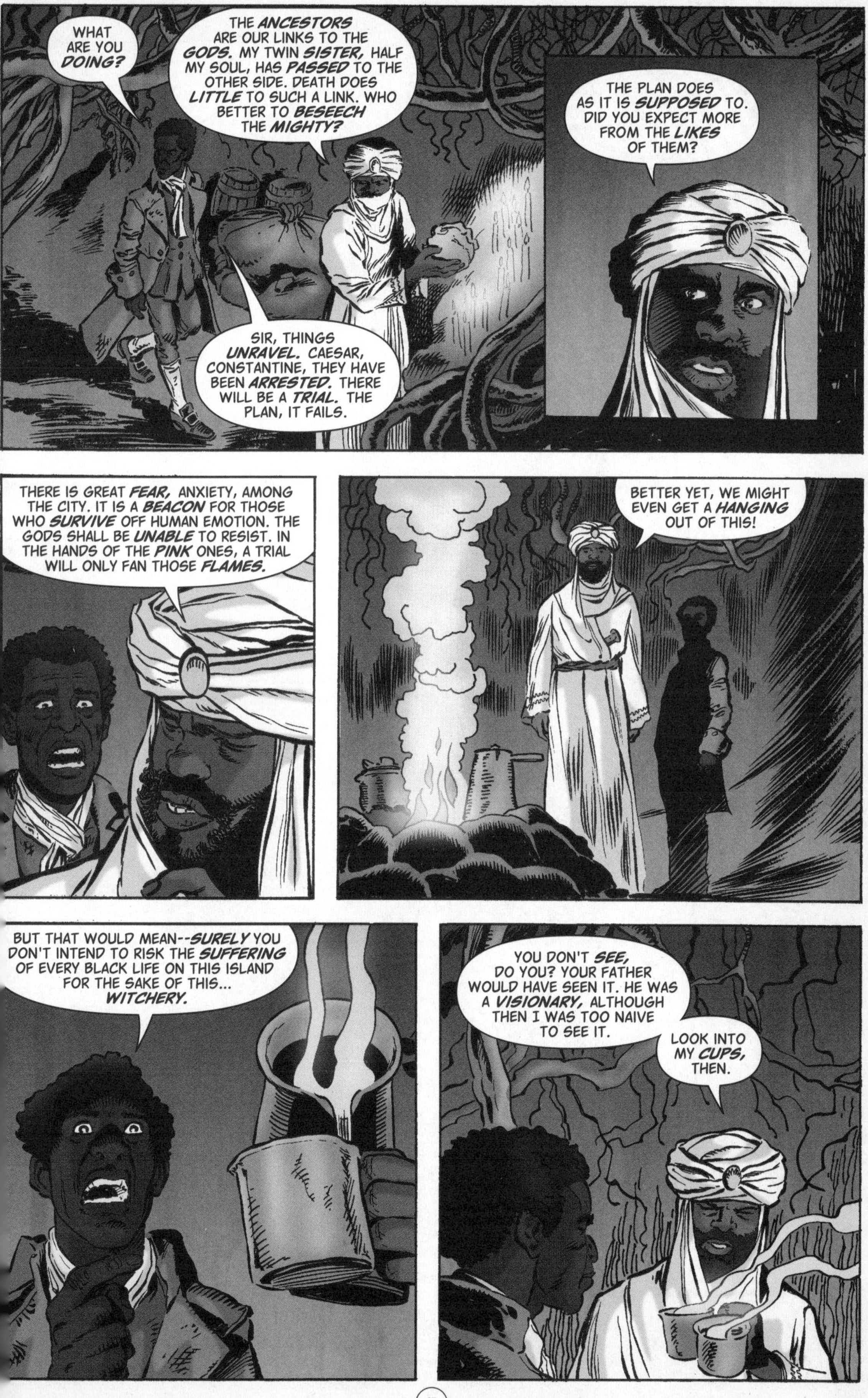
WHAT ARE YOU DOING?
THE ANCESTORS ARE OUR LINKS TO THE GODS. MY TWIN SISTER, HALF MY SOUL, HAS PASSED TO THE OTHER SIDE. DEATH DOES LITTLE TO SUCH A LINK. WHO BETTER TO BESEECH THE MIGHTY?
SIR, THINGS UNRAVEL. CAESAR, CONSTANTINE, THEY HAVE BEEN ARRESTED. THERE WILL BE A TRIAL. THE PLAN, IT FAILS.
THE PLAN DOES AS IT IS SUPPOSED TO. DID YOU EXPECT MORE FROM THE LIKES OF THEM?
THERE IS GREAT FEAR, ANXIETY, AMONG THE CITY. IT IS A BEACON FOR THOSE WHO SURVIVE OFF HUMAN EMOTION. THE GODS SHALL BE UNABLE TO RESIST. IN THE HANDS OF THE PINK ONES, A TRIAL WILL ONLY FAN THOSE FLAMES.
BETTER YET, WE MIGHT EVEN GET A HANGING OUT OF THIS!
BUT THAT WOULD MEAN--SURELY YOU DON'T INTEND TO RISK THE SUFFERING OF EVERY BLACK LIFE ON THIS ISLAND FOR THE SAKE OF THIS... WITCHERY.
YOU DON'T SEE, DO YOU? YOUR FATHER WOULD HAVE SEEN IT. HE WAS A VISIONARY, ALTHOUGH THEN I WAS TOO NAIVE TO SEE IT.
LOOK INTO MY CUPS, THEN.

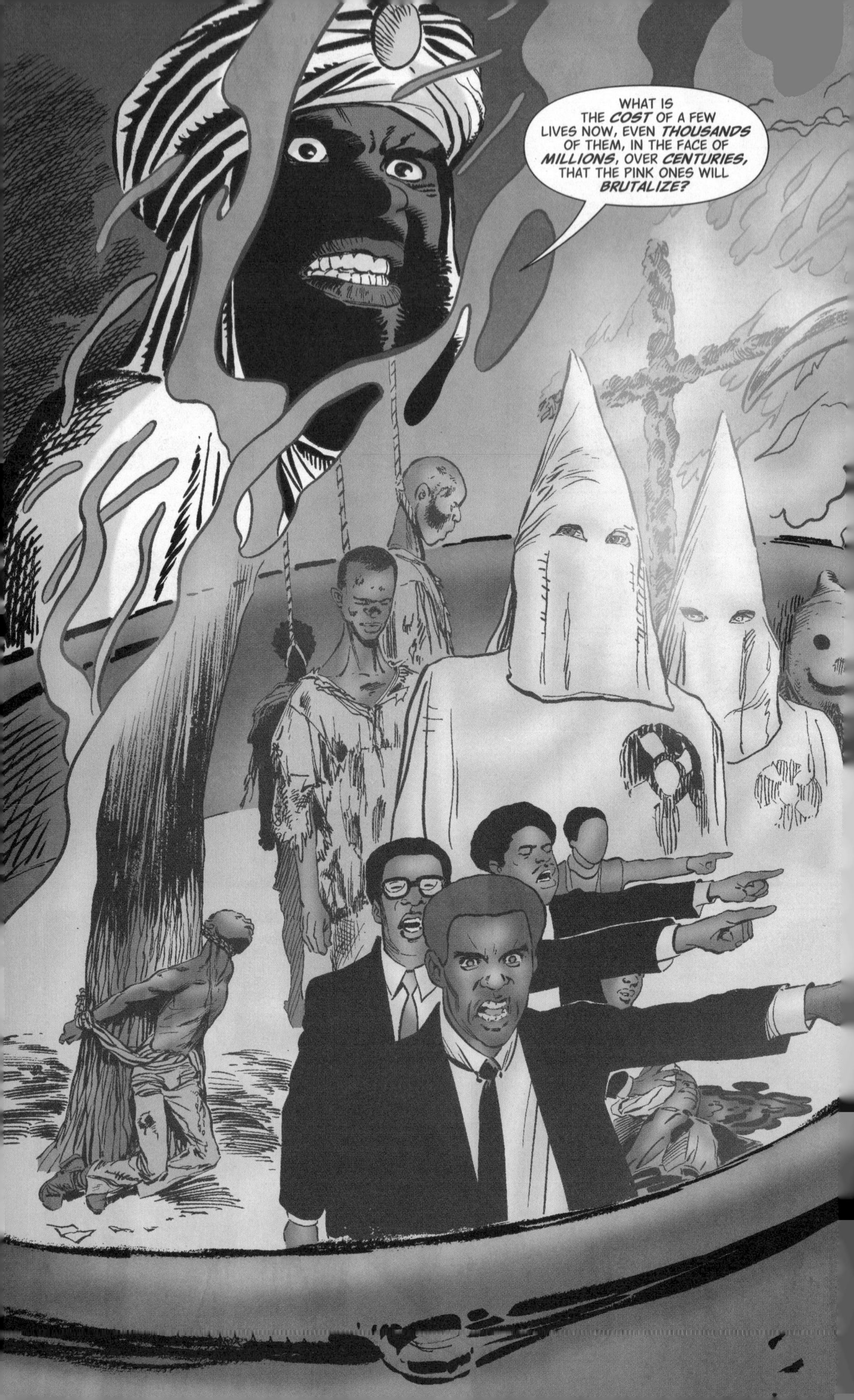
WHAT IS THE COST OF A FEW LIVES NOW, EVEN THOUSANDS OF THEM, IN THE FACE OF MILLIONS, OVER CENTURIES, THAT THE PINK ONES WILL BRUTALIZE?

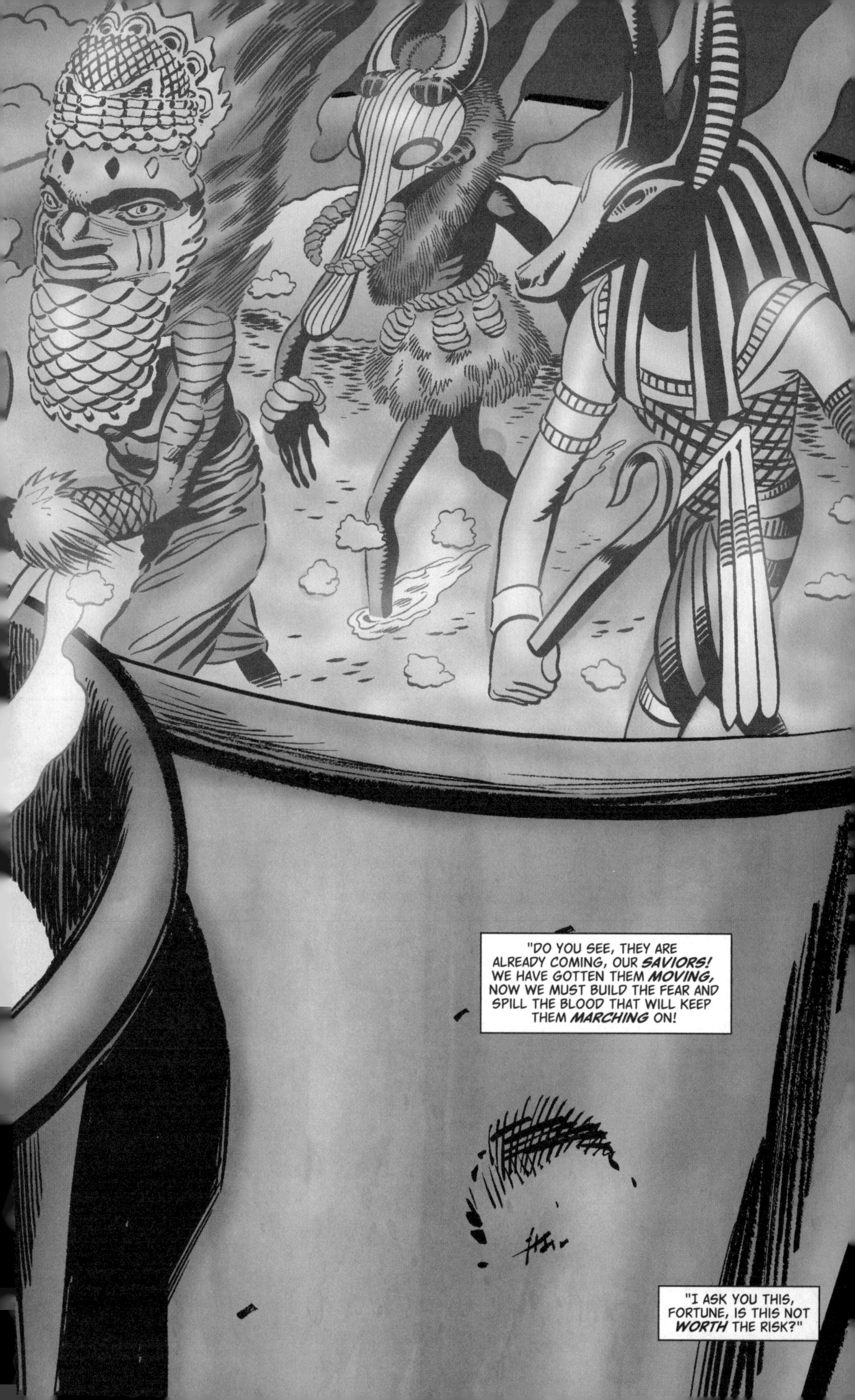
"DO YOU SEE, THEY ARE ALREADY COMING, OUR SAVIORS! WE HAVE GOTTEN THEM MOVING, NOW WE MUST BUILD THE FEAR AND SPILL THE BLOOD THAT WILL KEEP THEM MARCHING ON!
"I ASK YOU THIS, FORTUNE, IS THIS NOT WORTH THE RISK?"

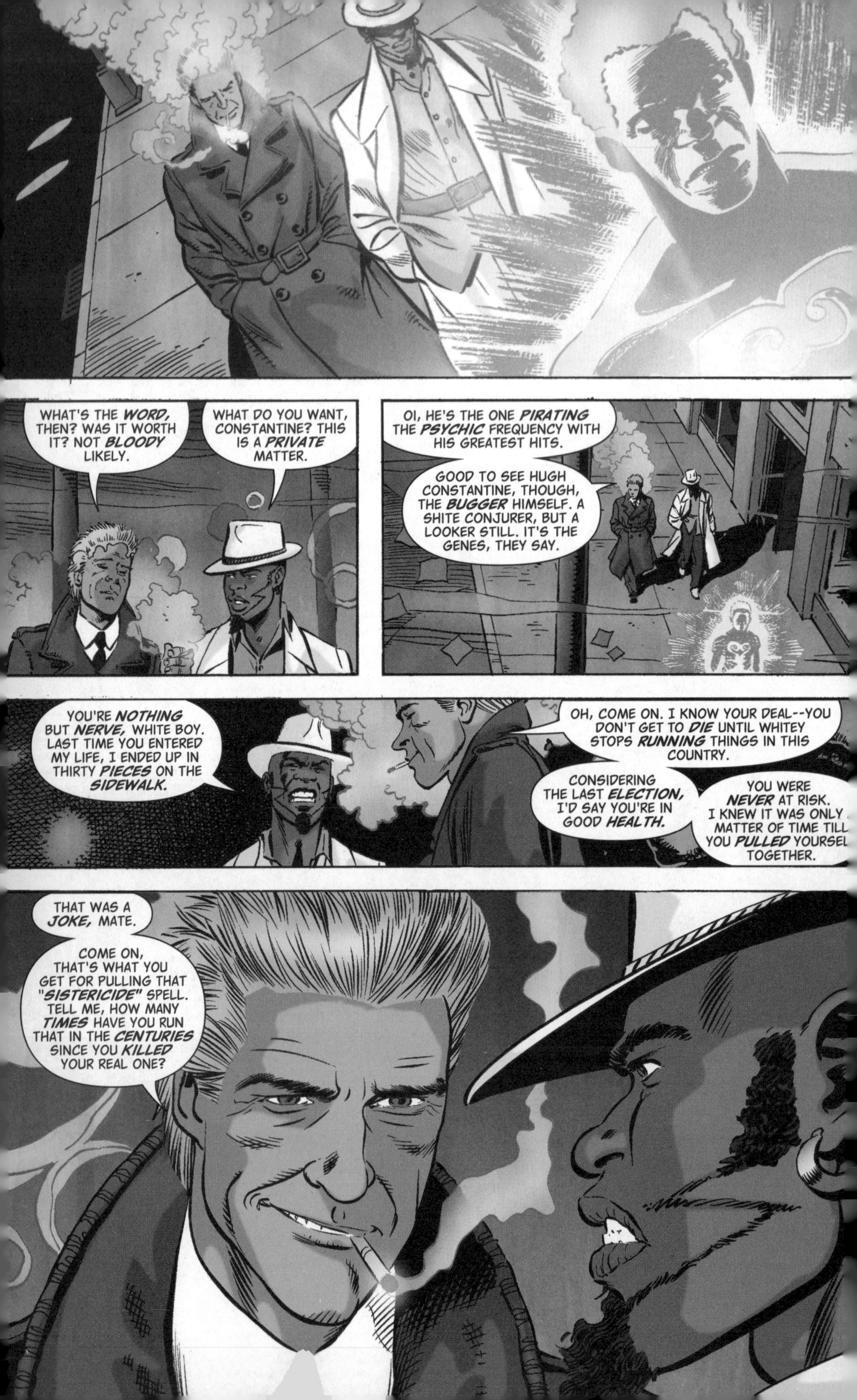

WHAT'S THE WORD, THEN? WAS IT WORTH IT? NOT BLOODY LIKELY.
WHAT DO YOU WANT, CONSTANTINE? THIS IS A PRIVATE MATTER.
OI, HE'S THE ONE PIRATING THE PSYCHIC FREQUENCY WITH HIS GREATEST HITS.
GOOD TO SEE HUGH CONSTANTINE, THOUGH, THE BUGGER HIMSELF. A SHITE CONJURER, BUT A LOOKER STILL. IT'S THE GENES, THEY SAY.
YOU'RE NOTHING BUT NERVE, WHITE BOY. LAST TIME YOU ENTERED MY LIFE, I ENDED UP IN THIRTY PIECES ON THE SIDEWALK.
OH, COME ON. I KNOW YOUR DEAL--YOU DON'T GET TO DIE UNTIL WHITEY STOPS RUNNING THINGS IN THIS COUNTRY.
CONSIDERING THE LAST ELECTION, I'D SAY YOU'RE IN GOOD HEALTH.
YOU WERE NEVER AT RISK. I KNEW IT WAS ONLY MATTER OF TIME TILL YOU PULLED YOURSEL TOGETHER.
THAT WAS A JOKE, MATE.
COME ON, THAT'S WHAT YOU GET FOR PULLING THAT "SISTERICIDE" SPELL. TELL ME, HOW MANY TIMES HAVE YOU RUN THAT IN THE CENTURIES SINCE YOU KILLED YOUR REAL ONE?

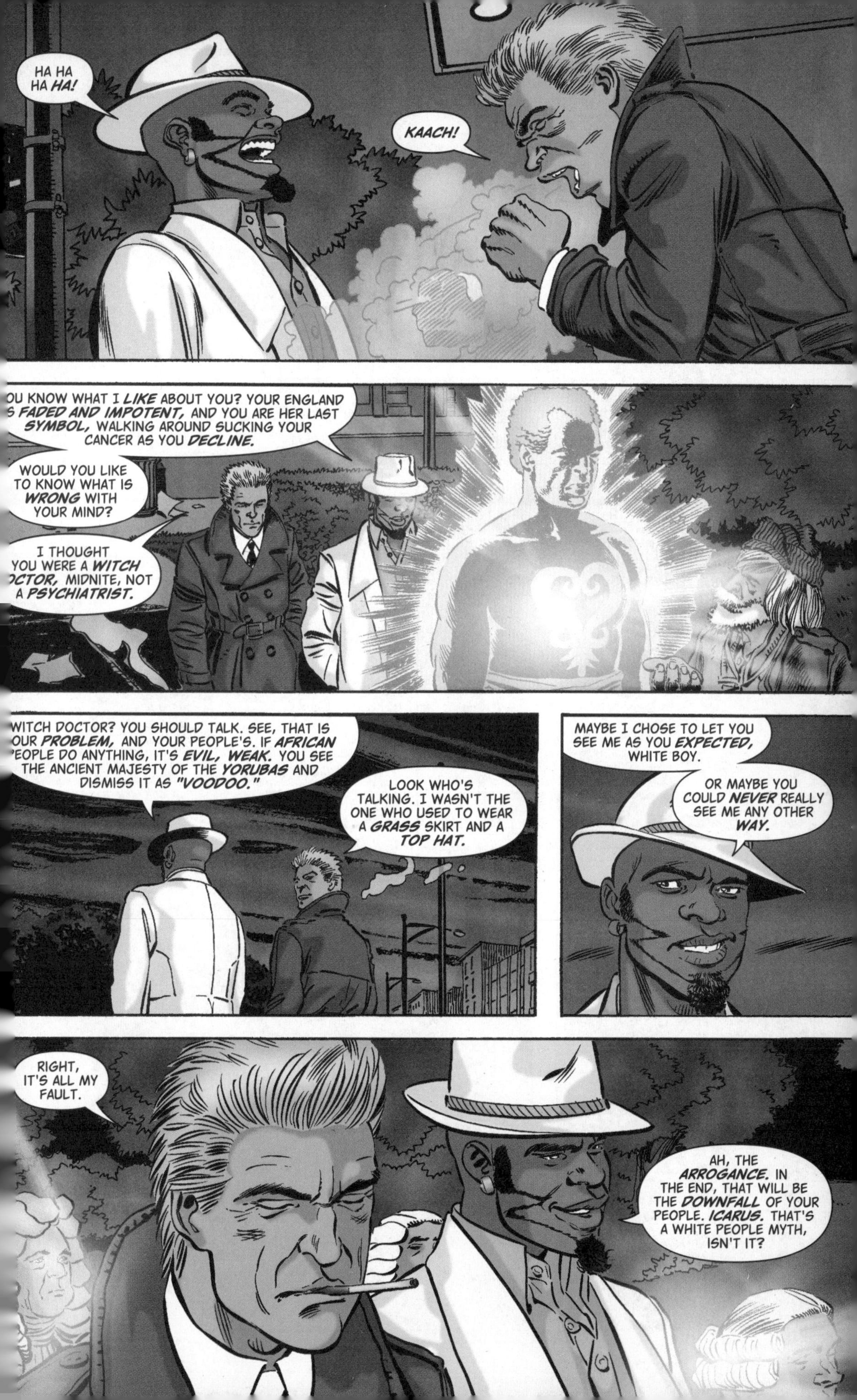

HA HA HA HA!
KAACH!
OU KNOW WHAT I LIKE ABOUT YOU? YOUR ENGLAND S FADED AND IMPOTENT, AND YOU ARE HER LAST SYMBOL, WALKING AROUND SUCKING YOUR CANCER AS YOU DECLINE.
WOULD YOU LIKE TO KNOW WHAT IS WRONG WITH YOUR MIND?
I THOUGHT YOU WERE A WITCH OCTOR, MIDNITE, NOT A PSYCHIATRIST.
WITCH DOCTOR? YOU SHOULD TALK. SEE, THAT IS OUR PROBLEM, AND YOUR PEOPLE'S. IF AFRICAN EOPLE DO ANYTHING, IT'S EVIL, WEAK. YOU SEE THE ANCIENT MAJESTY OF THE YORUBAS AND DISMISS IT AS "VOODOO."
LOOK WHO'S TALKING. I WASN'T THE ONE WHO USED TO WEAR A GRASS SKIRT AND A TOP HAT.
MAYBE I CHOSE TO LET YOU SEE ME AS YOU EXPECTED, WHITE BOY.
OR MAYBE YOU COULD NEVER REALLY SEE ME ANY OTHER WAY.
RIGHT, IT'S ALL MY FAULT.
AH, THE ARROGANCE. IN THE END, THAT WILL BE THE DOWNFALL OF YOUR PEOPLE. ICARUS. THAT'S A WHITE PEOPLE MYTH, ISN'T IT?

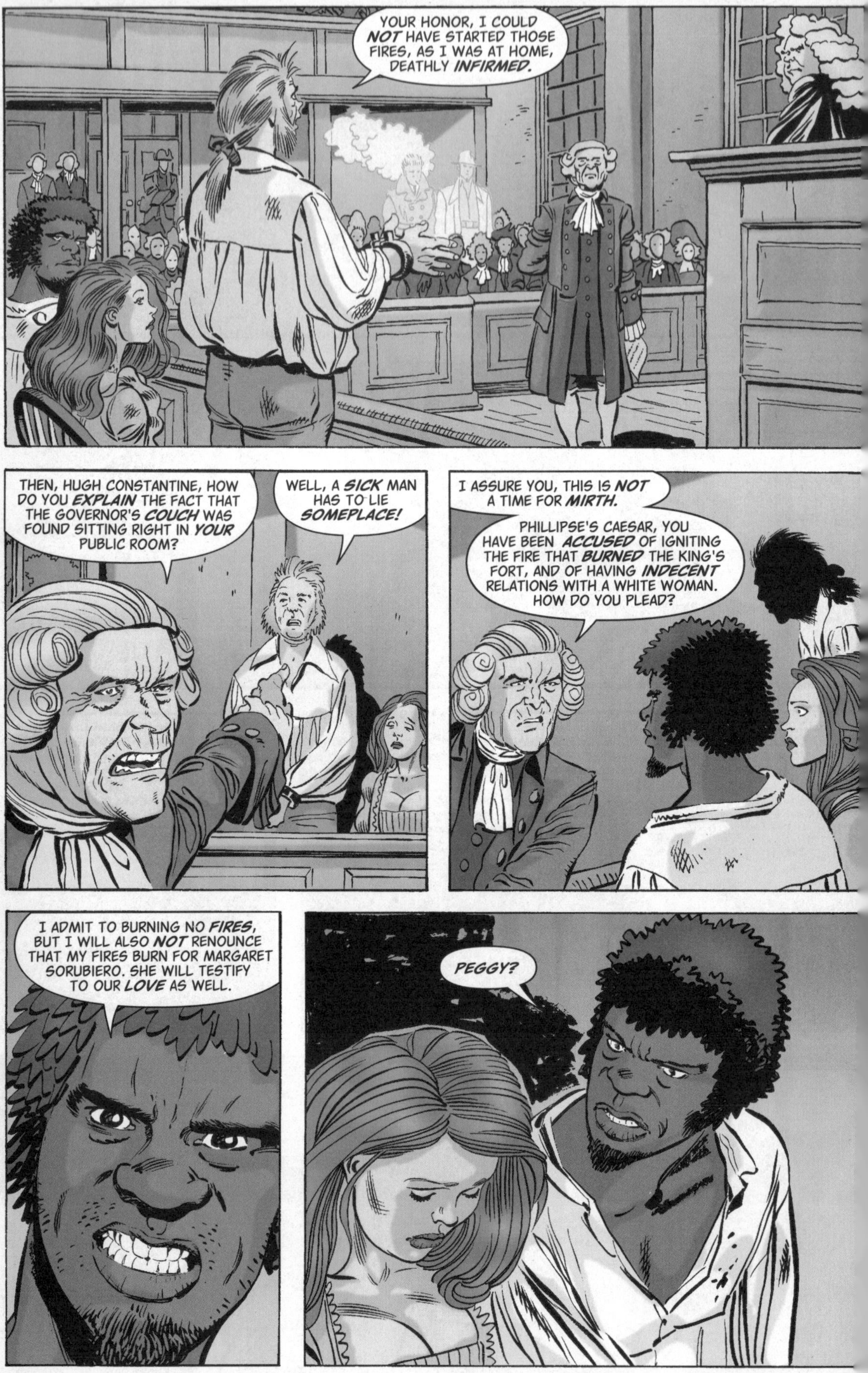
YOUR HONOR, I COULD NOT HAVE STARTED THOSE FIRES, AS I WAS AT HOME, DEATHLY INFIRMED.
THEN, HUGH CONSTANTINE, HOW DO YOU EXPLAIN THE FACT THAT THE GOVERNOR'S COUCH WAS FOUND SITTING RIGHT IN YOUR PUBLIC ROOM?
WELL, A SICK MAN HAS TO LIE SOMEPLACE!
I ASSURE YOU, THIS IS NOT A TIME FOR MIRTH.
PHILLIPSE'S CAESAR, YOU HAVE BEEN ACCUSED OF IGNITING THE FIRE THAT BURNED THE KING'S FORT, AND OF HAVING INDECENT RELATIONS WITH A WHITE WOMAN. HOW DO YOU PLEAD?
I ADMIT TO BURNING NO FIRES, BUT I WILL ALSO NOT RENOUNCE THAT MY FIRES BURN FOR MARGARET SORUBIERO. SHE WILL TESTIFY TO OUR LOVE AS WELL.
PEGGY?

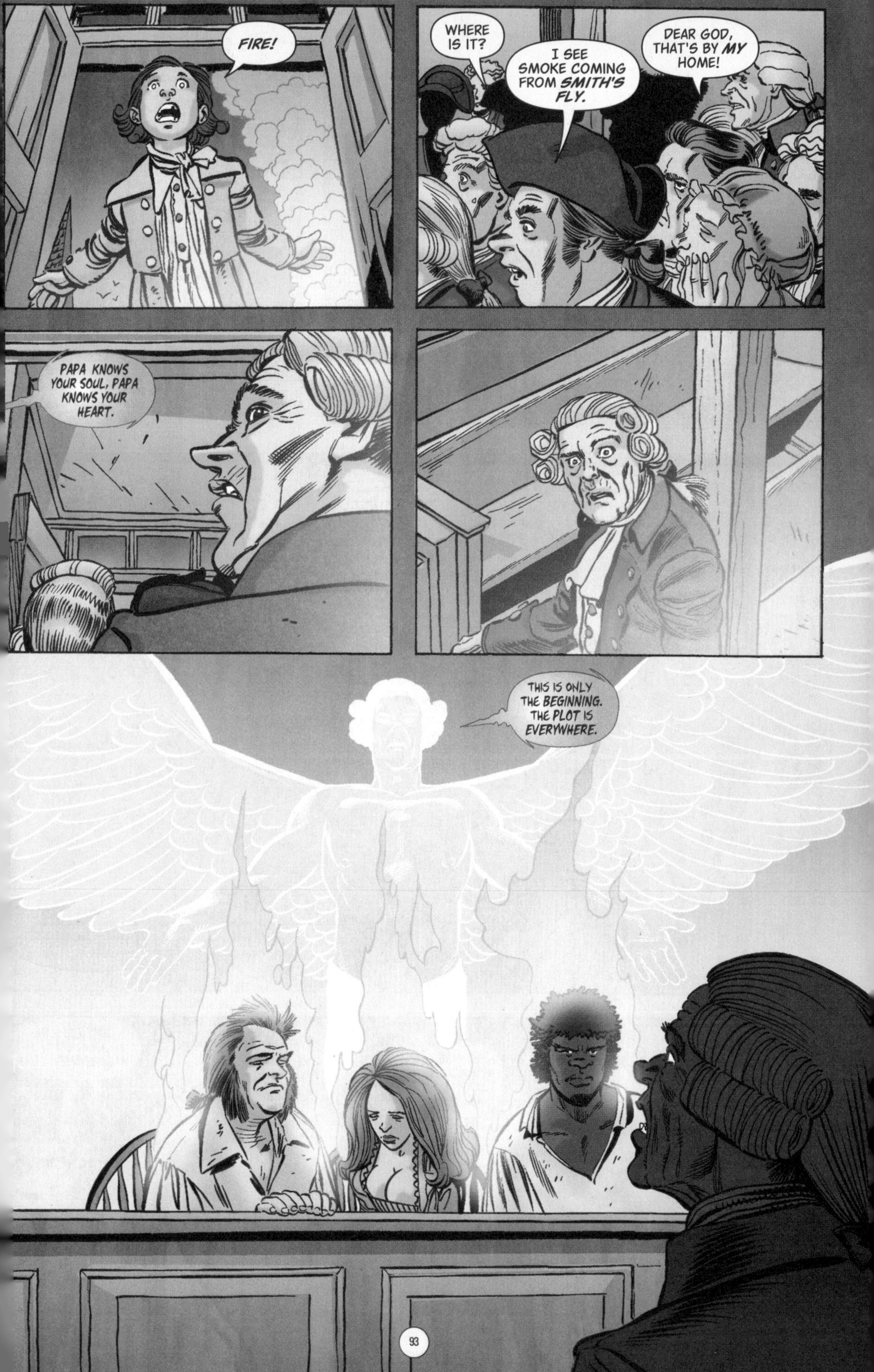
FIRE!
WHERE IS IT?
I SEE SMOKE COMING FROM SMITH'S FLY.
DEAR GOD, THAT'S BY MY HOME!
PAPA KNOWS YOUR SOUL, PAPA KNOWS YOUR HEART.
THIS IS ONLY THE BEGINNING. THE PLOT IS EVERYWHERE.

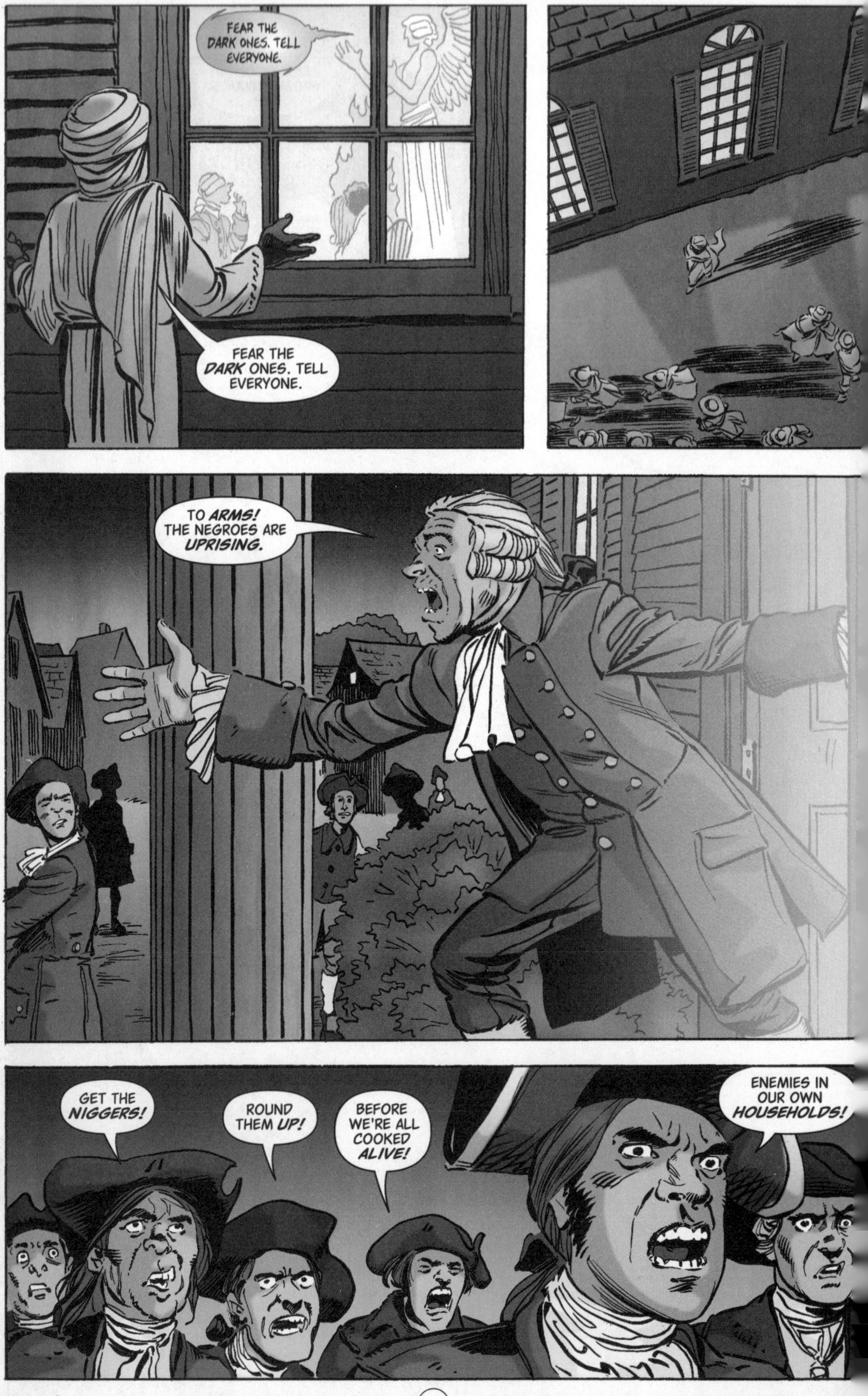
FEAR THE DARK ONES. TELL EVERYONE.
FEAR THE DARK ONES. TELL EVERYONE.
TO ARMS! THE NEGROES ARE UPRISING.
GET THE NIGGERS!
ROUND THEM UP!
BEFORE WE'RE ALL COOKED ALIVE!
ENEMIES IN OUR OWN HOUSEHOLDS!

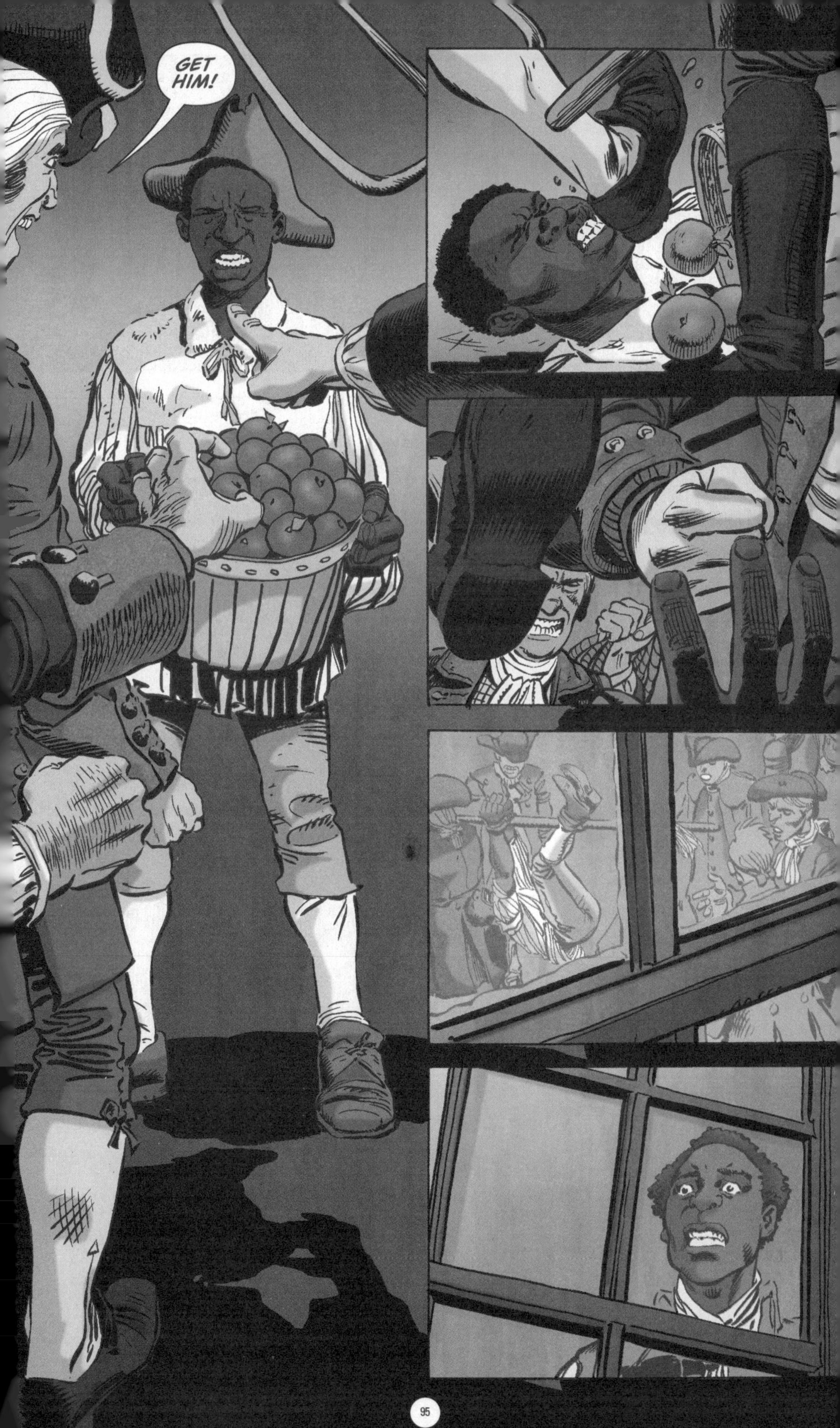
GET HIM!

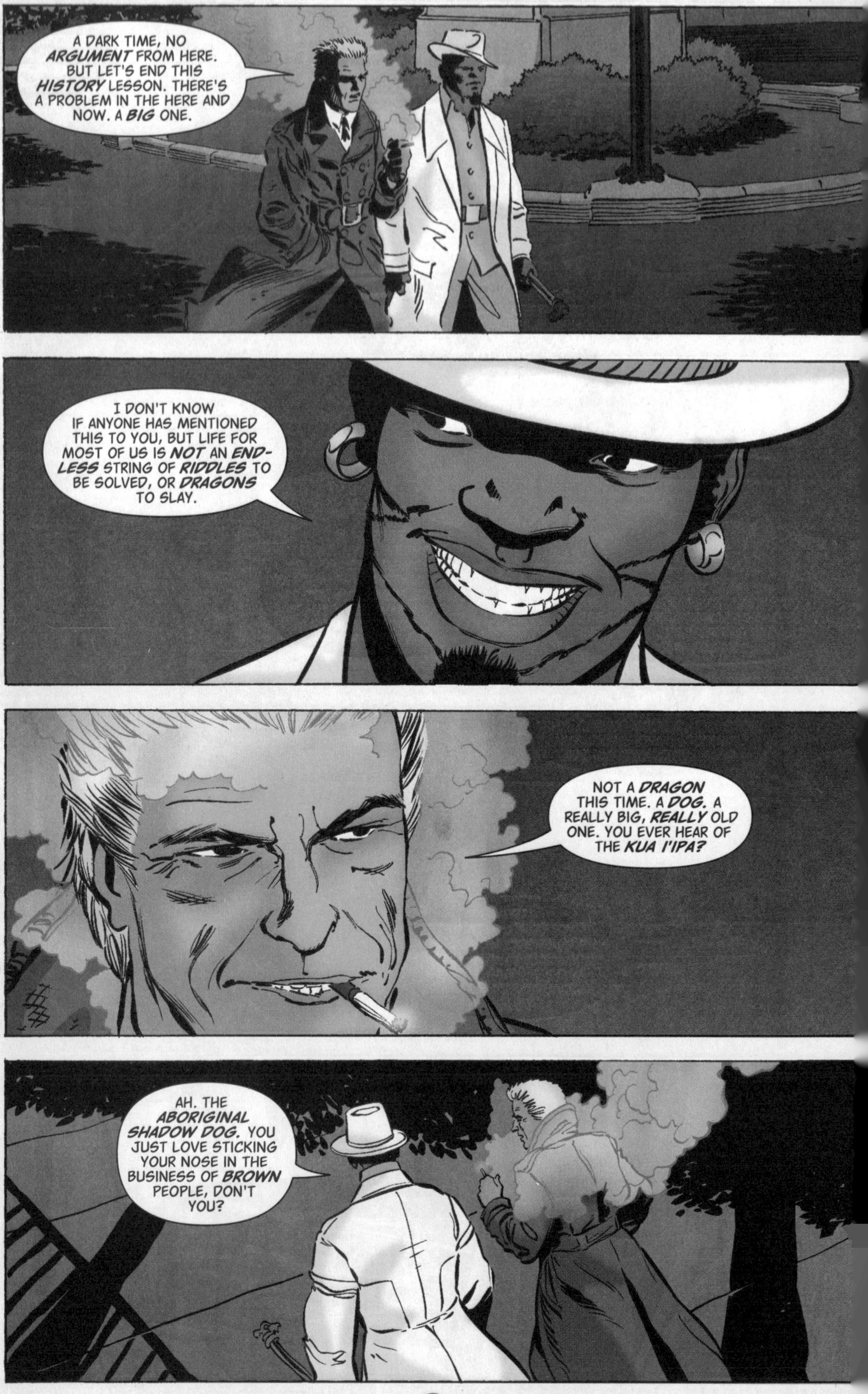
A DARK TIME, NO ARGUMENT FROM HERE. BUT LET'S END THIS HISTORY LESSON. THERE'S A PROBLEM IN THE HERE AND NOW. A BIG ONE.
I DON'T KNOW IF ANYONE HAS MENTIONED THIS TO YOU, BUT LIFE FOR MOST OF US IS NOT AN END-LESS STRING OF RIDDLES TO BE SOLVED, OR DRAGONS TO SLAY.
NOT A DRAGON THIS TIME. A DOG. A REALLY BIG, REALLY OLD ONE. YOU EVER HEAR OF THE KUA I'IPA?
AH. THE ABORIGINAL SHADOW DOG. YOU JUST LOVE STICKING YOUR NOSE IN THE BUSINESS OF BROWN PEOPLE, DON'T YOU?

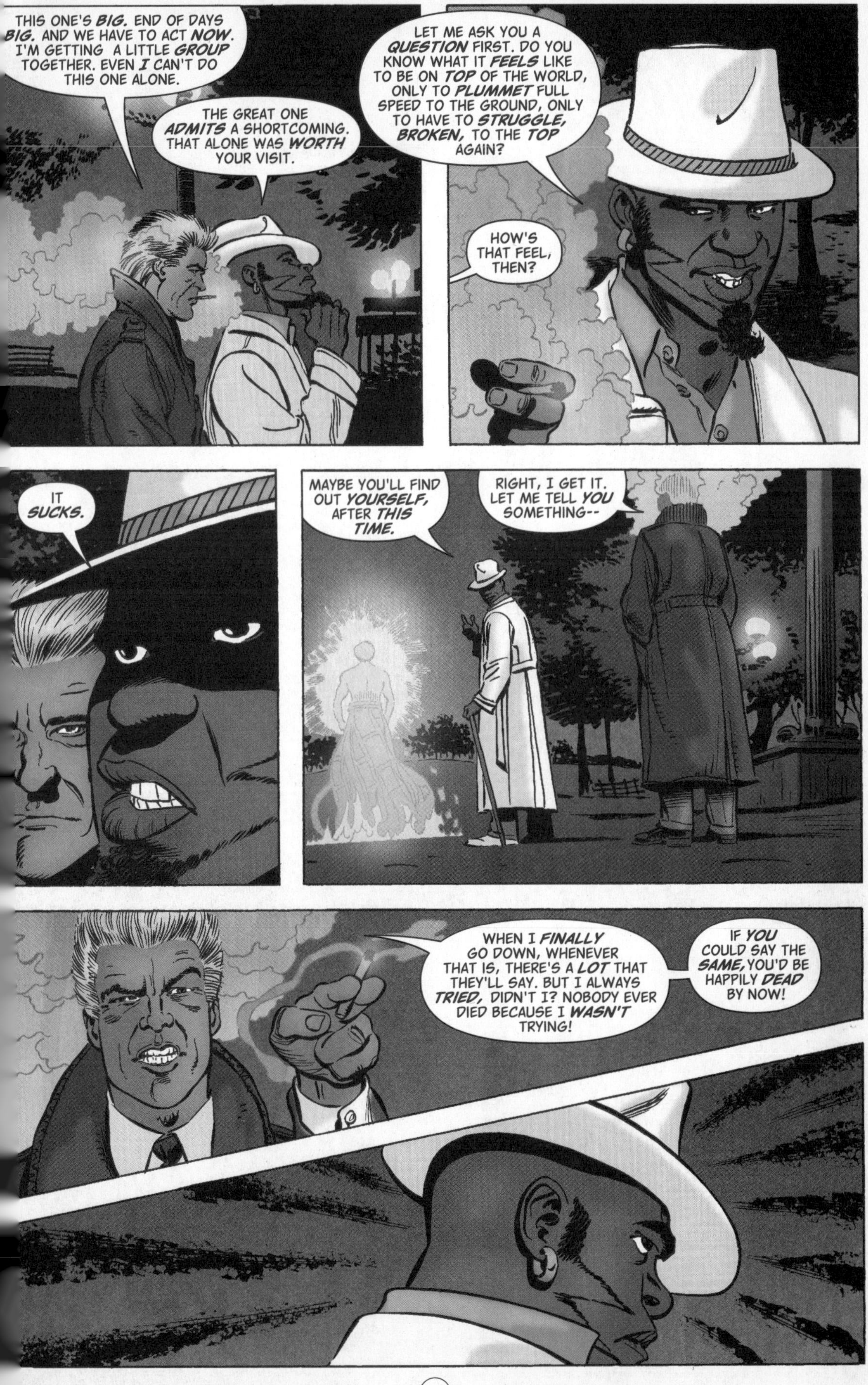
THIS ONE'S BIG. END OF DAYS BIG. AND WE HAVE TO ACT NOW. I'M GETTING A LITTLE GROUP TOGETHER. EVEN I CAN'T DO THIS ONE ALONE.
THE GREAT ONE ADMITS A SHORTCOMING. THAT ALONE WAS WORTH YOUR VISIT.
LET ME ASK YOU A QUESTION FIRST. DO YOU KNOW WHAT IT FEELS LIKE TO BE ON TOP OF THE WORLD, ONLY TO PLUMMET FULL SPEED TO THE GROUND, ONLY TO HAVE TO STRUGGLE, BROKEN, TO THE TOP AGAIN?
HOW'S THAT FEEL, THEN?
IT SUCKS.
MAYBE YOU'LL FIND OUT YOURSELF, AFTER THIS TIME.
RIGHT, I GET IT. LET ME TELL YOU SOMETHING--
WHEN I FINALLY GO DOWN, WHENEVER THAT IS, THERE'S A LOT THAT THEY'LL SAY. BUT I ALWAYS TRIED, DIDN'T I? NOBODY EVER DIED BECAUSE I WASN'T TRYING!
IF YOU COULD SAY THE SAME, YOU'D BE HAPPILY DEAD BY NOW!

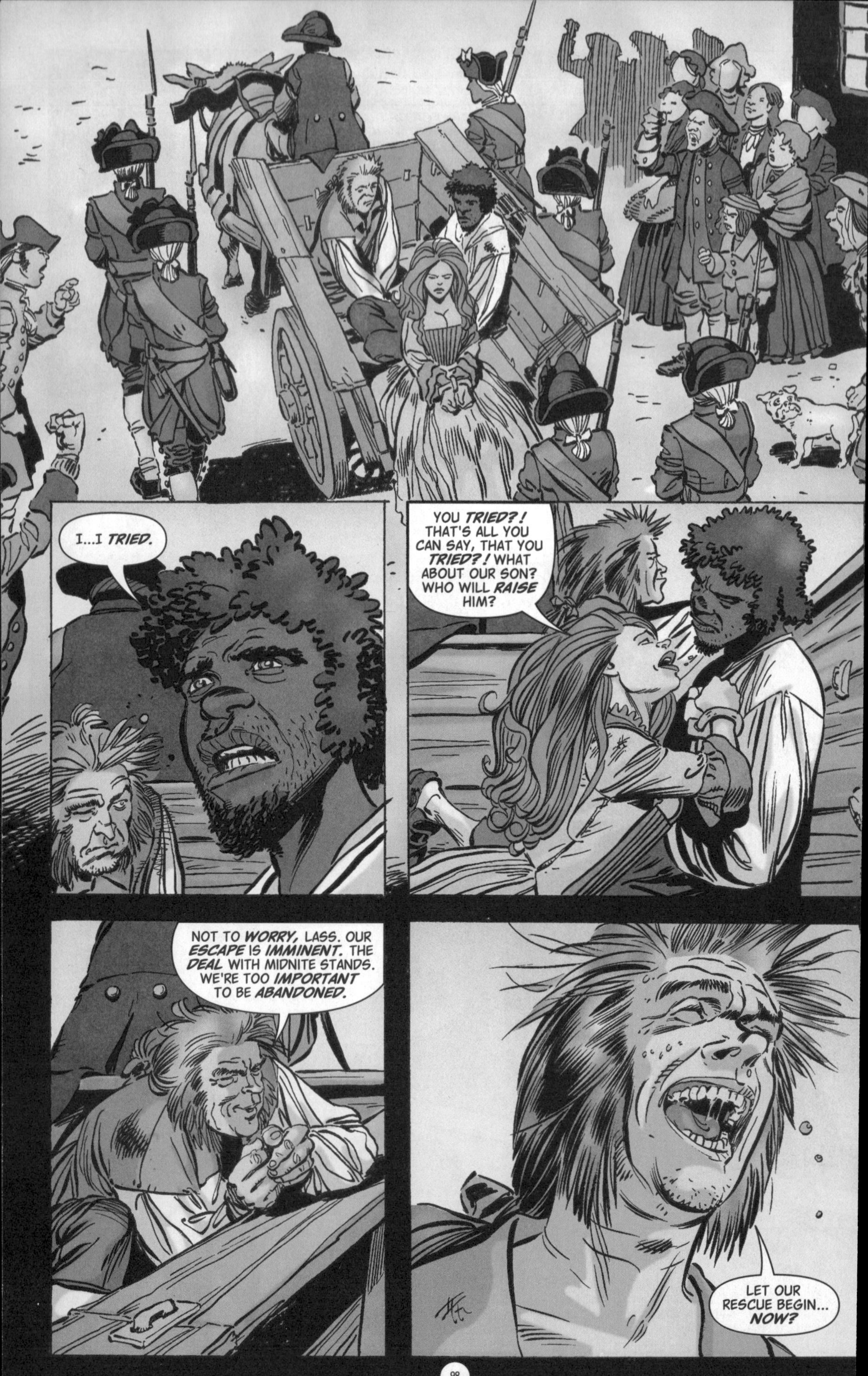
I...I TRIED.
YOU TRIED?! THAT'S ALL YOU CAN SAY, THAT YOU TRIED?! WHAT ABOUT OUR SON? WHO WILL RAISE HIM?
NOT TO WORRY, LASS. OUR ESCAPE IS IMMINENT. THE DEAL WITH MIDNITE STANDS. WE'RE TOO IMPORTANT TO BE ABANDONED.
LET OUR RESCUE BEGIN... NOW?

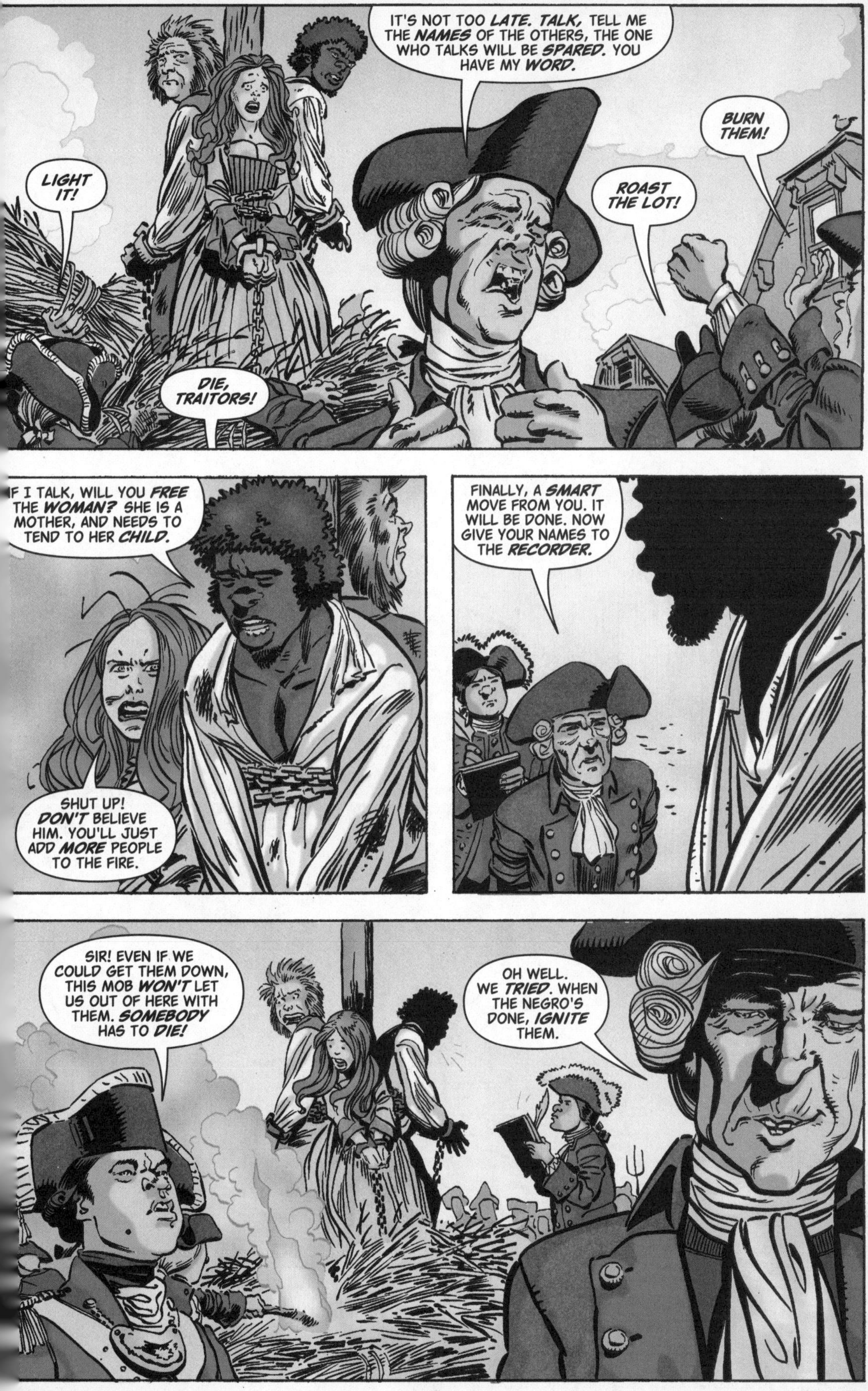
IT'S NOT TOO LATE. TALK, TELL ME THE NAMES OF THE OTHERS, THE ONE WHO TALKS WILL BE SPARED. YOU HAVE MY WORD.
LIGHT IT!
DIE, TRAITORS!
ROAST THE LOT!
BURN THEM!
IF I TALK, WILL YOU FREE THE WOMAN? SHE IS A MOTHER, AND NEEDS TO TEND TO HER CHILD.
SHUT UP! DON'T BELIEVE HIM. YOU'LL JUST ADD MORE PEOPLE TO THE FIRE.
FINALLY, A SMART MOVE FROM YOU. IT WILL BE DONE. NOW GIVE YOUR NAMES TO THE RECORDER.
SIR! EVEN IF WE COULD GET THEM DOWN, THIS MOB WON'T LET US OUT OF HERE WITH THEM. SOMEBODY HAS TO DIE!
OH WELL. WE TRIED. WHEN THE NEGRO'S DONE, IGNITE THEM.

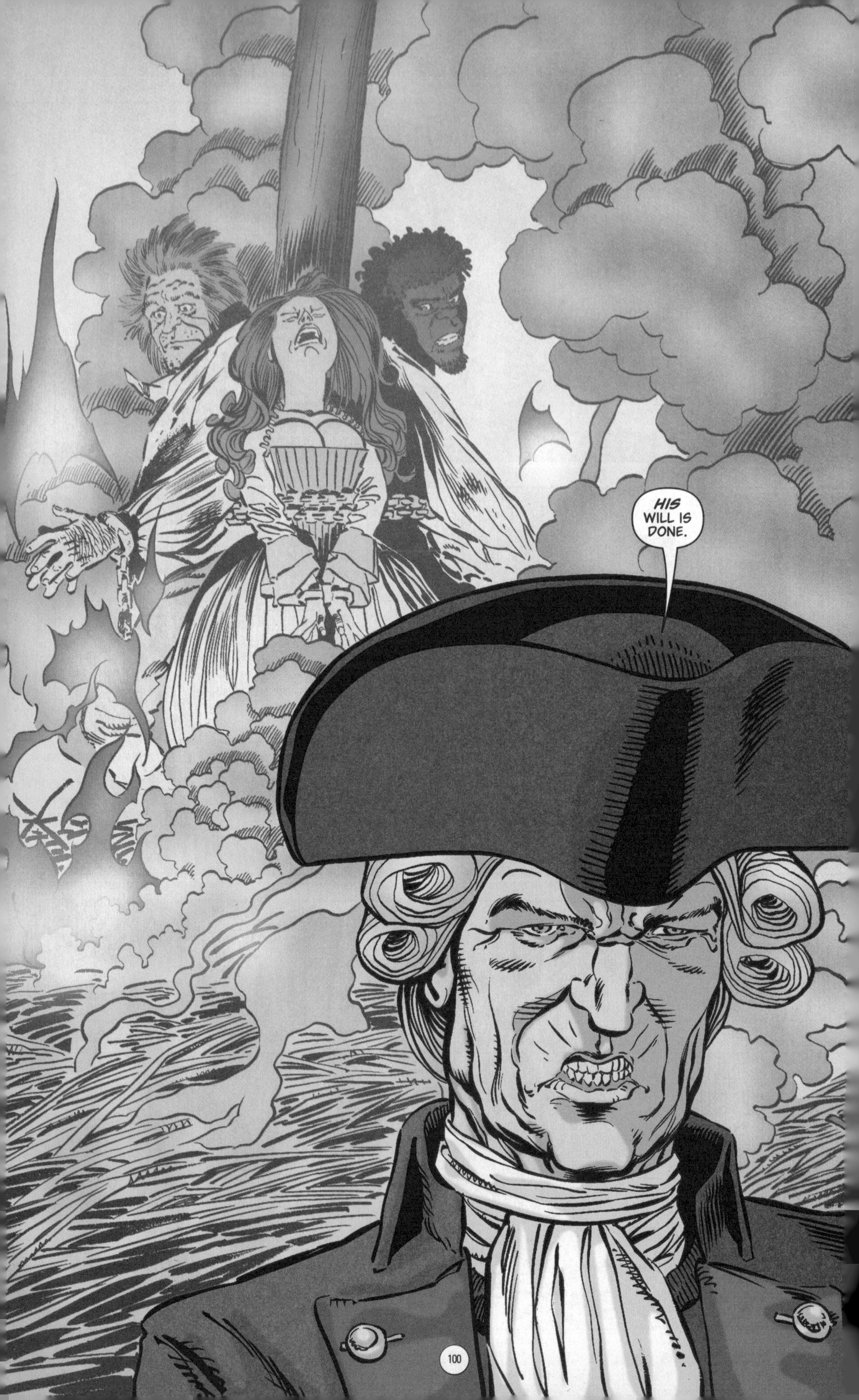
HIS WILL IS DONE.

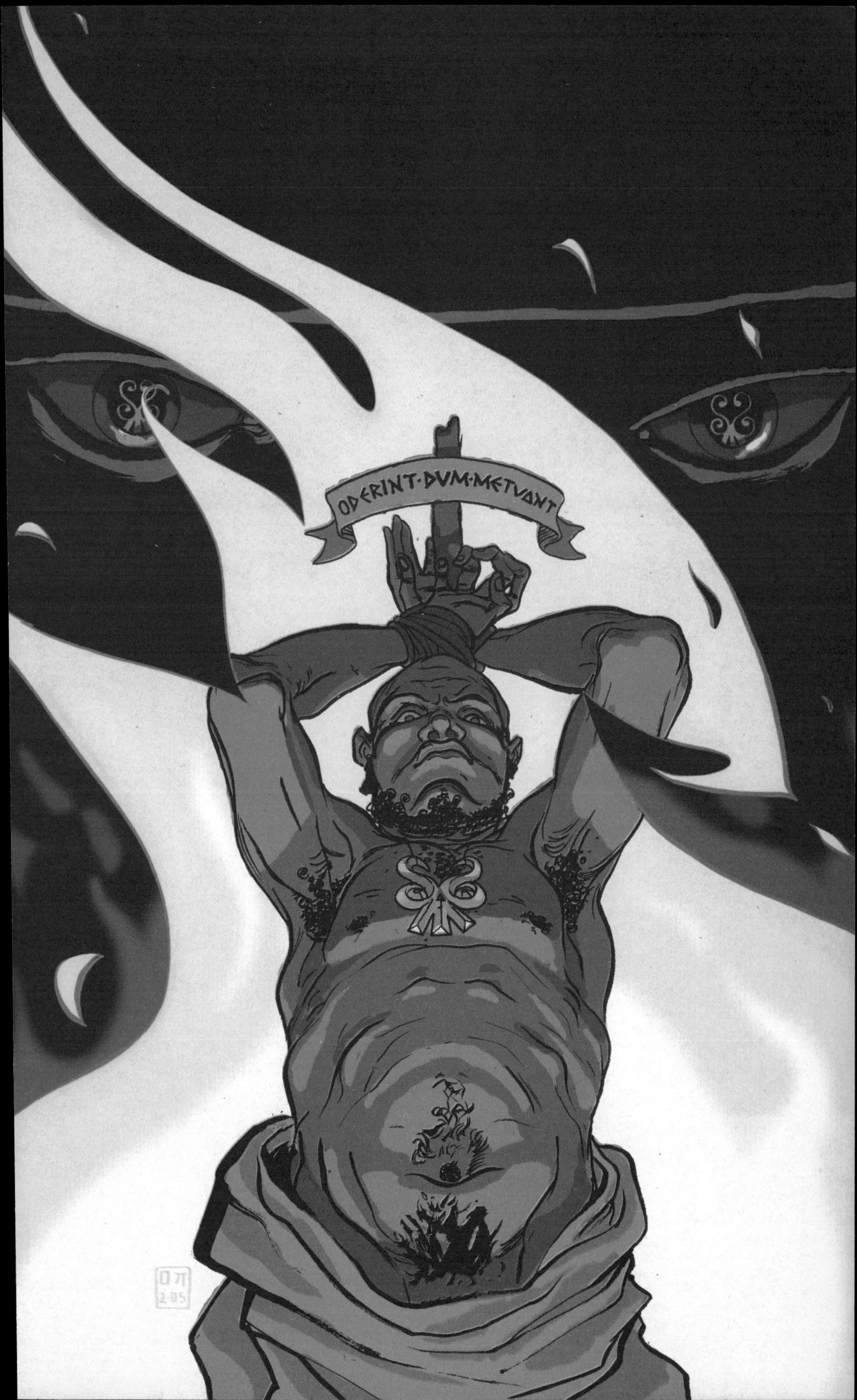
ODERINT·DVM·METVANT

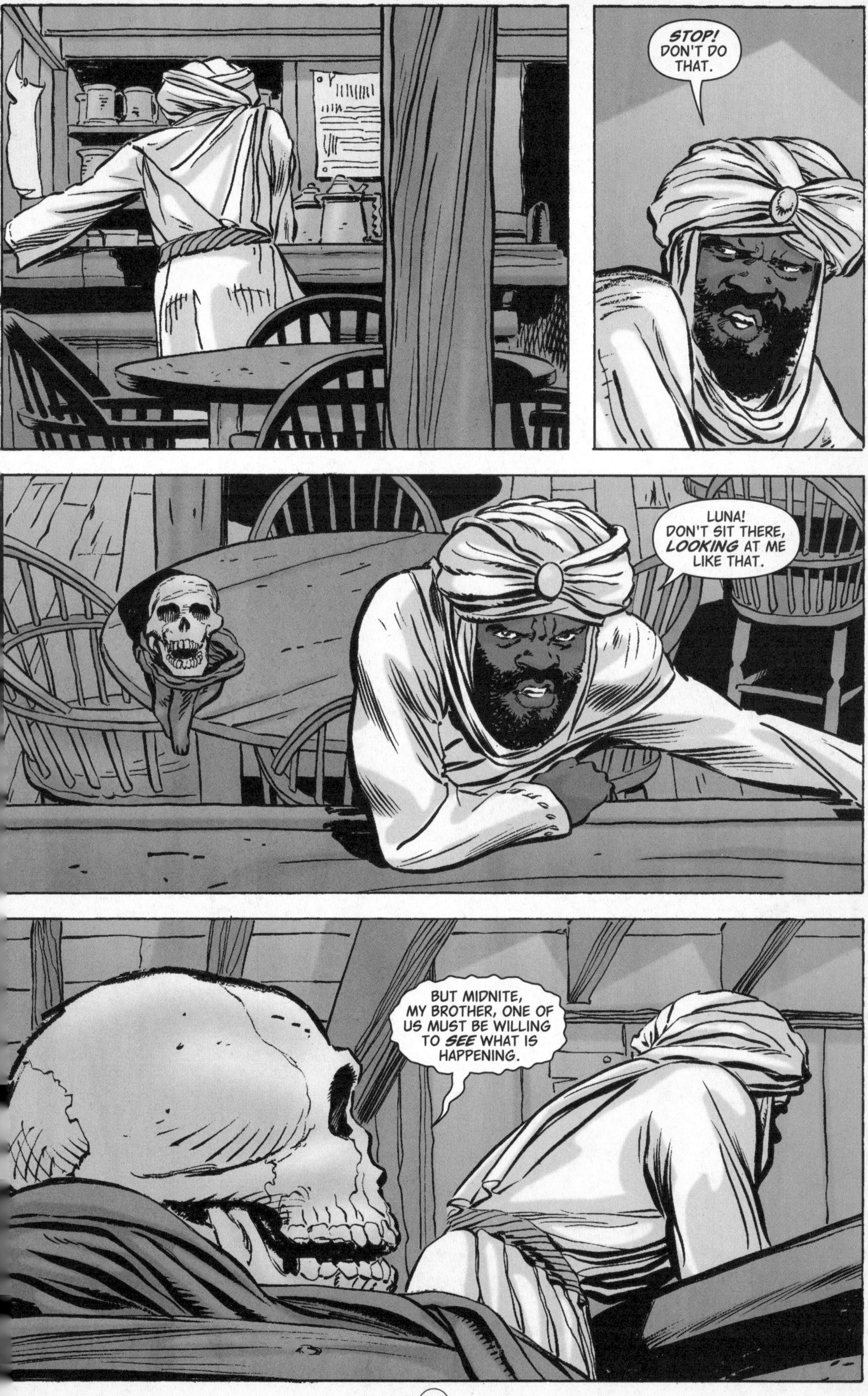
STOP! DON'T DO THAT.
LUNA! DON'T SIT THERE, LOOKING AT ME LIKE THAT.
BUT MIDNITE, MY BROTHER, ONE OF US MUST BE WILLING TO SEE WHAT IS HAPPENING.

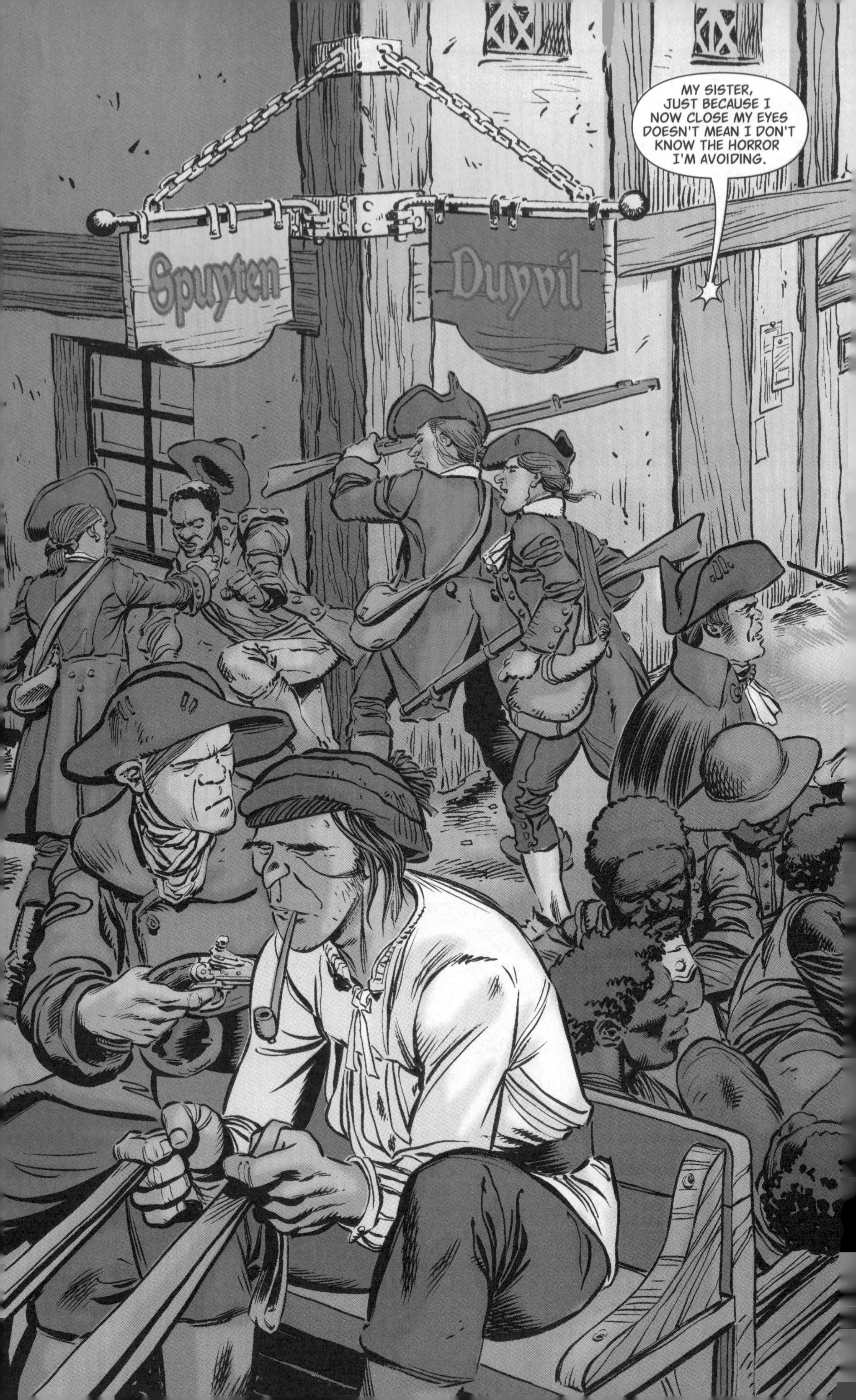
Spuyten
Duyvil
MY SISTER, JUST BECAUSE I NOW CLOSE MY EYES DOESN'T MEAN I DON'T KNOW THE HORROR I'M AVOIDING.

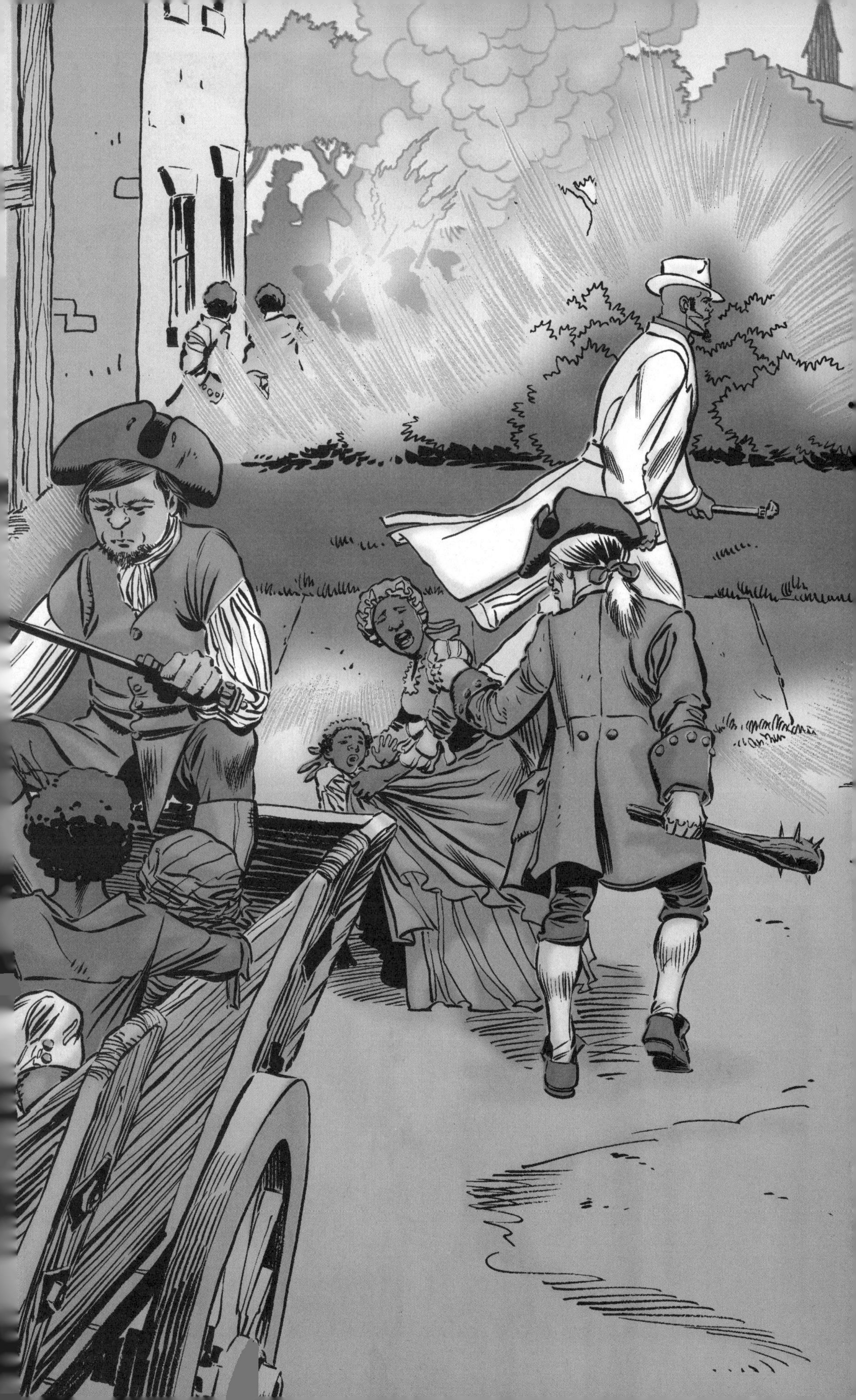

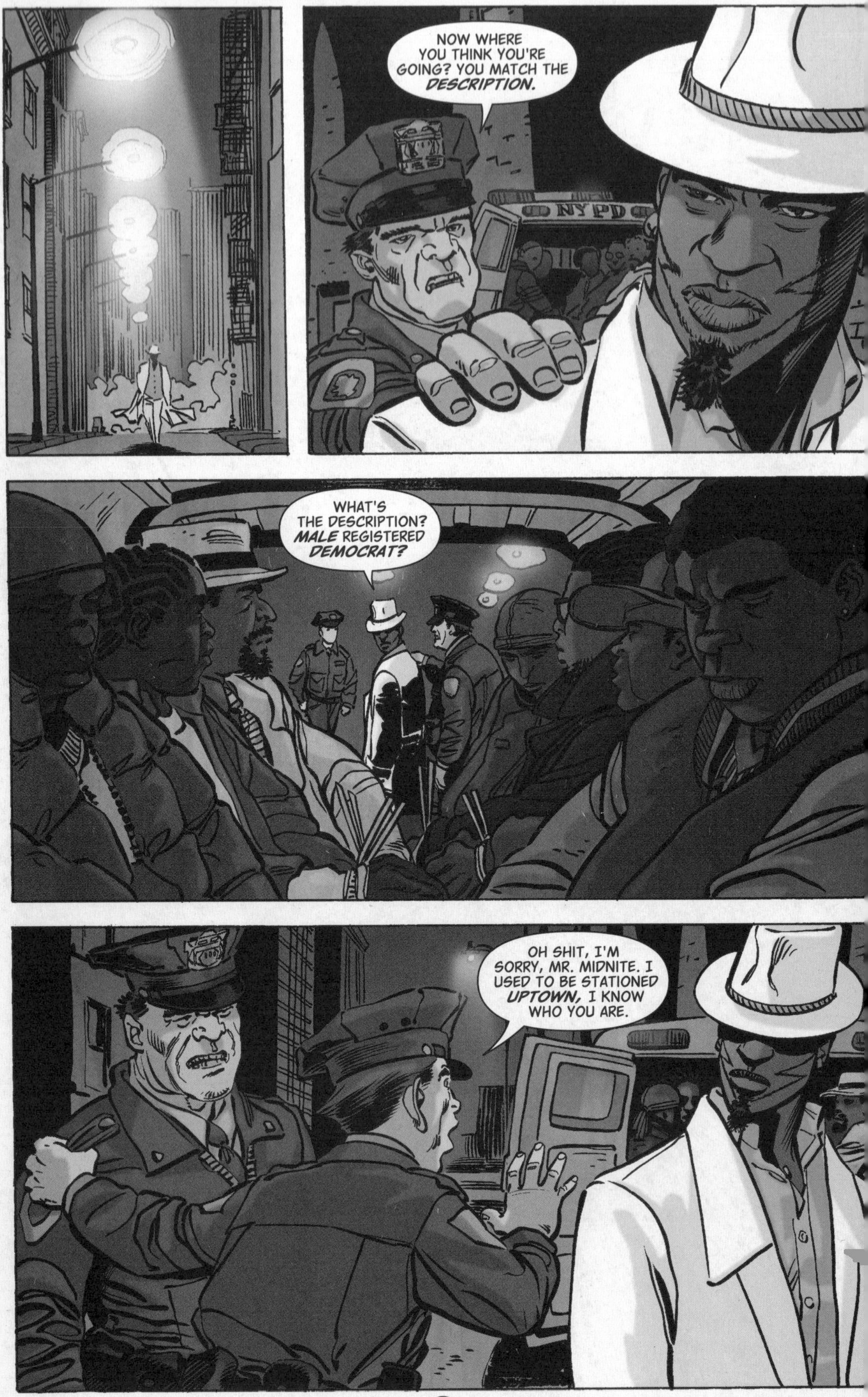
NOW WHERE YOU THINK YOU'RE GOING? YOU MATCH THE DESCRIPTION.
NYPD
WHAT'S THE DESCRIPTION? MALE REGISTERED DEMOCRAT?
OH SHIT, I'M SORRY, MR. MIDNITE. I USED TO BE STATIONED UPTOWN, I KNOW WHO YOU ARE.

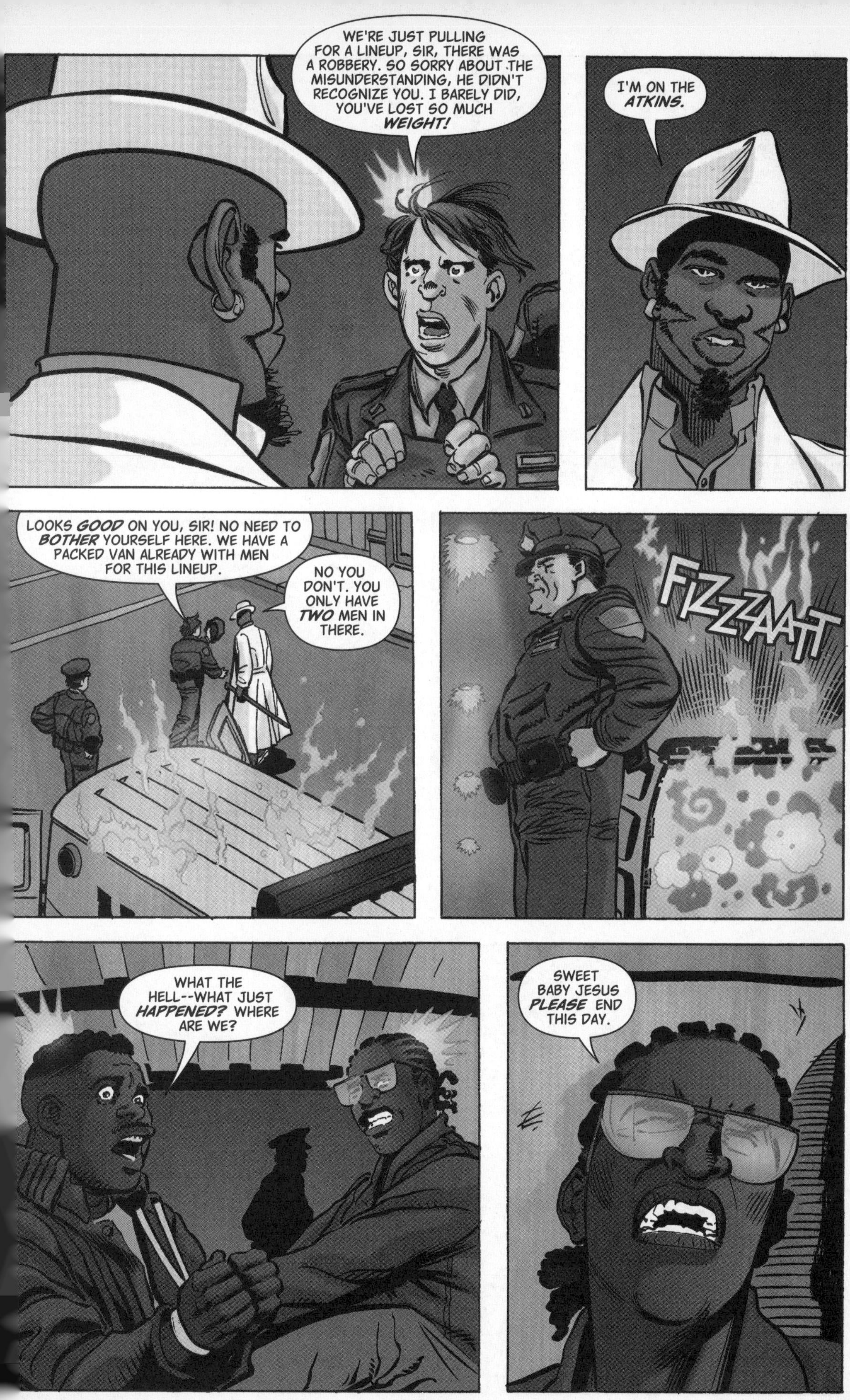
WE'RE JUST PULLING FOR A LINEUP, SIR, THERE WAS A ROBBERY. SO SORRY ABOUT THE MISUNDERSTANDING, HE DIDN'T RECOGNIZE YOU. I BARELY DID, YOU'VE LOST SO MUCH *WEIGHT!*
I'M ON THE *ATKINS.*
LOOKS *GOOD* ON YOU, SIR! NO NEED TO *BOTHER* YOURSELF HERE. WE HAVE A PACKED VAN ALREADY WITH MEN FOR THIS LINEUP.
NO YOU DON'T. YOU ONLY HAVE *TWO* MEN IN THERE.
FIZZZAATT
WHAT THE HELL--WHAT JUST *HAPPENED?* WHERE ARE WE?
SWEET BABY JESUS *PLEASE* END THIS DAY.

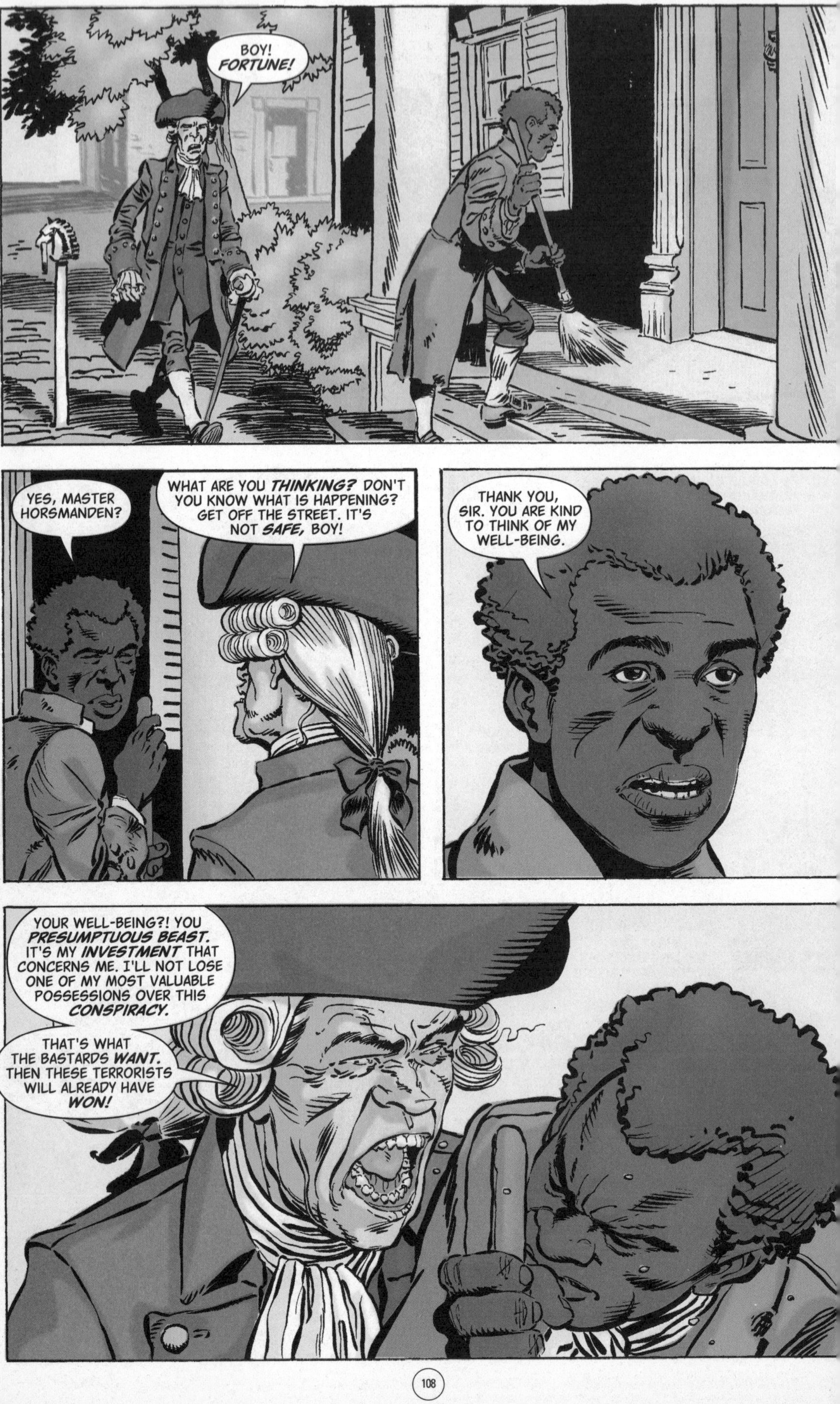

BOY! *FORTUNE!*
YES, MASTER HORSMANDEN?
WHAT ARE YOU *THINKING?* DON'T YOU KNOW WHAT IS HAPPENING? GET OFF THE STREET. IT'S NOT *SAFE,* BOY!
THANK YOU, SIR. YOU ARE KIND TO THINK OF MY WELL-BEING.
YOUR WELL-BEING?! YOU *PRESUMPTUOUS BEAST.* IT'S MY *INVESTMENT* THAT CONCERNS ME. I'LL NOT LOSE ONE OF MY MOST VALUABLE POSSESSIONS OVER THIS *CONSPIRACY.*
THAT'S WHAT THE BASTARDS *WANT.* THEN THESE TERRORISTS WILL ALREADY HAVE *WON!*

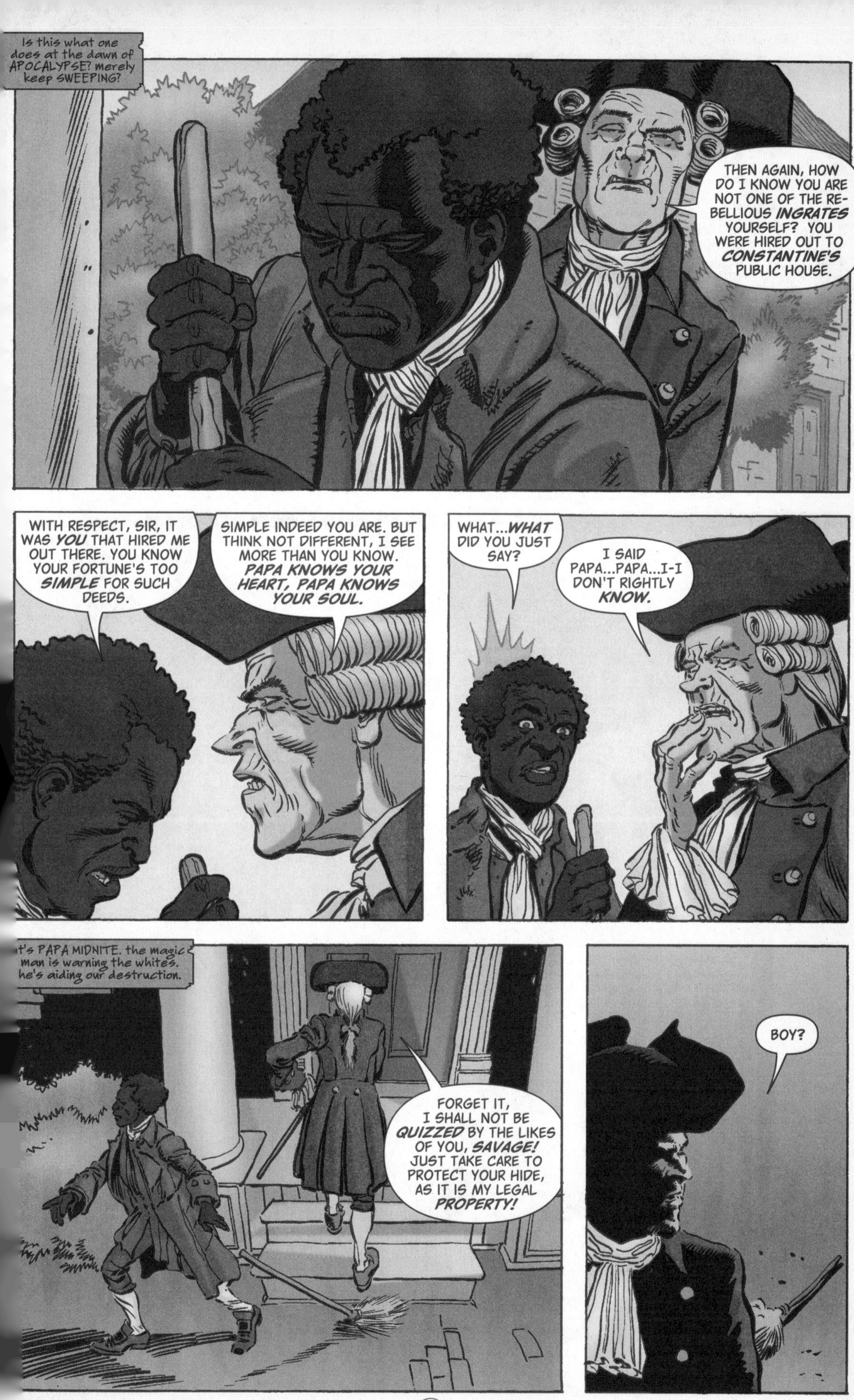
Is this what one does at the dawn of APOCALYPSE? merely keep SWEEPING?
THEN AGAIN, HOW DO I KNOW YOU ARE NOT ONE OF THE REBELLIOUS INGRATES YOURSELF? YOU WERE HIRED OUT TO CONSTANTINE'S PUBLIC HOUSE.
WITH RESPECT, SIR, IT WAS YOU THAT HIRED ME OUT THERE. YOU KNOW YOUR FORTUNE'S TOO SIMPLE FOR SUCH DEEDS.
SIMPLE INDEED YOU ARE. BUT THINK NOT DIFFERENT, I SEE MORE THAN YOU KNOW. PAPA KNOWS YOUR HEART, PAPA KNOWS YOUR SOUL.
WHAT...WHAT DID YOU JUST SAY?
I SAID PAPA...PAPA...I-I DON'T RIGHTLY KNOW.
t's PAPA MIDNITE. the magic man is warning the whites. he's aiding our destruction.
FORGET IT, I SHALL NOT BE QUIZZED BY THE LIKES OF YOU, SAVAGE! JUST TAKE CARE TO PROTECT YOUR HIDE, AS IT IS MY LEGAL PROPERTY!
BOY?

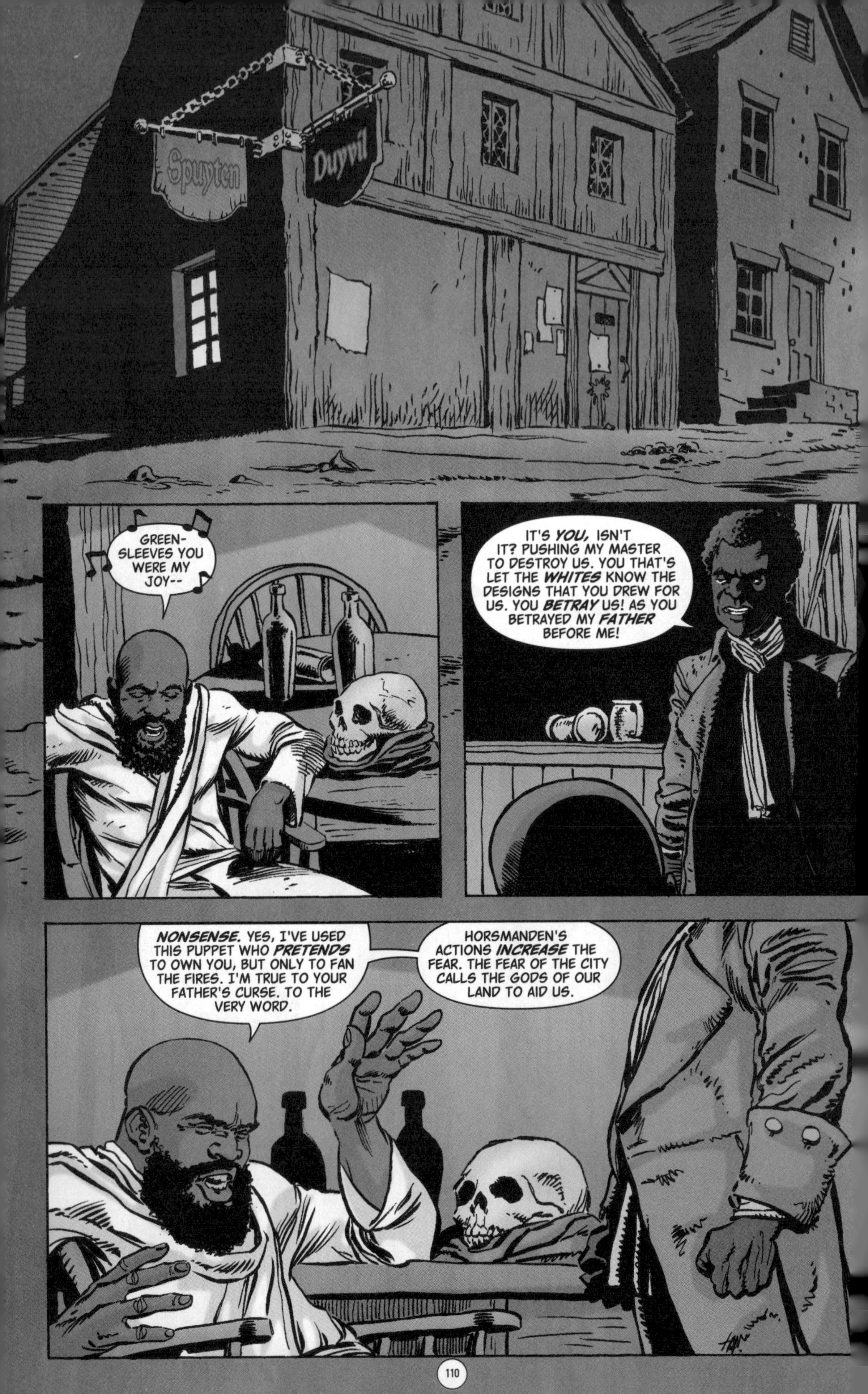
Spuyten
Duyvil
GREEN-SLEEVES YOU WERE MY JOY--
IT'S YOU, ISN'T IT? PUSHING MY MASTER TO DESTROY US. YOU THAT'S LET THE WHITES KNOW THE DESIGNS THAT YOU DREW FOR US. YOU BETRAY US! AS YOU BETRAYED MY FATHER BEFORE ME!
NONSENSE. YES, I'VE USED THIS PUPPET WHO PRETENDS TO OWN YOU, BUT ONLY TO FAN THE FIRES. I'M TRUE TO YOUR FATHER'S CURSE. TO THE VERY WORD.
HORSMANDEN'S ACTIONS INCREASE THE FEAR. THE FEAR OF THE CITY CALLS THE GODS OF OUR LAND TO AID US.

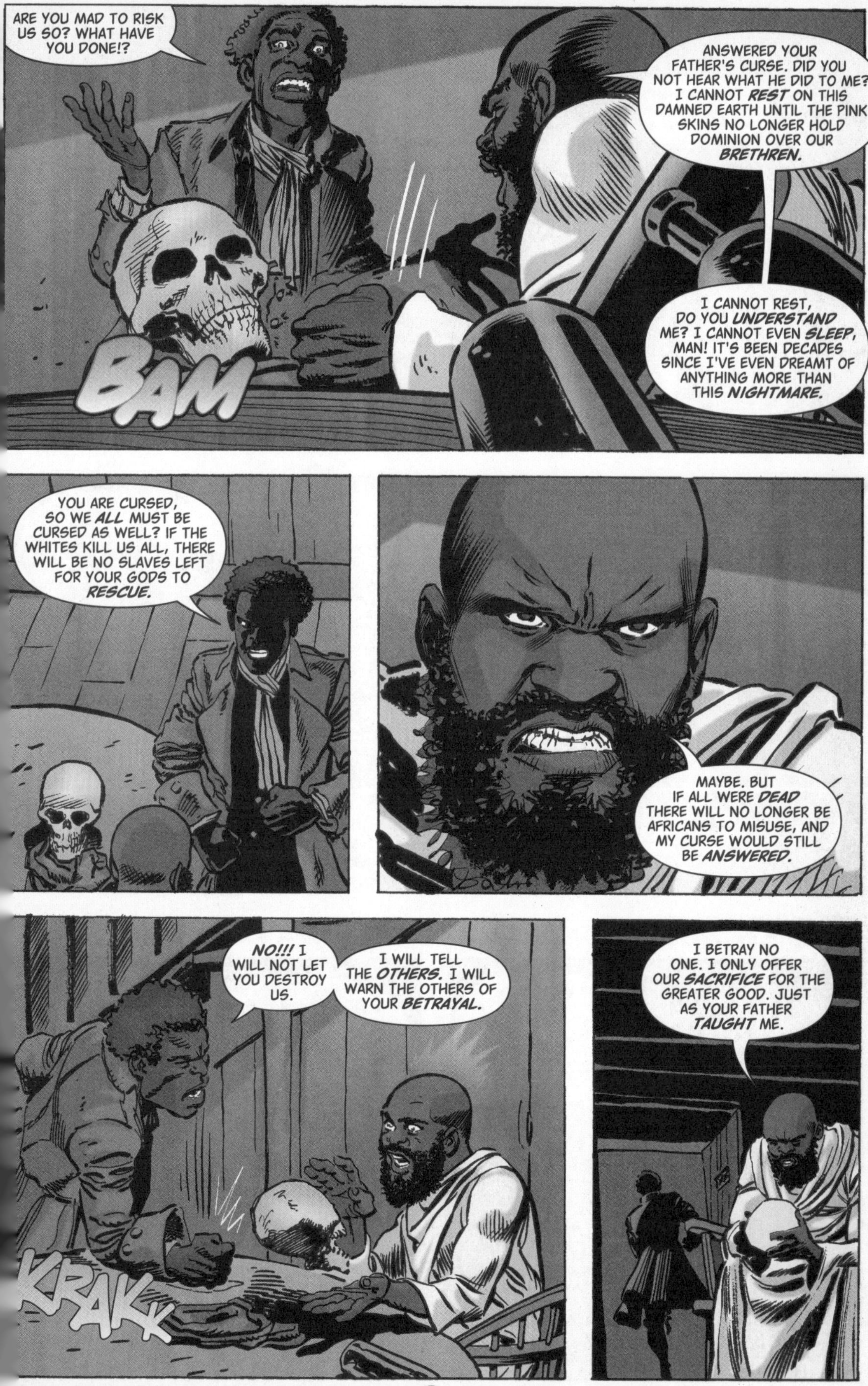

ARE YOU MAD TO RISK US SO? WHAT HAVE YOU DONE!?
ANSWERED YOUR FATHER'S CURSE. DID YOU NOT HEAR WHAT HE DID TO ME? I CANNOT REST ON THIS DAMNED EARTH UNTIL THE PINK SKINS NO LONGER HOLD DOMINION OVER OUR BRETHREN.
I CANNOT REST, DO YOU UNDERSTAND ME? I CANNOT EVEN SLEEP, MAN! IT'S BEEN DECADES SINCE I'VE EVEN DREAMT OF ANYTHING MORE THAN THIS NIGHTMARE.
BAM
YOU ARE CURSED, SO WE ALL MUST BE CURSED AS WELL? IF THE WHITES KILL US ALL, THERE WILL BE NO SLAVES LEFT FOR YOUR GODS TO RESCUE.
MAYBE. BUT IF ALL WERE DEAD THERE WILL NO LONGER BE AFRICANS TO MISUSE, AND MY CURSE WOULD STILL BE ANSWERED.
NO!!! I WILL NOT LET YOU DESTROY US.
I WILL TELL THE OTHERS. I WILL WARN THE OTHERS OF YOUR BETRAYAL.
KRAKK
I BETRAY NO ONE. I ONLY OFFER OUR SACRIFICE FOR THE GREATER GOOD. JUST AS YOUR FATHER TAUGHT ME.

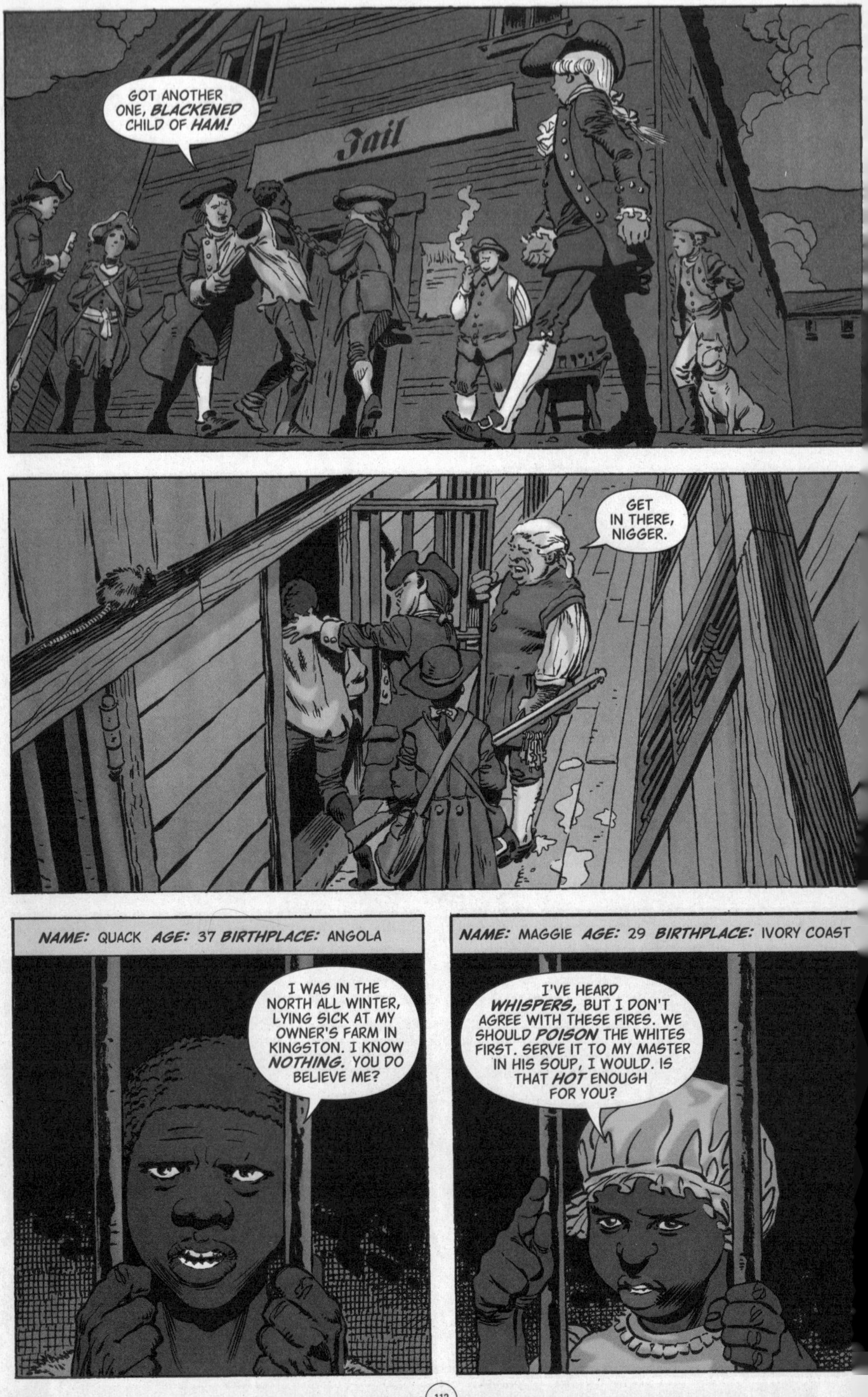
GOT ANOTHER ONE, BLACKENED CHILD OF HAM!
Jail
GET IN THERE, NIGGER.
NAME: QUACK AGE: 37 BIRTHPLACE: ANGOLA
I WAS IN THE NORTH ALL WINTER, LYING SICK AT MY OWNER'S FARM IN KINGSTON. I KNOW NOTHING. YOU DO BELIEVE ME?
NAME: MAGGIE AGE: 29 BIRTHPLACE: IVORY COAST
I'VE HEARD WHISPERS, BUT I DON'T AGREE WITH THESE FIRES. WE SHOULD POISON THE WHITES FIRST. SERVE IT TO MY MASTER IN HIS SOUP, I WOULD. IS THAT HOT ENOUGH FOR YOU?

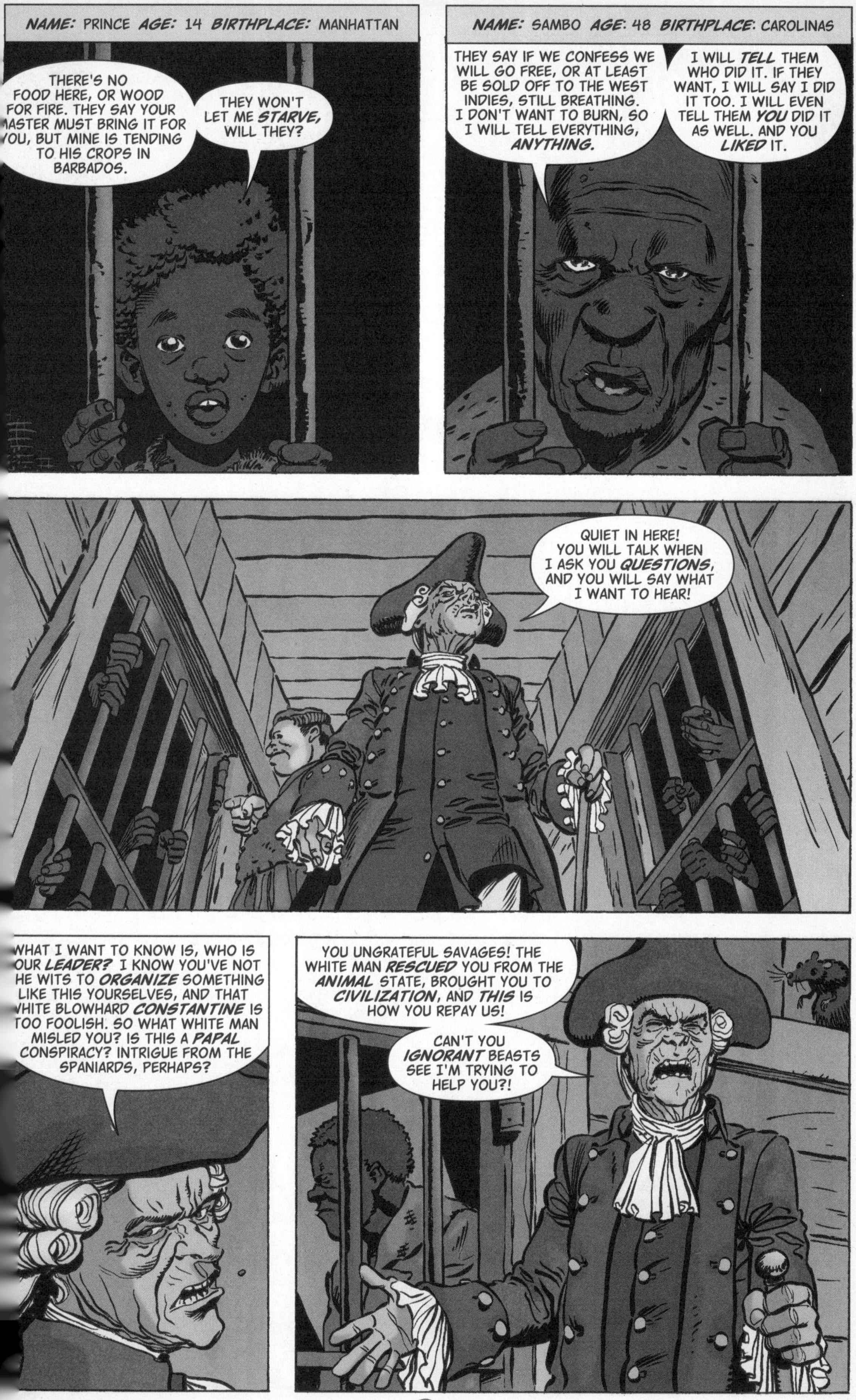
NAME: PRINCE AGE: 14 BIRTHPLACE: MANHATTAN
THERE'S NO FOOD HERE, OR WOOD FOR FIRE. THEY SAY YOUR ASTER MUST BRING IT FOR OU, BUT MINE IS TENDING TO HIS CROPS IN BARBADOS.
THEY WON'T LET ME STARVE, WILL THEY?
NAME: SAMBO AGE: 48 BIRTHPLACE: CAROLINAS
THEY SAY IF WE CONFESS WE WILL GO FREE, OR AT LEAST BE SOLD OFF TO THE WEST INDIES, STILL BREATHING. I DON'T WANT TO BURN, SO I WILL TELL EVERYTHING, ANYTHING.
I WILL TELL THEM WHO DID IT. IF THEY WANT, I WILL SAY I DID IT TOO. I WILL EVEN TELL THEM YOU DID IT AS WELL. AND YOU LIKED IT.
QUIET IN HERE! YOU WILL TALK WHEN I ASK YOU QUESTIONS, AND YOU WILL SAY WHAT I WANT TO HEAR!
WHAT I WANT TO KNOW IS, WHO IS OUR LEADER? I KNOW YOU'VE NOT HE WITS TO ORGANIZE SOMETHING LIKE THIS YOURSELVES, AND THAT HITE BLOWHARD CONSTANTINE IS TOO FOOLISH. SO WHAT WHITE MAN MISLED YOU? IS THIS A PAPAL CONSPIRACY? INTRIGUE FROM THE SPANIARDS, PERHAPS?
YOU UNGRATEFUL SAVAGES! THE WHITE MAN RESCUED YOU FROM THE ANIMAL STATE, BROUGHT YOU TO CIVILIZATION, AND THIS IS HOW YOU REPAY US!
CAN'T YOU IGNORANT BEASTS SEE I'M TRYING TO HELP YOU?!

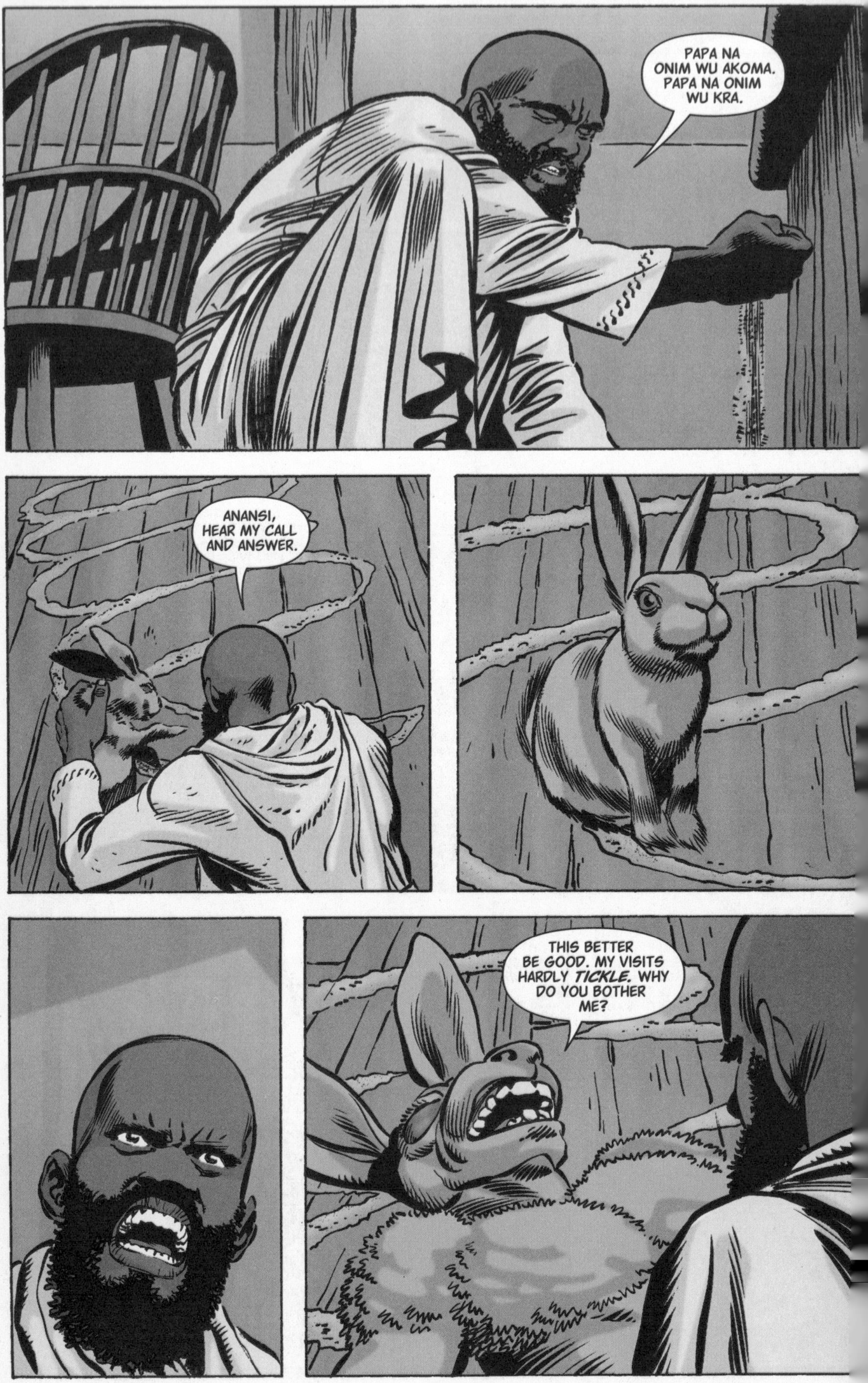
PAPA NA ONIM WU AKOMA. PAPA NA ONIM WU KRA.
ANANSI, HEAR MY CALL AND ANSWER.
THIS BETTER BE GOOD. MY VISITS HARDLY *TICKLE*. WHY DO YOU BOTHER ME?

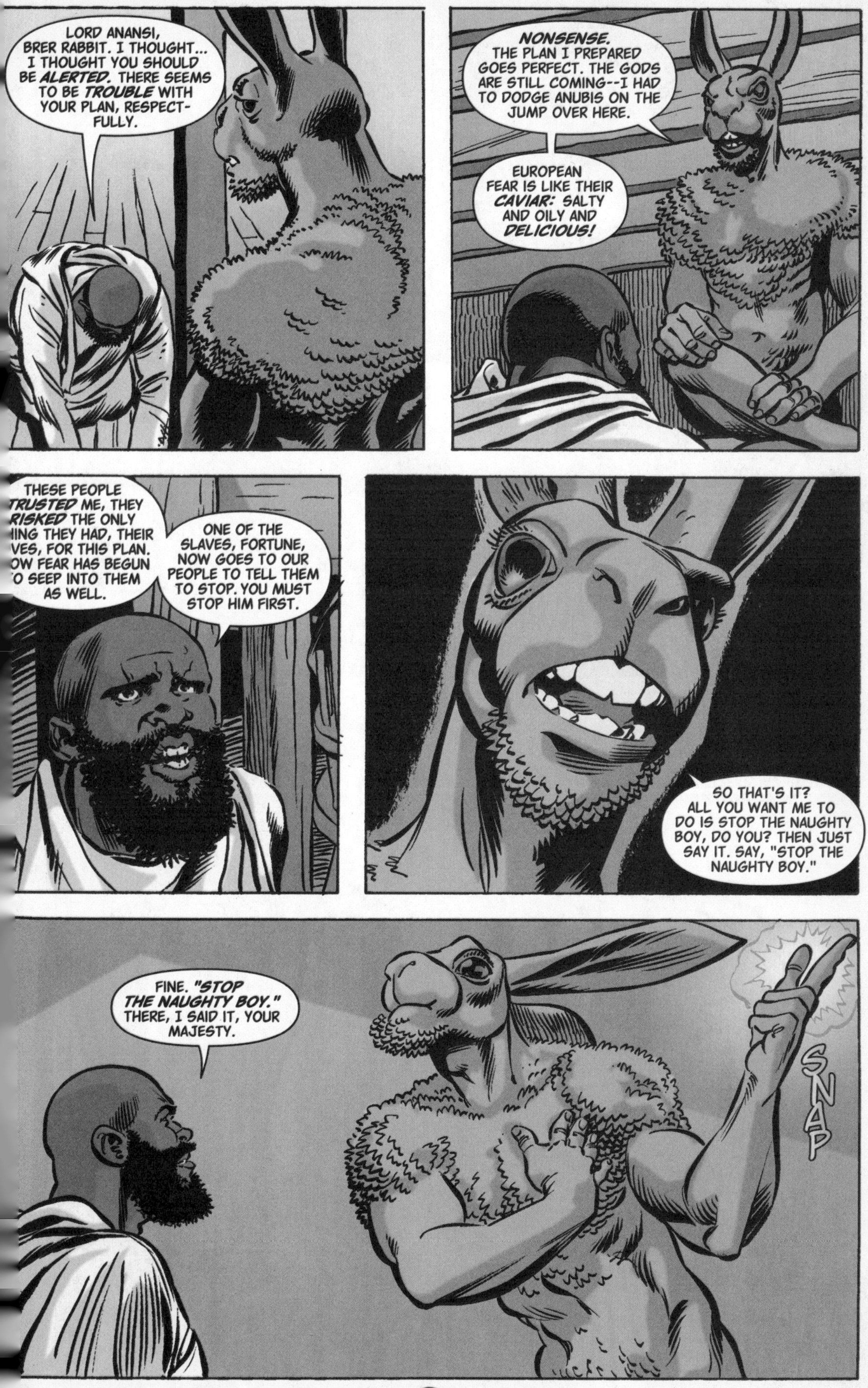
LORD ANANSI, BRER RABBIT. I THOUGHT... I THOUGHT YOU SHOULD BE ALERTED. THERE SEEMS TO BE TROUBLE WITH YOUR PLAN, RESPECT-FULLY.
NONSENSE. THE PLAN I PREPARED GOES PERFECT. THE GODS ARE STILL COMING--I HAD TO DODGE ANUBIS ON THE JUMP OVER HERE.
EUROPEAN FEAR IS LIKE THEIR CAVIAR: SALTY AND OILY AND DELICIOUS!
THESE PEOPLE TRUSTED ME, THEY RISKED THE ONLY HING THEY HAD, THEIR VES, FOR THIS PLAN. OW FEAR HAS BEGUN O SEEP INTO THEM AS WELL.
ONE OF THE SLAVES, FORTUNE, NOW GOES TO OUR PEOPLE TO TELL THEM TO STOP. YOU MUST STOP HIM FIRST.
SO THAT'S IT? ALL YOU WANT ME TO DO IS STOP THE NAUGHTY BOY, DO YOU? THEN JUST SAY IT. SAY, "STOP THE NAUGHTY BOY."
FINE. "STOP THE NAUGHTY BOY." THERE, I SAID IT, YOUR MAJESTY.
SNAP

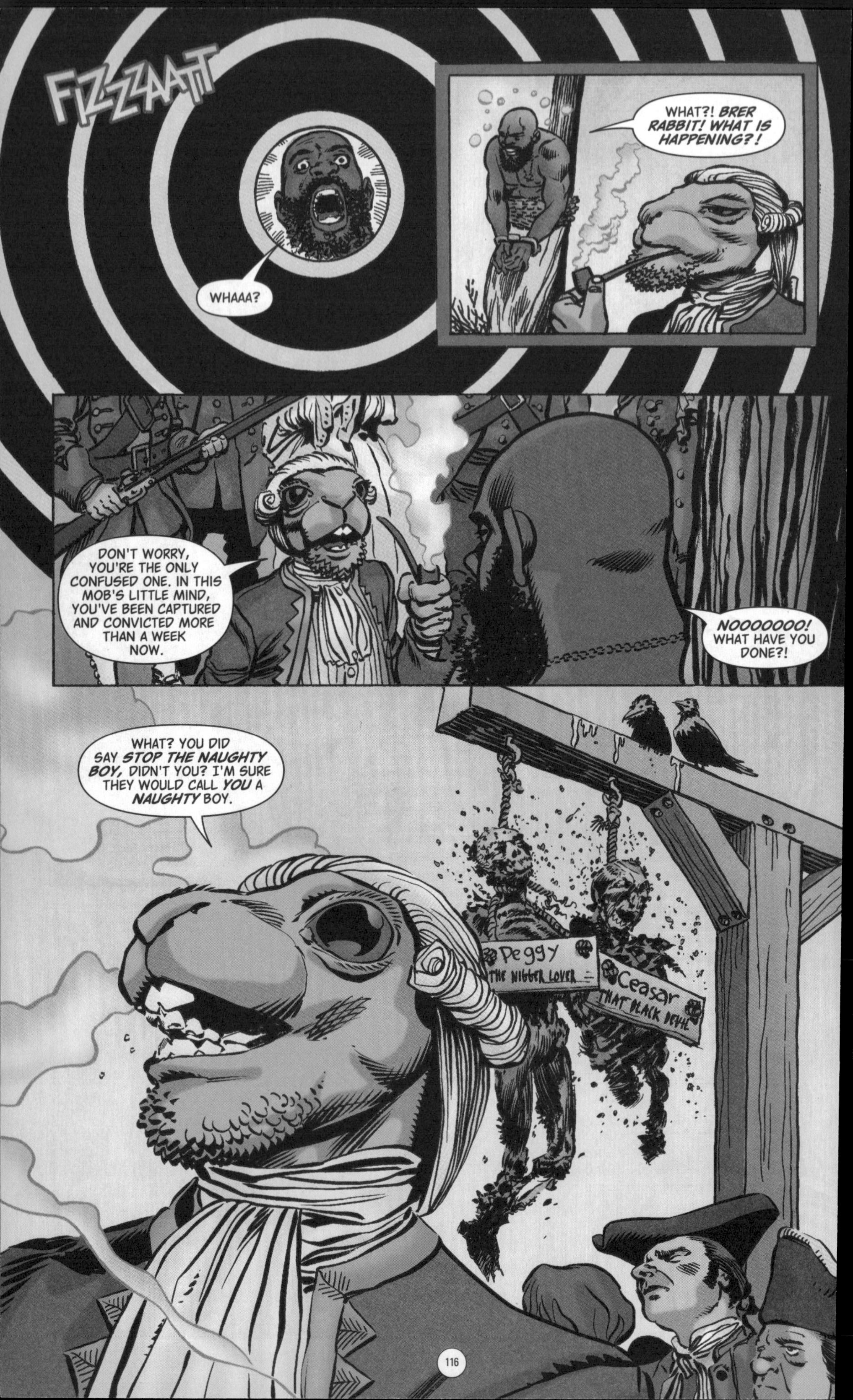
FIZZZAATT
WHAAA?
WHAT?! BRER RABBIT! WHAT IS HAPPENING?!
DON'T WORRY, YOU'RE THE ONLY CONFUSED ONE. IN THIS MOB'S LITTLE MIND, YOU'VE BEEN CAPTURED AND CONVICTED MORE THAN A WEEK NOW.
NOOOOOOO! WHAT HAVE YOU DONE?!
WHAT? YOU DID SAY STOP THE NAUGHTY BOY, DIDN'T YOU? I'M SURE THEY WOULD CALL YOU A NAUGHTY BOY.
Peggy THE NIGGER LOVER
Ceasar THAT BLACK DEVIL

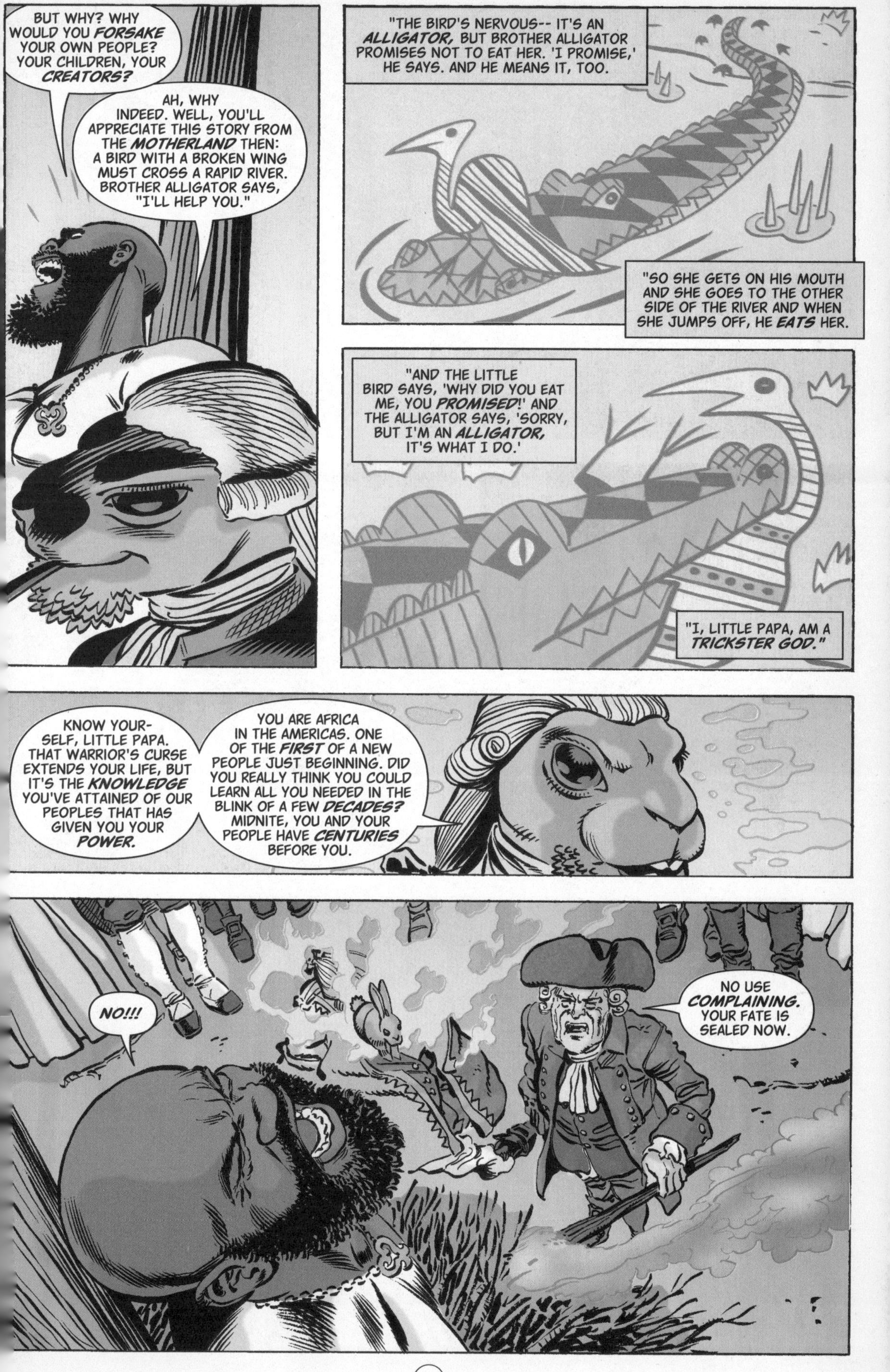
BUT WHY? WHY WOULD YOU FORSAKE YOUR OWN PEOPLE? YOUR CHILDREN, YOUR CREATORS?
AH, WHY INDEED. WELL, YOU'LL APPRECIATE THIS STORY FROM THE MOTHERLAND THEN: A BIRD WITH A BROKEN WING MUST CROSS A RAPID RIVER. BROTHER ALLIGATOR SAYS, "I'LL HELP YOU."
"THE BIRD'S NERVOUS-- IT'S AN ALLIGATOR, BUT BROTHER ALLIGATOR PROMISES NOT TO EAT HER. 'I PROMISE,' HE SAYS. AND HE MEANS IT, TOO.
"SO SHE GETS ON HIS MOUTH AND SHE GOES TO THE OTHER SIDE OF THE RIVER AND WHEN SHE JUMPS OFF, HE EATS HER.
"AND THE LITTLE BIRD SAYS, 'WHY DID YOU EAT ME, YOU PROMISED!' AND THE ALLIGATOR SAYS, 'SORRY, BUT I'M AN ALLIGATOR, IT'S WHAT I DO.'
"I, LITTLE PAPA, AM A TRICKSTER GOD."
KNOW YOURSELF, LITTLE PAPA. THAT WARRIOR'S CURSE EXTENDS YOUR LIFE, BUT IT'S THE KNOWLEDGE YOU'VE ATTAINED OF OUR PEOPLES THAT HAS GIVEN YOU YOUR POWER.
YOU ARE AFRICA IN THE AMERICAS. ONE OF THE FIRST OF A NEW PEOPLE JUST BEGINNING. DID YOU REALLY THINK YOU COULD LEARN ALL YOU NEEDED IN THE BLINK OF A FEW DECADES? MIDNITE, YOU AND YOUR PEOPLE HAVE CENTURIES BEFORE YOU.
NO!!!
NO USE COMPLAINING. YOUR FATE IS SEALED NOW.

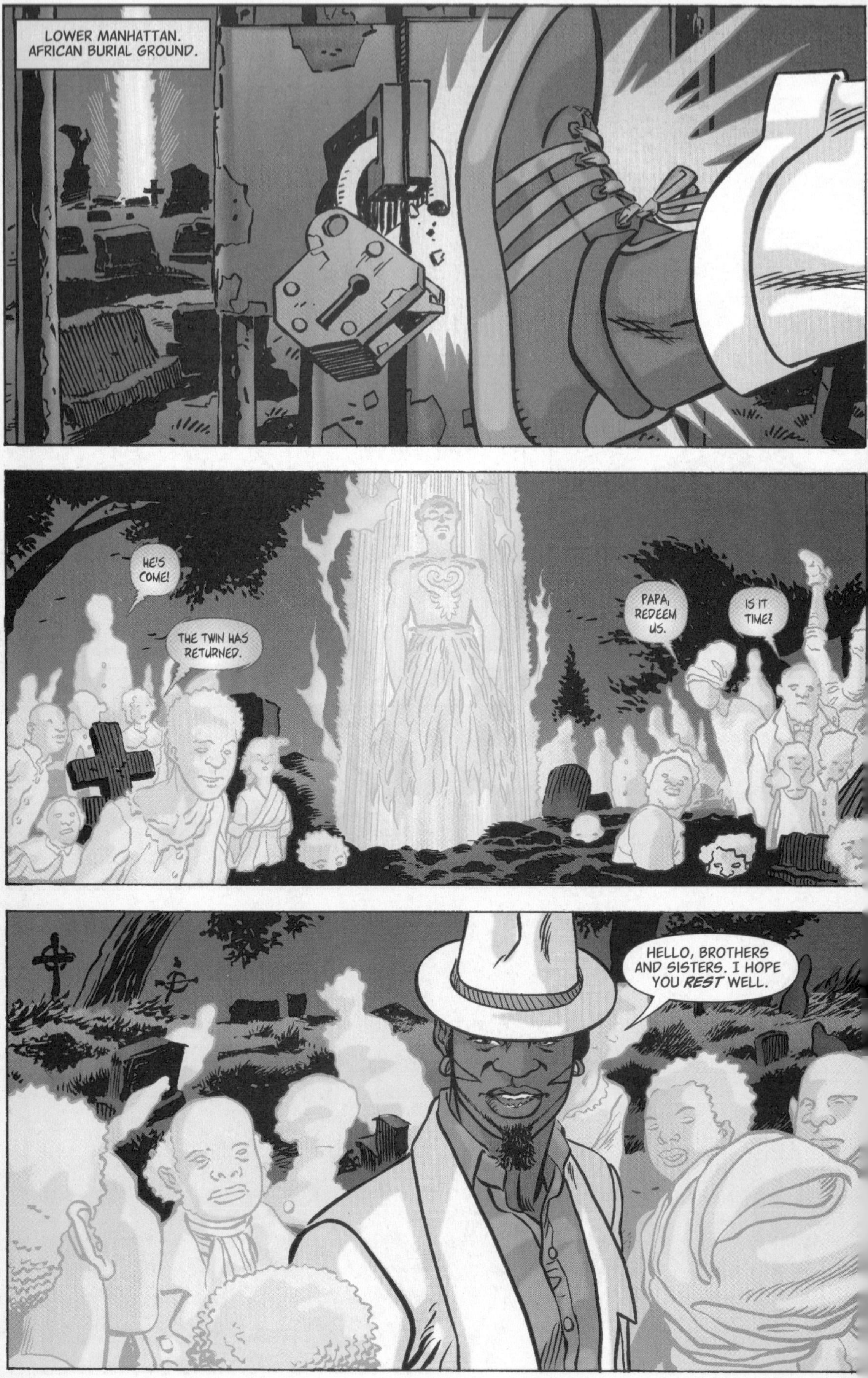
LOWER MANHATTAN. AFRICAN BURIAL GROUND.
HE'S COME!
THE TWIN HAS RETURNED.
PAPA, REDEEM US.
IS IT TIME?
HELLO, BROTHERS AND SISTERS. I HOPE YOU *REST* WELL.

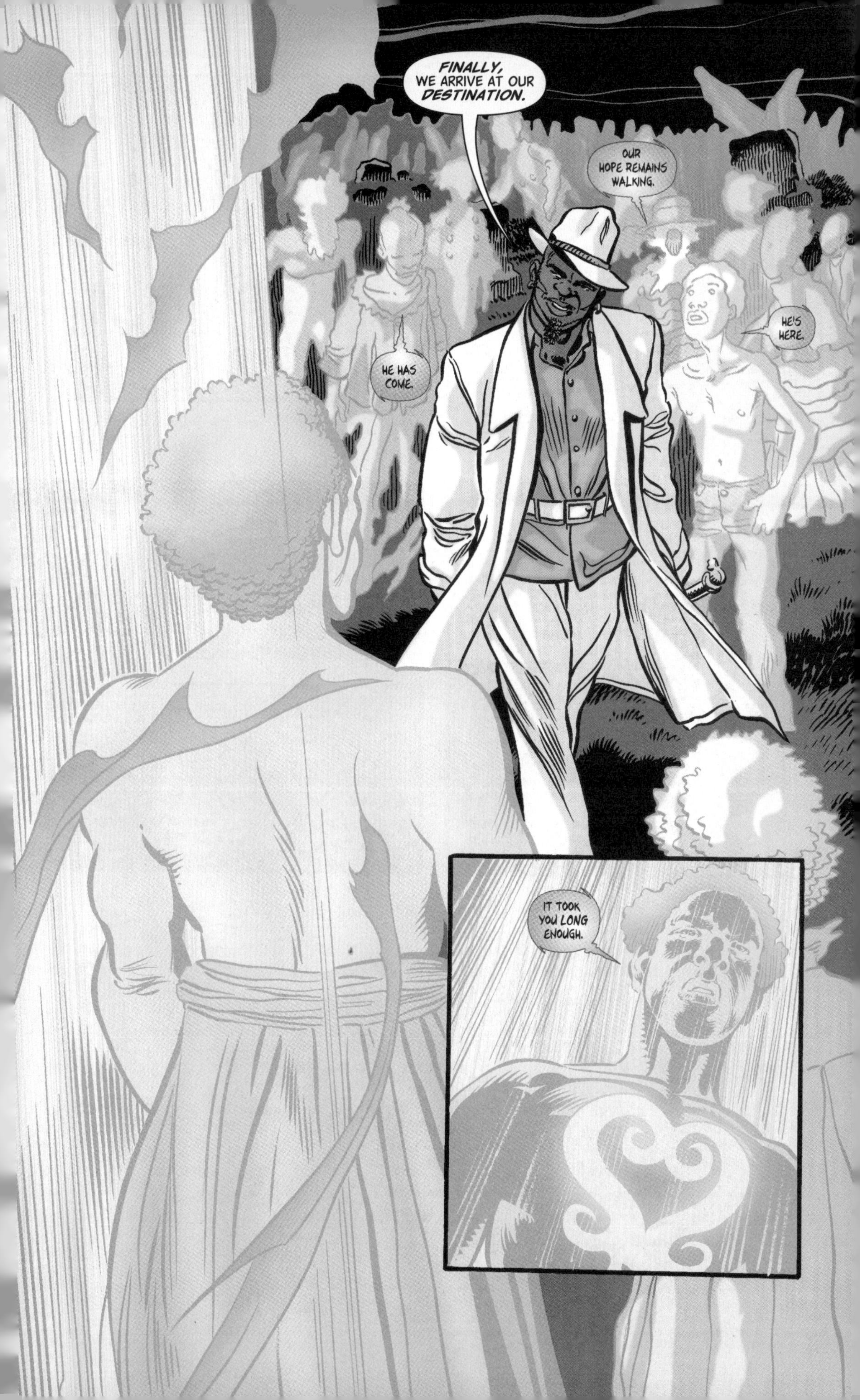
FINALLY, WE ARRIVE AT OUR DESTINATION.
OUR HOPE REMAINS WALKING.
HE'S HERE.
HE HAS COME.
IT TOOK YOU LONG ENOUGH.

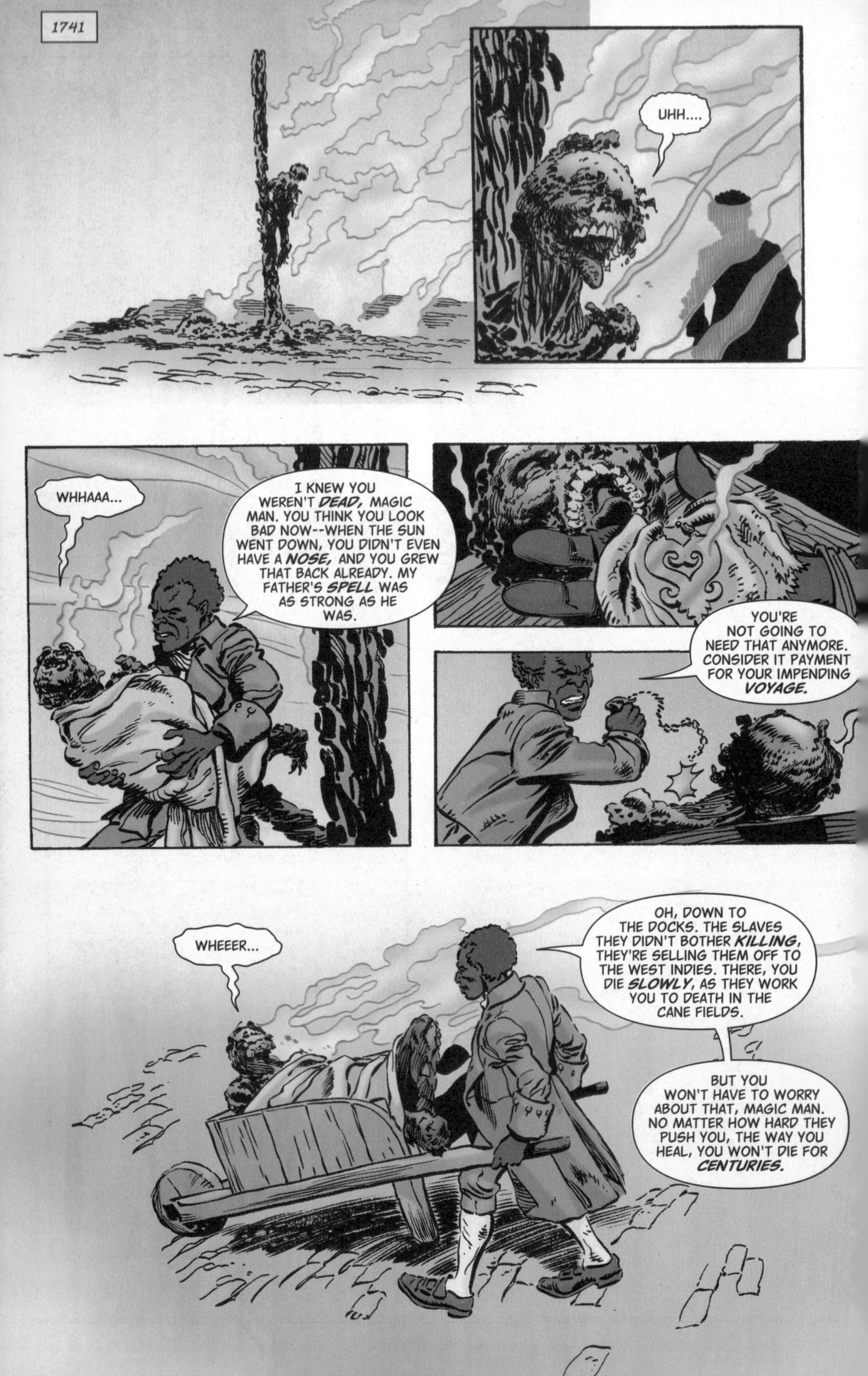
1741
UHH....
WHHAAA...
I KNEW YOU WEREN'T DEAD, MAGIC MAN. YOU THINK YOU LOOK BAD NOW--WHEN THE SUN WENT DOWN, YOU DIDN'T EVEN HAVE A NOSE, AND YOU GREW THAT BACK ALREADY. MY FATHER'S SPELL WAS AS STRONG AS HE WAS.
YOU'RE NOT GOING TO NEED THAT ANYMORE. CONSIDER IT PAYMENT FOR YOUR IMPENDING VOYAGE.
WHEEER...
OH, DOWN TO THE DOCKS. THE SLAVES THEY DIDN'T BOTHER KILLING, THEY'RE SELLING THEM OFF TO THE WEST INDIES. THERE, YOU DIE SLOWLY, AS THEY WORK YOU TO DEATH IN THE CANE FIELDS.
BUT YOU WON'T HAVE TO WORRY ABOUT THAT, MAGIC MAN. NO MATTER HOW HARD THEY PUSH YOU, THE WAY YOU HEAL, YOU WON'T DIE FOR CENTURIES.

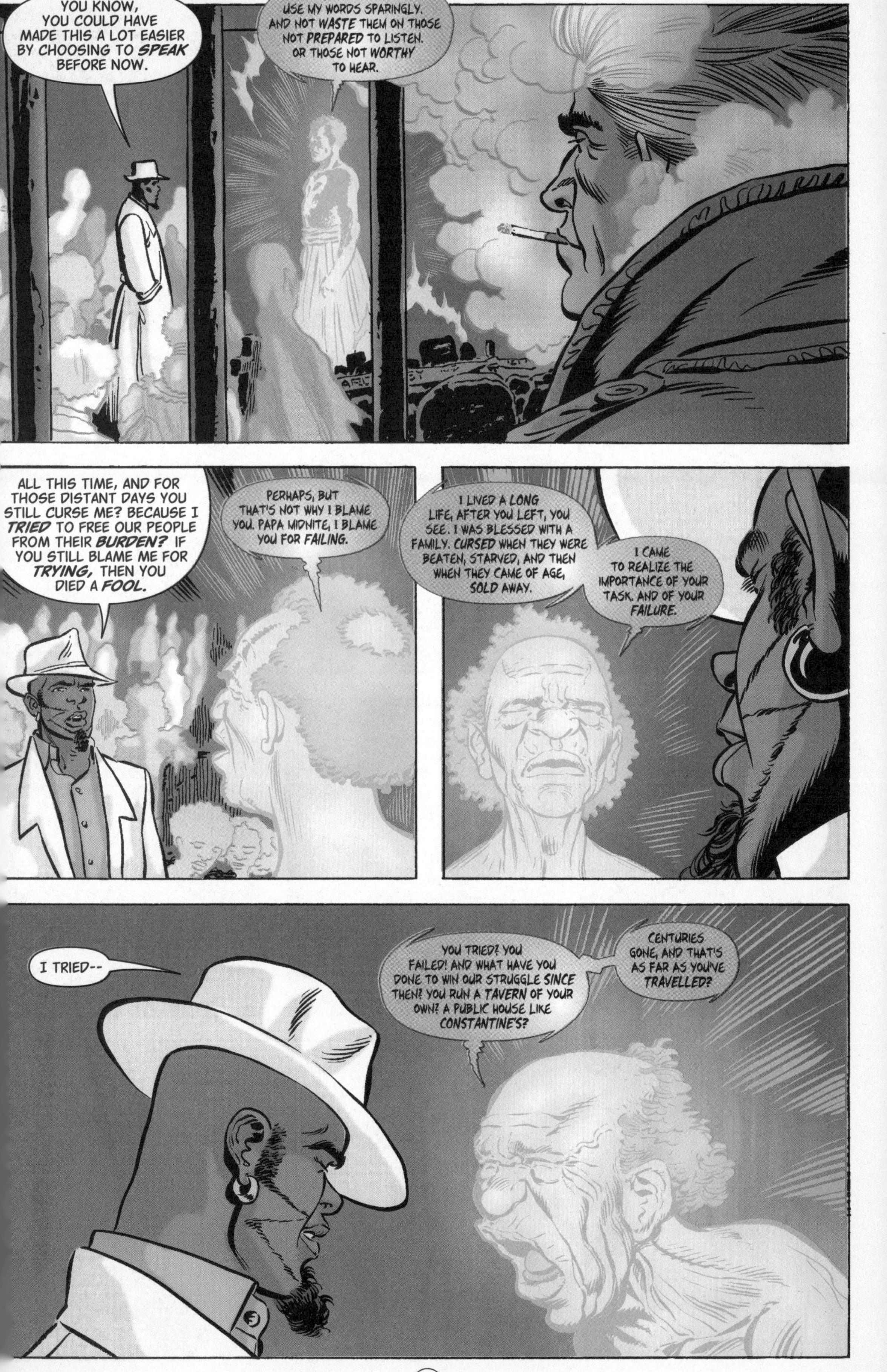
YOU KNOW, YOU COULD HAVE MADE THIS A LOT EASIER BY CHOOSING TO SPEAK BEFORE NOW.
I LEARNED TO USE MY WORDS SPARINGLY. AND NOT WASTE THEM ON THOSE NOT PREPARED TO LISTEN. OR THOSE NOT WORTHY TO HEAR.
ALL THIS TIME, AND FOR THOSE DISTANT DAYS YOU STILL CURSE ME? BECAUSE I TRIED TO FREE OUR PEOPLE FROM THEIR BURDEN? IF YOU STILL BLAME ME FOR TRYING, THEN YOU DIED A FOOL.
PERHAPS, BUT THAT'S NOT WHY I BLAME YOU. PAPA MIDNITE, I BLAME YOU FOR FAILING.
I LIVED A LONG LIFE, AFTER YOU LEFT, YOU SEE. I WAS BLESSED WITH A FAMILY. CURSED WHEN THEY WERE BEATEN, STARVED, AND THEN WHEN THEY CAME OF AGE, SOLD AWAY.
I CAME TO REALIZE THE IMPORTANCE OF YOUR TASK. AND OF YOUR FAILURE.
I TRIED--
YOU TRIED? YOU FAILED! AND WHAT HAVE YOU DONE TO WIN OUR STRUGGLE SINCE THEN? YOU RUN A TAVERN OF YOUR OWN? A PUBLIC HOUSE LIKE CONSTANTINE'S?
CENTURIES GONE, AND THAT'S AS FAR AS YOU'VE TRAVELLED?

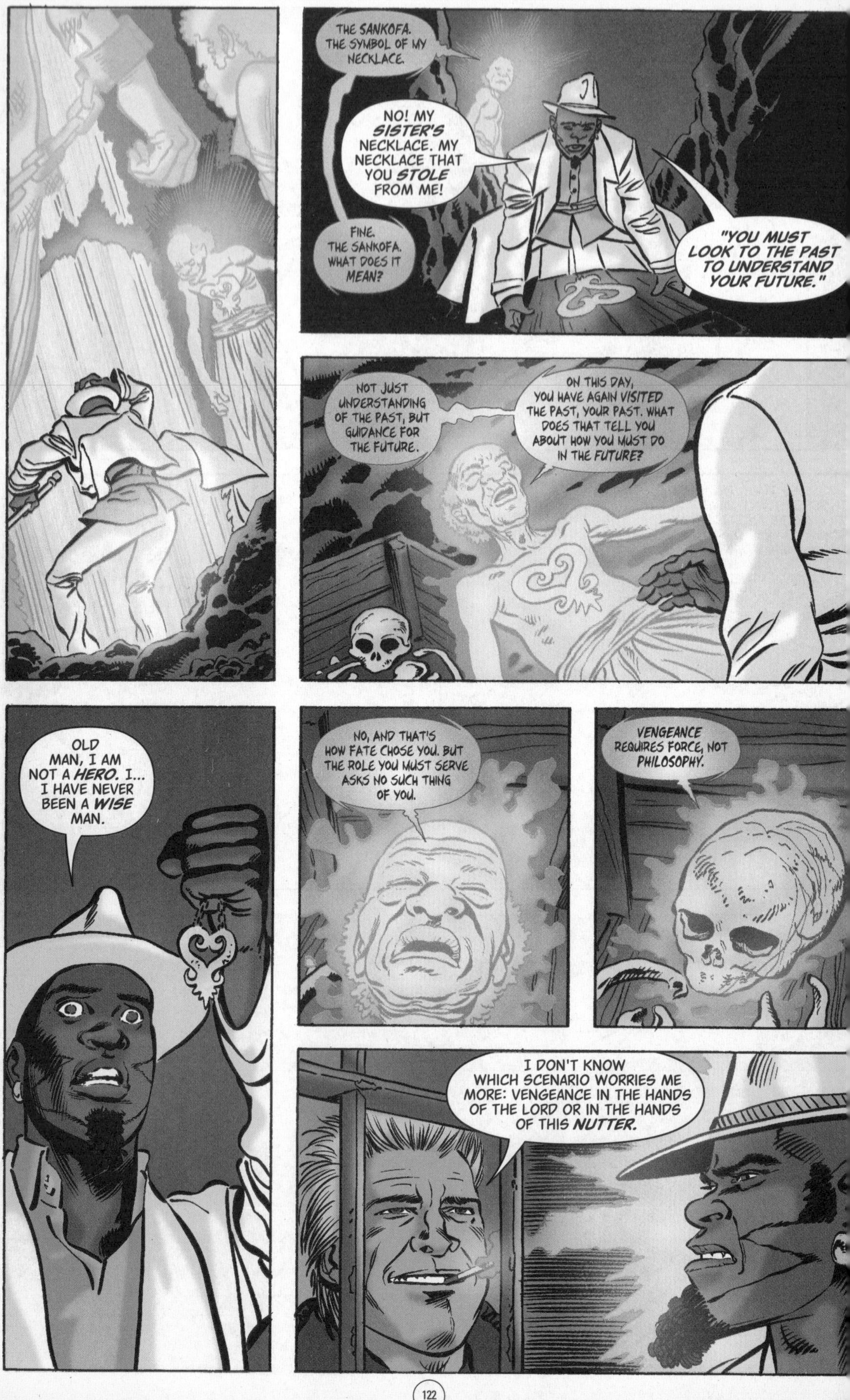

THE SANKOFA. THE SYMBOL OF MY NECKLACE.
NO! MY SISTER'S NECKLACE. MY NECKLACE THAT YOU STOLE FROM ME!
FINE. THE SANKOFA. WHAT DOES IT MEAN?
"YOU MUST LOOK TO THE PAST TO UNDERSTAND YOUR FUTURE."
NOT JUST UNDERSTANDING OF THE PAST, BUT GUIDANCE FOR THE FUTURE.
ON THIS DAY, YOU HAVE AGAIN VISITED THE PAST, YOUR PAST. WHAT DOES THAT TELL YOU ABOUT HOW YOU MUST DO IN THE FUTURE?
OLD MAN, I AM NOT A HERO. I... I HAVE NEVER BEEN A WISE MAN.
NO, AND THAT'S HOW FATE CHOSE YOU. BUT THE ROLE YOU MUST SERVE ASKS NO SUCH THING OF YOU.
VENGEANCE REQUIRES FORCE, NOT PHILOSOPHY.
I DON'T KNOW WHICH SCENARIO WORRIES ME MORE: VENGEANCE IN THE HANDS OF THE LORD OR IN THE HANDS OF THIS NUTTER.

1741

HUGH CONSTANTINE WHITE TRAITOR

POOONININN

CRUMBLE

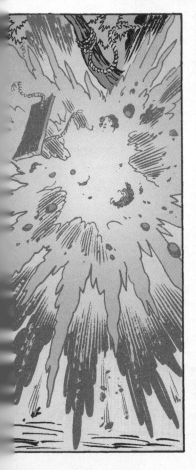

THAT BASTARD MIDNITE! NEW *BLOODY* YORK, I'LL TELL YOU. BUGGER THIS, I'M ON THE FIRST FREIGHT TO *BRISTOL*.

A TRAGEDY. BREAKS ME HEART, IT DOES.

SORRY I HAD TO *SUCK* UP YOUR LIFE FORCE AT THE END THERE TO BOOST ME *OWN*.

AT LEAST YOU DIDN'T DIE IN *VAIN*, RIGHT?

AW, SOD IT. MY *MATES*, YOU DESERVED BETTER.

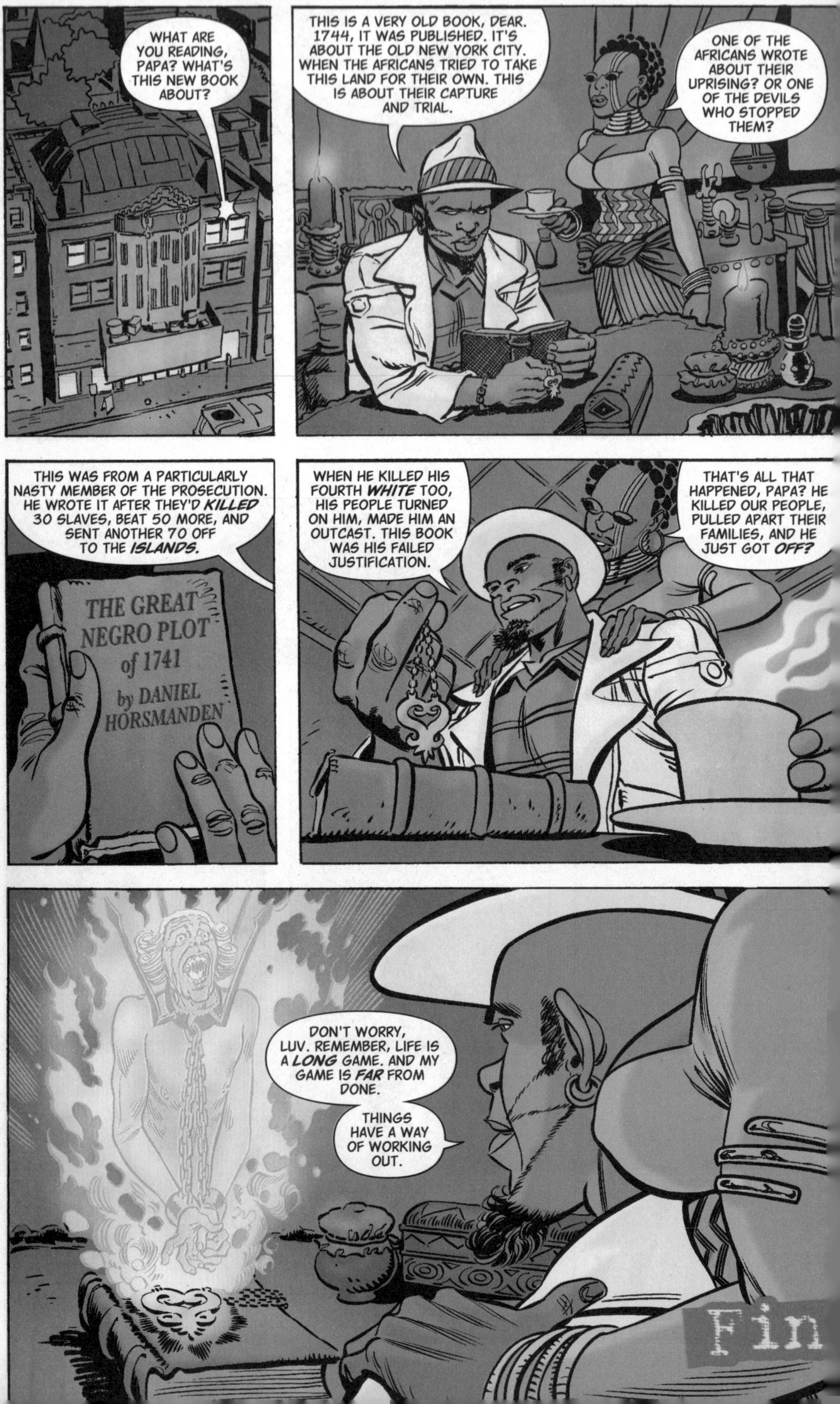
WHAT ARE YOU READING, PAPA? WHAT'S THIS NEW BOOK ABOUT?
THIS IS A VERY OLD BOOK, DEAR. 1744, IT WAS PUBLISHED. IT'S ABOUT THE OLD NEW YORK CITY. WHEN THE AFRICANS TRIED TO TAKE THIS LAND FOR THEIR OWN. THIS IS ABOUT THEIR CAPTURE AND TRIAL.
ONE OF THE AFRICANS WROTE ABOUT THEIR UPRISING? OR ONE OF THE DEVILS WHO STOPPED THEM?
THIS WAS FROM A PARTICULARLY NASTY MEMBER OF THE PROSECUTION. HE WROTE IT AFTER THEY'D KILLED 30 SLAVES, BEAT 50 MORE, AND SENT ANOTHER 70 OFF TO THE ISLANDS.
THE GREAT NEGRO PLOT of 1741 by DANIEL HORSMANDEN
WHEN HE KILLED HIS FOURTH WHITE TOO, HIS PEOPLE TURNED ON HIM, MADE HIM AN OUTCAST. THIS BOOK WAS HIS FAILED JUSTIFICATION.
THAT'S ALL THAT HAPPENED, PAPA? HE KILLED OUR PEOPLE, PULLED APART THEIR FAMILIES, AND HE JUST GOT OFF?
DON'T WORRY, LUV. REMEMBER, LIFE IS A LONG GAME. AND MY GAME IS FAR FROM DONE.
THINGS HAVE A WAY OF WORKING OUT.
Fin

REIMAGINED BY REVOLUTIONARY COMICS WRITER ALAN MOORE, THIS CLASSIC GOTHIC NIGHTMARE BLOSSOMS INTO A MASTERPIECE OF LYRICAL FANTASY, TELLING THE HORRIFYING YET POIGNANT STORY OF A MAN REBORN AS THE LIVING AVATAR OF ALL THE GREEN LIFE ON EARTH.

SWAMP THING

VOLUME 1:
SAGA OF THE SWAMP THING

ALSO AVAILABLE:
VOL. 2: LOVE & DEATH
VOL. 3: THE CURSE
VOL. 4: A MURDER OF CROWS
VOL. 5: EARTH TO EARTH
VOL. 6: REUNION
VOL. 7: REGENESIS
VOL. 8: SPONTANEOUS GENERATION

SWAMP THING: DARK GENESIS
SWAMP THING: BAD SEED
SWAMP THING: LOVE IN VAIN
SWAMP THING: HEALING THE BREACH

VERTIGO
BOOK 1

SAGA OF THE
SWAMP THING

alan moore
steve bissette
john totleben